P9-EMB-729

DISCARDED

Notes from a Kidwatcher

Notes from a Kidwatcher

Selected Writings of Yetta M. Goodman

edited by
Sandra Wilde

Heinemann
Portsmouth, NH

HEINEMANN
A division of Reed Elsevier Inc.
361 Hanover Street
Portsmouth, NH 03801-3912
Offices and agents throughout the world

This collection copyright 1996 by Heinemann. All rights reserved. No part of this book may be reproduced in any form or by any electronic or mechanical means, including information storage and retrieval systems, without permission in writing from the publisher, except by a reviewer, who may quote brief passages in a review.

Credits for previously published material appear on the first page of the article.

Library of Congress Cataloging-in-Publication Data
Goodman, Yetta M.
    Notes from a kidwatcher: selected writings of Yetta M. Goodman/
edited by Sandra Wilde.
        p.   cm.
    Includes bibliographical references (p.).
    ISBN 0-435-08868-8
    1. Goodman, Yetta M.   2. Language arts.   3. Miscue
analysis.   4. Language experience approach in education.   I. Wilde,
Sandra.   II. Title.
LB1576.G719   1996
372.6—dc20   96-11841
                                                                    CIP

Editors: Toby Gordon and Alan Huisman
Cover Design: Jenny Jensen Greenleaf
Manufacturing: Louise Richardson

Printed in the United States of America on acid-free paper.
00 99 98 97 96   DA   1 2 3 4 5

To my parents
William Trachtman and Dora Shapiro Trachtman

To my professors
Marion Edman and E. B. Smith
They would be surprised!

Yetta M. Goodman

Contents

Preface

In selecting work for this anthology from well over a hundred published articles and book chapters, our guiding principle was to choose work that is of historical importance, that is central to Yetta's body of work, that is not widely available, and/or that is of ongoing relevance to teachers. Many of the articles we chose, of course, fit more than one of these criteria. Yetta is also the author or coauthor of a number of books; we have included the most important of these in a brief curriculum vitae.

We have grouped the articles to reflect major themes, arranged roughly in the order of their emergence in Yetta's writing; the articles within each section are arranged chronologically.

Minor changes from the form in which the articles were originally published represent corrections, clarifications, and the elimination of repetition. (Yetta requested that the generic *he* and *man* in some of the earlier articles not be changed, since they reflect the language usage of that time.)

For their help on this book, we would like to thank Terry Green, Debra Jacobson, Prisca Martens, Marie Ruiz, and Monica Taylor, all at the University of Arizona; Jan Allen, at Portland State University; Helen Shaw at Colophon; and Toby Gordon, Alan Huisman, Mike Gibbons and his staff, Renée Le Verrier, and Melissa Inglis, at Heinemann.

A portion of Sandra Wilde's royalties from this book are being donated to the Adult Day Treatment Center at Portland Providence Medical Center in Portland, Oregon. This program, under the direction of Bill Kruger, does important work in helping the those who struggle with severe and persistent emotional problems create happier lives for themselves.

Notes from a Kidwatcher

Introduction

Yetta Goodman:
Past, Present, and Future

In July 1995, Yetta Goodman and I sat down for an hour at the Whole Language Umbrella conference in Windsor, Ontario, and she talked with me about her early years of working with children, her current work with teachers and doctoral students, and her future plans for research and writing. We have chosen to use that interview as the introduction to this book, since the writing that Yetta has done over the years is so much a reflection of her personal history.

Sandra Wilde

What led you to be a teacher?
I think I always wanted to be a teacher because I never remember wanting to be anything else. Maybe it had something to do with my sister, who was a lot older than me, who became a teacher.

[After high school] I became a camp counselor, and I loved being a counselor, I loved working with kids in outdoor settings. I became a song leader and learned how to play the guitar.

And weren't you part of a whole socially conscious camp tradition?
The Jewish Centers Association in California considered itself a social work-oriented camp. And we used to make fun of the camp groups

that were activity-oriented, we'd make fun of the people who just made lanyards or took the kids horseback riding. It really was, theoretically, very different, because we were social group-oriented. So we would sit around and have conversations, and we would do all those other activities too, but those were secondary to kids' building a social community within a camp setting. And it was a Jewish camp, but it didn't have a very religious orientation, and many of the counselors were social workers.

I worked in camps for fourteen years, and I moved from being a counselor to being a camp director and eventually I supervised all the Jewish Centers camps in Los Angeles for about four or five years. We had a few hundred counselors all over the area and a couple thousand kids. At that time I used to run counselor sessions; we used to have overnights for counselors and learn how to work with kids. The focus was on self-esteem and learning to feel good about yourself as a swimmer, learning to feel good about yourself as a hiker. I started out a very good teacher; not everybody has that fortunate beginning, and I think it was because I had this background where I felt that learning in camping situations was fun and exciting, that you could take kids that didn't enjoy living in some ways, who were "Sad Sack" kinds of kids, and turn them into kids that would go skipping down the mountainside when you went on a hike.

What was your teacher education program like?
My work was in Los Angeles, and in some ways that was fortunate too. I went to L. A. City College, and the conceptualizations in the teacher education courses there were innovative, although certainly not as innovative as they are today. Language experience was very strong then. That was a major part of my language arts and reading program, and progressive education was still alive and well.

Was that where you were introduced to Hilda Taba's work?
Although I didn't know about her and her curriculum at that time, we were, in our social studies and science methods courses, doing big projects with our kids, thematic units; we would be involved in setting up our classroom as a model United Nations and things like that, and I'm sure that came out of Hilda Taba's work. Basically we were progressively oriented.

What grade did you teach first?
I started out in a middle school, except at that time it was an intermediate school; it was a new experiment, we were going to "self-contain" middle-school kids. I started out with eighth graders and worked

with seventh and eighth graders for a while. That was in Redondo Beach, California, and we were the first set of teachers that worked in the Redondo Beach Intermediate School. They probably call it a middle school now. But it was the same concept of integrating subjects. I taught every subject—except homemaking, shop, and PE—in an integrated fashion.

And then I spent years in upper elementary. But my own kids were young, and I decided that rather than teach full-time I would substitute teach, and that's when I spent a lot of time in primary classrooms. I really learned to love subbing too, because I've always been successful coming into a group of kids and involving them in some way. I used music, I used my guitar, and I never had a lot of problems with discipline, though I wasn't always sure why.

Do you consider yourself as always having been a whole language teacher even though the term wasn't being used at that point?
Yes, the only tradition I've known is a classroom where you integrate curriculum, where you work with other faculty members. And I always was supported by my principals, who were all men, though they did know I was different. I remember when I wanted to do a unit on "Negro history," during Negro History Week, in Brotherhood Month, and suggested that we do this as a whole school. My principal said, you go ahead and do that, that's fine with me, but let's not worry about the rest of the teachers.

This was during the McCarthy period, and I got in trouble because of that. My kids sent letters to the Julius Rosenwald Foundation, which had many materials on Negro history. Julius Rosenwald was the president of the Sears Roebuck Company at that time. And so my kids all wrote letters and sent letters off, and then I got a call, and the principal said, "The superintendent wants to see you." I got very nervous.

I went into the superintendent's office, and he had a tape recorder on his desk. There were some people dressed in business suits sitting off to the side, but I didn't know who they were or why they were there. I looked down at the desk, and there were all the letters my kids had sent to the Julius Rosenwald Foundation, and the superintendent said to me, "Why are your kids writing these letters?" and I said, "Well, they're writing for information on Negro history," and he said, "And who are they writing to?" I said, "Well, you know that's a special foundation that's set up by Sears Roebuck," and he looked at me and said "Sears Roebuck?" He thought the letters were being sent to [convicted Communist spy] Julius Rosen*berg*. And the postman who collected the school mail also thought it was Julius Rosenberg and had reported it to the superintendent of schools.

So that was the era. It would have been easy for me to have been scared off, and not even try it, but I've always been the kind of person who tries things. There's an old Jewish saying, "If you ask questions, it's never kosher." So I learned not to ask questions. And if somebody questioned me, I'd say, "I'm sorry, I won't do it again."

Who have been the biggest influences on your thinking and career?
It's very hard for me to identify them. I know I was interested in progressive education before I met Ken [Goodman], interested in teaching. Certainly Ken and I have had an impact on each other all of our lives. There are certain professors who stand out, and they're not education professors necessarily. I had a sociology professor named Gordon Alexander at L.A. City College. He was obviously being spied on by the FBI, because he'd say, "I think, those of you who are taking notes in this class, this is what they'll want to know." He had wonderful attitudes about kids, about teaching, so I know I took ideas from him. Then there was a woman by the name of Rita Hanson, in language arts, just like some of the women we read about like Lucy Sprague Mitchell, that kind of educator. There was a whole group of women like that in California, a whole group of progressive educators. I wasn't part of that movement, but somehow those influences had to be there. And then another woman, Helen Lodge, who is still alive. She introduced us to something called American English. It was the first course where I started to think about language in a different way. That was influential too, my camping was influential, and my doctoral program was probably the next big step, the people I met at Wayne State University.

And when you think back more recently, who have you read in the last ten or twenty years that have been very influential?
The most important people I keep reading, of course. I'm still reading Vygotsky and Piaget, for example, and I started those in my early doctoral program. I did a report in my first doctoral class comparing Piaget, Vygotsky, and Bruner. That was 1963, I think. The last few years I've been doing a lot of going back to history. Also Emilia Ferreiro has been influential, in terms of my early literacy work, a psychologist who began to ask questions about early literacy the same way that I was asking questions, that was very important. There are probably others, but those come quickly to mind.

What do you think are the most important things teachers today need to know, need to do, need to be reading?
I think teachers need to know a lot about language and learning. They

have to think about what they believe about how kids learn and they have to think about how language works. All of us have to be constantly looking into what we know about language, what are the arguments in the language field, in linguistics and stuff like that. The same thing is true of learning theory. There's constructivist learning, which is certainly the way I would go, but even within constructivist learning theory, we have constructivists like the Piagetians and the Vygotskians, who sometimes sound like they don't even talk to each other, or they don't want to talk to each other! I think that teachers need to look into those areas.

Teachers need to know that they're learners, that being a teacher is a lifelong learning process and you never stop. You want kids to believe that you can only be a learner when you have decided you want to learn and get excited about learning. Teachers need to approach learning this way too. Each one of us starts at a different place. Some of us have a stronger background in one area than another. But we always have to keep learning, asking ourselves questions about what learning *is*. Certainly I'm very supportive of the role of inquiry, the role of asking questions, whether it's in science or social studies or math.

What kinds of things are really important for teachers to be doing in the classroom?
I don't know! I want teachers to begin to ask themselves what *they* think is important. You can't clone a teacher. No two teachers, even within a set curriculum, are going to be alike. And if you don't believe in a set curriculum, then you have to say to yourself, Okay, how do I build curriculum? That doesn't mean that I'm against people sitting down and talking in a school or in a school district, to say, Here's a few things we think our kids should be thinking about or wondering about. But there should always be an opportunity to negotiate, because the most important parts of learning are not directly related to any specific content. Now I do think content is important, I don't want to negate that, but once you realize that learning is cyclical, that you're going to come back to things over and over, you're not so nervous about covering curriculum. As Hilda Taba said, it's much more important to *un*cover knowledge.

Also, teachers should strive to create a democratic community. You can't become a person who believes in democracy after you've lived in autocratic classrooms for twelve years. You've got to have lived democratically. So certainly that would be another thing I think teachers would want to consider. But I have a hard time anymore saying what teachers need to know or *must* know.

And what about issues such as culture in the classroom, multicultural curriculum?
I'm glad you mentioned that, because of course I take that so for granted, that a classroom is going to be diverse. Yesterday, at the Whole Language Umbrella, Sharon Murphy, the incoming president, was asking us to think about what diversity means for whole language teachers. One of the things I thought about is that diversity is embedded in whole language teaching; we *want* our classrooms to be diverse. I don't believe there's a homogeneous group anywhere in the world anyway, so why do we even pretend that we're going to have homogeneous groups in classrooms? So if every classroom is diverse, every diverse person in your classroom is a resource for every other kid. We should be thrilled to have a deaf kid in the classroom, and thrilled to have a kid from Greece who doesn't speak English, and thrilled to have a couple of Hmong kids. Because not only are *they* resources, but their families, their parents, their communities, are resources. And their cultures are resources. And so to me, I just sort of take that for granted, and I know I shouldn't. But it's got to be there. If you believe in kids, you have to believe in who they are, and they're going to be diverse, so you take them with what their language is, with what their culture is, with what their background is, and we want to expand on everybody's language.

I want kids who speak the language that's closer to mine—and I don't even think mine is whatever people would call standard—I want those kids to be respectful of, and celebrate, the language of Appalachia, the language of African Americans from rural Mississippi, the language of New Yorkers, the language from New Jersey. And the only way we can begin to celebrate those languages is to begin to use the informants we have and help kids realize the richness that we all share.

And that goes back to the teacher's knowledge base.
Yes, and not to be afraid and think that somehow you're negating language development because you're not teaching a standard.

You've made the statement, "Everything I know about reading I've learned from kids." What are some of the most exciting things you've learned from kids and from kidwatching?
I learned most of what I know about grammar from miscue analysis. When you see a kid reading a book, and a kid comes to the word *v-e-r-y*, I rarely have seen a kid look at the picture for *v-e-r-y*. But when a kid comes to the word *m-o-n-k-e-y*, he'll look over at the pictures. And by watching kids you can begin to see that they know "nounness," as

opposed to intensifiers or adjectives or whatever people want to call *very*. So that's one of the things that miscue analysis has taught me a lot about.

I learned another thing a long, long time ago. In the old basals the notion was that you put the same word in as many times as you can in any context. Well, kids taught me that they treat those words differently. For example, one story that the kids read for me, called "The Singing River," was about a man who had a boat that went down the Singing River. And then kids fell into the river. And the man who took care of the boat that went down the Singing River was the river man. So you had *river* in an adjectival slot, you had *river* in its noun sense in a prepositional phrase, and you had *River* as part of a title. Kids miscued differently on each one. For "The Singing River," we got the Singing *Rivay*, but then for *river man*, we always got an *er* ending, because they know something about adjectives in those positions. And the kids didn't get it right because *river* isn't usually an adjective. So they might say *fiver*, or *live-er*, or *rive-er*. And the same kids who had just miscued on that, all of a sudden when the rive-er man fell into the river, there they got it, because there it is in its most common syntactic form.

What are some of your favorite children's books?
Today? [laughs]

Or ones that you remember from your own childhood.
I did go to the library regularly when I was a kid. I don't remember specific books so much as I remember sets of books. I read all the color fairy tales, the *Pink Fairy Tale Book*, the *Red Fairy Tale Book* [compiled by Andrew Lang]. I read *The Dutch Twins*, all the twin books. Remember those? They were terrible, stereotypic books.

Lately I've been looking at sets of books that teach people about schooling, so that we can have a unit about schooling and help kids realize that there are all kinds of things about schools. So things pop into my head like *My Great-Aunt Arizona*, by Gloria Houston, and *Children of the Dust Bowl*, by Jerry Stanley, about a California school organized for migrant kids from Oklahoma, who were not welcome in Calfornia's public schools of the time, books like that where you can explore schooling with kids and let them talk about the kinds of schools they went to, or that they would like, or do interviews with their parents about the kinds of schools they went to. So I've been collecting a whole set of those, even those little books by Miriam Cohen and Lillian Hoban, *When Will I Read?* and *First Grade Takes a Test*. But I'm sure that if you asked me tomorrow I'd give you another list.

In your work with teachers, what principles guide you?
Respect has got to be the main thing, and of course I believe that about learners too. I'm not just saying that. Sometimes people say to me, Oh, you're always saying such nice things about teachers! And I want to make it clear that I'm not just saying it, I really mean that the teachers that I work with, people who call themselves whole language teachers, who work hard at teaching, and there are large numbers of teachers like that, they teach me a lot about what should happen in classrooms. I haven't spent eight to four in a classroom all day long, five days a week, nine, ten months a year, in a long time. They work very hard, and they know so much, and I've been impressed with the fact that teachers can write their stories, write what they're doing, support their knowledge base. In working with teachers I'm constantly helping them find those strengths in themselves.

It sounds like respect and admiration.
And admiration, absolutely admiration. I don't think I could spend all day in a classroom anymore, five days a week. Even though I think I work very hard, it's a very different kind of intensity.

When you think back to the beginning of your career and where you are now, what's the same and what's different?
I'm much more confident. I was never very confident in myself, I was not very confident as a kid, as a learner. And although I was always confident as a teacher, I was never confident with people I felt were more knowledgeable than me. I bought into the power issue; I thought that professors and administrators were smarter than me.

And how are you the same as when you started out?
Even early on, I always felt that if classrooms could be joyful, kids would want to learn more and motivation wouldn't be an issue. And although I do still think that, I try to supplement it with the notion that learning is still a struggle, that you sometimes fail along the way. Going through disequilibrium may be tough, but coming out of it makes you a more capable person, so you feel better about it, and you're more willing to take those challenges as you go along.

What are you working on now?
Three things. One of them is my lifelong interest, since about 1970, in early literacy. I want to go back to that. I really would like to write my own thesis about literacy development, and I'm playing with pulling together everything I've ever done in the area. Maybe write my model of literacy development.

Another is retrospective miscue analysis. I'm just so excited about that, because it puts strengths into the learner, it gives the learner power. It gives learners the opportunity to revalue themselves.

The third is, I'm trying to write a book about what language study should look like in classrooms. I really want to put it into the whole language paradigm, where we do inquiry units about language, we study about language using children's literature. I think of a book like *I Hate English!* by Ellen Levine. What a wonderful book to sit around with kids and talk about: Do you hate the language you speak? How could you hate a language? Or to look at the Japanese scribbles that Taro Yashima uses in *Crow Boy* and talk about that with kids. The other part of language study would be helping kids be critical of what they read and critical of what they hear, critical pedagogy in relationship to literacy.

Anything else you want to talk about?
The most exciting thing to me has been my work with doctoral students. I've always been fortunate to have doctoral students who have been bright women (and some men too!) who challenge me and who don't sit there and just soak up things, who are thinkers themselves.

Part One

Culture
and
Community
(1969–1994)

My interest in culture and community comes directly from the importance my own culture has for me. I am a secular Jewish woman who grew up in an orthodox Jewish home. I am a child of the Depression, a junk peddler's daughter. My family was working class, and if it hadn't been for Franklin Roosevelt's Home Owners Loan Corporation, my parents would not just have been impoverished, we might have become part of the homeless masses roaming the United States in the 1930s. As it was, I grew up with little money in an African American ghetto in Cleveland, Ohio, always sensitive to the cultural differences of the people in my community. African American children and first-generation European American children like me made up my circle of friends. We were all poor, some of us were bilingual, and our teachers did not consider our future in school to be very bright. My sister and I were the culture brokers in our family. Whatever needed to be read or written in English for legal purposes was our responsibility. We were vulnerable to the system. I don't want to go on about my personal beginnings, but I set this as backdrop because I believe my interest in dialect, language variation, and cultural differences comes from my personal cultural history.

Given my concerns as I grew up, it isn't surprising that when I started my work with adolescents and children, I was always interested in youngsters who did not belong to the dominant cultural group in the United States. I've always had a mission to show that children and young people from all walks of life are capable learners. So my research with kids who represent a range of ethnic, racial, and cultural groups is no accident. Now I know from the work of anthropologists like my colleagues Denny Taylor and Teresa McCarty that my work fits the role of advocate for learners and their families. This is no romantic notion. It is a commitment to react to oppressive practices in educational institutions of learning and teaching, and in the educational research conventions that block teachers and the public from appreciating the capabilities of human beings with a wide range of backgrounds.

When I started in education, the focus was on individual differences. I appreciated that focus because it helped us as a profession to undo the perception that in public education students are treated as a mass where everyone does the same things, at the same time, quietly, in straight rows. In this perception, teachers were viewed as technicians in a factory assembly line delivering the same instruction to every student. Recently the strength of the influence of social aspects of the community on learning has become a major concept. Not only is the community of learners in classrooms considered important to learning, but educators are coming to understand the importance of families and cultures outside the classroom. This expands beyond understanding and respecting individual differences to providing learning opportunities through collaboration, discussion, debate, and argumentation in the social community.

From the beginning of my career in education, I have been concerned by our labeling learners from a position of prejudice and mythology, by our believing that once categorized, such students receive greater help. As a student, I was labeled bilingual, poor, from immigrant parents. I was in a middle track in high school, and it was obvious the teachers didn't consider us very worthy of attention. School counselors told me directly that I was not college material but would make a good secretary or could continue to work in a grocery.

When I entered education I heard the label *culturally deprived child.* Later, other terms—*slow learners, learning disabled, at risk*—identified those who come to learning along different paths. I have little doubt that such labels would be mine if the child I was were in school today.

Perhaps as we continue to appreciate the power of the community in the classroom, we will come to understand that knowledgeable professional teachers are capable of organizing safe classrooms involving everyone in the learning community, and that with the support of a group of children or adolescents, the special learner becomes an asset to the group. I remember my daughter Debi, in fifth grade, causing her math teacher some problems by suggesting that the work she was getting she had done the previous year and that she would like to work with some new ideas. Her teacher in exasperation said, "Who do you think you are, somebody special?" Debi at eleven replied, "Yes, of course. Every child is somebody special."

Good teaching based on an understanding of cultural significance and individual differences suggests that each child needs to be respected and treated in special ways and that a community of learners needs to be organized to help support the unique characteristics of every student. This is no easy task. We need to support the development of a community of teachers who are also learners and who have come to believe that they too are special and contribute to the greater good of society.

The Culturally Deprived Child: A Study in Stereotyping

Since the discovery of poverty by the American establishment, children living in low-income areas are a paramount concern to educators. Anyone seeking a federal grant tries to incorporate the term *culturally deprived child* or one of its many equivalent and successor terms in the study's proposal. However, *culturally deprived child* is a meaningless term that does not permit coordinated scientific study by educators, psychologists, and sociologists of many assumptions loosely stated as fact. In more recent years, the term has been replaced by *economically deprived, socially deprived, educationally deprived, culturally disadvantaged, socially disadvantaged,* or more general words—simply *deprived* or *disadvantaged.* Although new labels are created and in some writings three or four of the above are used interchangeably, the results are the same. The terms are not precisely defined. They are vague and their use promotes dangerous value judgments.

To begin, this article will examine the use of the term *culturally deprived,* since it was a base term first popularized by two widely quoted books: *Compensatory Education for Cultural Deprivation* (Bloom et al. 1965) and *The Culturally Deprived Child* (Riessman 1962). This is not an attempt to discredit the material presented or insights developed by these authors but rather an attempt to emphasize that much good work can become meaningless unless the major concept is carefully defined and the underlying assumptions are honestly presented.

Riessman's book is the work most frequently quoted by educators dealing with the problem of the "culturally deprived." The Bloom work is based on working papers contributed by well-known sociolo-

Originally published in *Integrated Education* 7 (1969), pp. 58–63. This journal is now defunct and copyright has reverted to Yetta M. Goodman.

gists, psychologists, and educators at the Research Conference on Education and Cultural Deprivation held in Chicago in June 1964. Riessman explains his use of terms:

> While lower socio-economic groups lack many of the advantages and disadvantages of middle-class culture, we do not think it is appropriate to describe them as "culturally deprived." As we shall see, they possess a culture of their own with many positive characteristics that have developed out of coping with a difficult environment. The term "culturally deprived" refers to those aspects of middle-class culture—such as education, books, formal language—from which these groups have not benefited. However, because it is a term in current usage, we will use "culturally deprived" interchangeably with "educationally deprived" to refer to members of lower socio-economic groups who have had limited access to education. (p. 3)

For some reason Riessman negates his own term, indicates that it is inappropriate, but goes on to capitalize on the "commonsense" use of the term. He compounds the confusion by introducing another term, *educationally deprived,* which he does not define. In essence, Riessman is saying, The term is inappropriate, perhaps even misleading, but we'll use it anyway!

This general lack of distinction among terms continues in more recent literature. In a 1967 article, a program is described for *"delinquency-prone* [my emphasis] seventh-grade boys" who were taught by teachers "selected for their . . . ability to work with pupils of low *socio-economic family status"* (Hall & Waldo 1967, p. 82). No attempt is made to suggest the differences found between *disadvantaged,* which appeared in the title of the article, *delinquency-prone,* or *low socio-economic,* nor why the terms are used interchangeably or what the terms have in common.

Consider the following two quotations from Riessman's book:

> The underprivileged boy's emphasis on masculinity derives from his patriarchal culture where the father is the "tough boss" of the home, and his authority is backed up by physical force. Even in the Negro subculture, the mother frequently plays a strong masculine type of role, and is prone to stress and utilize force. (p. 30)

> A large section of the Negro group has a matriarchal family structure where the mother and grandmother play powerful roles. The attitude toward sex is likely to be somewhat different in this setting than in the more typically patriarchal cultures. (p. 45)

The same phenomenon is presented to substantiate conflicting ideas. In one, the boys are masculine because both matriarchal and patriarchal subcultures have masculine overtones. In the other, the attitude toward sex is different because of the matriarchal influence. Terms such as *masculinity, patriarchal culture,* and *masculine type of mother* are not scientifically defined, but the wording sounds scientific and new stereotypes are developed that are widely quoted and believed. Two additional synonyms are carelessly tossed in to indicate the "culturally deprived child"—*underprivileged boy* and *Negro*—without any qualifiers.

Hidden value judgments of the term *culturally deprived* are evident as one examines the various subgroups included in the definition of *culturally deprived* in Bloom et al.:

1. Those students who "do not make normal progress in their school learning . . . [and] whose motivation for present learning and whose goals for the future are such as to handicap them in school work" (p. 4).

2. The one-third of the high school entrants who do not complete secondary school (p. 4).

3. Those who have "experiences in homes which do not transmit the cultural patterns necessary for the types of learning characteristics of the schools and the larger society" (p. 5).

4. Lower class and middle class are commonly contrasted to indicate differences between culturally deprived and non–culturally deprived.

5. Although the authors say "cultural deprivation should not be equated with race" (p. 5), there are complete separate sections devoted to the problems of Negroes without careful examination of Negro groups that are not "culturally deprived" leading the reader to conclude that *Negro* and *culturally deprived* are synonymous terms.

These five subgroups are not mutually inclusive because of the many variables that are different from one group to another. Yet they are all placed under the same term *culturally deprived.* The definitions are presented in terms of names of subgroups or types of subgroups as well as characteristics of the individuals within society. The term *culturally deprived* has various references that can only lead to confusion and can in no way develop a hypothesis for a scientific definition. It seems as if the term that is left is a value judgment of a group that is somewhat inferior to those doing the describing.

Fowler and Burnett (1967) present value judgments as assumptions to their research. They "assumed that the advantaged . . . would provide more complex models of social, verbal and other styles of functioning" and "assumed that certain qualities of what may be characterized as Negro folk-culture have much to offer members of the middle class. Among these qualities are simplicity, directness and potential for closeness in interpersonal relations" (p. 429).

Note the casual juxtaposition of *middle class* [white] and *advantaged* as opposed to *lower class, Negro,* and *disadvantaged.* What is the difference between culture and folk culture? How are qualities of complexity and simplicity measured? Are these not simply stereotyped value judgments?

I do not question the sincere motives of the people writing, researching, and teaching in the field of "cultural deprivation." I do, however, question their substituting quotes of each other's inadequate terms and poorly researched hypotheses for scientific investigation to answer significant researchable questions.

In a research report presented to the International Reading Association in Boston (Massad 1968), the researcher concludes that "the children from two different socio-economic levels appear to have different processes for creative thought." The conclusions, however, are based on accepting statements from others like "research has already indicated that the results of general intelligence measures may be affected by language and/or cultural deprivation" (p. 2).

The report also quotes Bloom et al.: "The culturally deprived child has not had the same opportunity as other children in using language in the home; the language of the culturally deprived child is not as complex as that of other children either" (p. 8).

In this report the labels *children with language differences, cultural deprivation, children from low socio-economic level, children from low-class families, and the culturally deprived child* and are all used and seem to be equated, since no attempt is made to show in what ways these groups are mutually inclusive or exclusive.

The loose use of terms in the literature leads to the following dangers:

1. The greatest is in cutting off inquiry by extending the term *culturally deprived* and its loose synonyms into every aspect of the life of children being described. Cohen (1969) complains about the cultural deprivation fallacy in schools. He believes that if "the content of learning [is made] relevant to children and we have applied pedagogies based on sound principles of learning," the children in ghettos will learn to read. Yet he also states: "Ghetto kids are deprived. Their deprivations make them more dependent than middle-class kids upon the school to learn to be literate" (p. 258). I submit that anyone who wants to make education relevant to children must know a great deal about those children and not prejudge children before they are taught.

Broad generalizations are made about home environment and social class, family structure, language, cognitive and learning processes, intelligence and aptitudes, personality and motivation, achievement, and the types of programs and personnel needed. In the area of language, for example, such quotes as the following are common:

> Children from lower-class homes have been found to be weak in auditory discrimination and visual discrimination; "disadvantaged children" lack abstract language; language usage is limited in deprived homes; communication is through gestures and other nonverbal means; language is terse and not necessarily grammatically correct. (Bloom et al., p. 70)

Inquiry into the language of the "culturally deprived" is cut off. A quest for adequate definition is abandoned, and to make matters worse, inquiry is not pursued into even more important questions such as What is auditory and visual discrimination? What is communication? and Can there be terse language that is not grammatically correct?

Much of the research done carefully controls all variables and uses control groups and adequate samples but never questions the basic assumption that one thousand youngsters tested from the lowest economic area of a metropolis are equally "deprived" when they may, in fact, be too variable to provide meaningful conclusions.

2. The possibility of institutionalizing segregation is becoming a very real one. This is ironic because it is the very opposite of the stated intention of the various writers. Yet Riessman calls for special teachers, specially trained for working with "culturally deprived" children, and Bloom et al. recommend that "nursery schools and kindergartens should be very different from the nursery schools and kindergartens commonly used for middle-class children" (p. 17).

In the catalogue of a state college serving a metropolitan community, the following course description occurred:

> *Art for the Culturally Disadvantaged.* Special problems in the teaching of art to children who vary markedly from others of the same age because of deprivations in home and community experiences.

The assumptions are made that children with such backgrounds exist, that such backgrounds are deprived, and that special training is needed to help teachers work with such children.

3. A process of developing new pseudoscientific stereotypes of subgroups within our society has begun. There has been an attempt by those studying "culturally deprived" children to eliminate old stereotypes like "inferior mentality," "primitive morality," "laziness," "gaudy, flashy dress," "don't care for their children," and so on. Without benefit of an adequate methodological approach to the defini-

tion of terms, Riessman presents a list of liabilities of the "culturally deprived" that include "narrowness of tradition," "pragmatic," "anti-intellectual," "limited development of individualism, self-expression and creativity" (p. 18). These terms carry the weight of authority and scholarship instead of the label of ignorant prejudice. Educators can now label children with great justification but with no evidence of the scientific method in use to justify these new labels.

4. Sociologists, psychologists, and educators are themselves attributing a general negative quality to a specific type of culture that cannot be evil in and of itself. Rosenthal and Jacobson (1968), in doing research on teacher expectations, indicate that programs directed at disadvantaged children are based on the premise that "the deficiencies are all in the child and the environment from which he comes." Their research rests on the premise that "at least some of the deficiencies and therefore at least some of the remedies might be in the schools and particularly in the attitudes of teachers toward disadvantaged children" (p. 23).

My father was a junk peddler, not a salvage dealer or a surplus dealer but a peddler who drove up and down city streets calling for "paper, rags, any junk" with a thick Eastern European dialect. My parents were certainly not literate in any language in any academic sense. My background was culturally deprived using any of the criteria advanced in the contemporary literature about the subject (except color). Yet, I do not want to forget or expunge my cultural heritage. I could not do it if I wished. In the zeal to bring better conditions to the poverty-stricken of our society, we have created a group who must either completely reject the values that are being held out to them or be ashamed of their own culture, their heritage, and their mother tongue, in their desire for upward mobility.

The so-called culturally deprived of our country have in contemporary times as well as in times past produced people who are committed to American democracy and are actively involved in programs dedicated to social change and progress. How shall we interpret *e pluribus unum*, from many to one? Must we become a monolithic, homogenized one? Or can we be a pluralistic but united society?

References

Bloom, Benjamin S., Davis, Allison & Hess, Robert. 1965. *Compensatory education for cultural deprivation*. New York: Holt, Rinehart & Winston.

Champlin, Nathaniel. 1965. The search for the human. Unpublished manuscript, Wayne State University, Detroit, MI.

Cohen, S. Alan. 1969. Local control and the cultural deprivation fallacy. *Grade Teacher, 86,* 255–58.

Fowler, William & Burnett, Alice. 1967. Models for learning in an integrated preschool. *The Elementary School Journal, 67,* 428–41.

Hall, Nason E. & Walso, Gordon P. 1967. Remedial reading for the disadvantaged. *Journal of Reading, 11,* 81–92.

Massad, Carolyn E. 1968, May. *Language-thought processes in children from differing socio-economic levels.* Paper presented at the annual meeting of the International Reading Association, Boston, MA. (ERIC Document Reproduction Service No. ED 022 636)

Riessman, Frank. 1962. *The culturally deprived child.* New York: Harper.

Rosenthal, Robert & Jacobson, Lenore F. 1968, April. Teacher expectations for the disadvantaged. *Scientific American,* 19–23.

The Culture of the Culturally Deprived

About five years ago, I walked into an elementary school in an almost all black, lower-economic area in Detroit ready to perform my responsibilities as a college supervisor of a number of student teachers. The principal greeted me warmly and asked whether I was not the person who often led folk singing for some functions at the university. "Could we impose on you to do this for our children sometime?" she graciously asked. "They could really benefit from such a broadening experience."

Eager to get directly involved with children, I accepted. A few weeks later, I came back to the school with my guitar. The children were responsive. In one sixth-grade class, I began singing "Hush Little Baby," a widely known folk song for children. The children began singing with me, but after a few lines I realized that we were not all singing the same words. I stopped and said: "Some of you know different verses than I do. That often happens when we sing folk songs. Would some of you like to sing me your verses?" I got no response. I suggested that perhaps they wanted to share their verses with their own teacher. I could come back and add them to my collection. I took time to talk about the dignity of the oral tradition in folk music. Before I left, I made arrangements with the teacher to encourage the children to bring in their verses.

A few weeks later, I returned with my tape recorder. The teacher told me that several girls and boys were willing to exchange songs with me. Six children, the sixth-grade teacher, and I went to the gym, which was not being used at that hour, and began taping folk material. The

Originally published in *Elementary School Journal* 71 (1971), pp. 376–83. Copyright 1971 by the University of Chicago Press. Reprinted with permission.

gym teacher was of great help: "Sing her the one you do jumping rope. What about the hand-clapping one?" he shouted. I collected the "culture of the culturally deprived."

If the phrase sounds contradictory, it is. One of the conclusions of my research in this area is that cultural deprivation is an impossibility—unless we all agree that all people are culturally deprived in certain situations and at certain times.

The kind of research I was doing in this sixth grade is not often done in educational and psychological fields, although it is considered a perfectly good approach in linguistics and anthropology. It is important to bring few preconceptions or value judgments to the study of a people or a language. A scientist goes into a community, lives among the people, and tries to become involved in their lives. He may have to live in a community for many months or years to understand the values, the mores, and the history of the people who live there. The more time he spends living in a community, studying it from within its own culture, the more valid his research is likely to be. Anthropologists, in their wanderings over the earth, have studied many peoples in places both remote and nearby. In all their years of study, anthropologists and linguists have found no groups without language, no groups without culture.

Yet in educational research, in our sincere attempt to improve the lives of the poor in our own society, we have set up a hypothetical model of correctness instead of making our research value free. We are so tied to the mores and the values of one particular group—our own—that research studies are based on the preconception that the adult model, the researcher, is the right model. Children who do not measure up to children who are most like the adult model, we proclaim, have poor language or no language, are culturally deprived or lack culture. We talk about remediation, diagnosing their problems as if they were sicknesses, and then prescribe medicine or courses of actions to solve these problems.

Rosenthal and Jacobson (1968), who have studied teachers' expectations of children, indicate that programs directed at disadvantaged children are based on the premise that "the deficiencies are all in the child and the environment from which he comes" (p. 20). Rosenthal and Jacobson's conclusions suggest that in our research we produce the results we expect.

However, when one approaches a group of children without preconceived notions, it is possible to discover strengths as well as weaknesses, a different cultural pattern rather than a deprived one, different language patterns rather than no language. This is what I began to understand as I collected samples of children's "play party games" and songs. These games and songs are made up by the children and passed on within the child community. They are not passed on by adults, for most adults have only vague memories of the games and songs they knew as children. I found the best informants to be fifth and sixth graders.

I wish to present some of the games and songs so that others may become aware of the culture I encountered. Most of the games and songs present evidence of the very characteristics my informants were accused of lacking according to standardized tests. Many of the children had low scores on tests for auditory and visual discrimination. The children were variously labeled *perceptually handicapped, linguistically disadvantaged,* or *mentally retarded.* However, as I watched and listened to these children in an environment in which they were comfortable, I began to have grave doubts about the results of tests designed to label children who have handicaps. I began to question research that has put children like these into positions of deprivation and inferiority.

I often use one of the songs I collected as an auditory memory test for adults. I call it a dictated-sentence test. The words and music are presented in Figure 1. I sing or say one line and the adults, often teachers, repeat each line. In such a test, every sound, every word, and every intonation pattern must be repeated exactly as it is pro-

Figure 1.
Dictated Memory Test

(The phrases to be repeated vocally do not coincide with the musical bars. The end of each phrase is designated by a wavy line that extends above and below the staff.)

duced by the tester. Any departure proves that the listener has some type of handicap. There is no repeating of any section for the listener.

Remember that each phrase has to be repeated perfectly to be considered correct. If the person taking the test says "caught you" for "cau cha," the response is incorrect. "What's his name" would be unacceptable for "wassis name."

No one has ever passed this test. Does that prove that the adults, often teachers, lack auditory discrimination and that they need remediation? Or perhaps the adults are just out of it? They just don't dig!

Researchers like Drake (1964) have concluded that "ability to reproduce a simple rhythm is highly correlated with a child's ability to blend letter sounds." He suggests that "rhythmic performance of motor skills is related to reading and handwriting" (p. 202). Oral coding tests based on this type of research have been developed. Children are asked to repeat rhythm patterns tapped by the researcher. If children are unable to repeat the pattern, it is an indication that they may not be able to learn to read. Yet, when I observed children's play party games, I found that their play was often accompanied by intricate hand-clap, footwork, and body-rhythm patterns as well as songs.

To digress for a moment, it seems ironic that at one time a stereotype of Negroes suggested that all of them could sing and dance. Since someone has concluded that the ability to reproduce rhythm patterns may be related to the ability to read, it has been discovered that the variously labeled poor of our country—a large percent of whom are black—just ain't got rhythm.

It is often said that these children know no nursery rhymes. A trip around the school playground during recess may turn up several old English folk rhymes. The words may not be exactly like those in the "official" Mother Goose, and the rhythms are altered, because the oral tradition in folk material has been at work.

"London Bridge" has been changed to a chant rhythm. The children stand in a circle, and one child is in the center. The children in the circle call:

London Bridge is
Oo–watcha ku my baby
Oo–watcha ku my baby
Oo–watcha ku my baby
London Bridge is
Oo–watcha ku my baby
Work out Care'line.

At this point Caroline, in the middle, begins a rhythmic body movement, whatever is popular at the time. The children in the circle follow her movement, and all continue to chant:

Figure 2.
"Little Sally Walker"

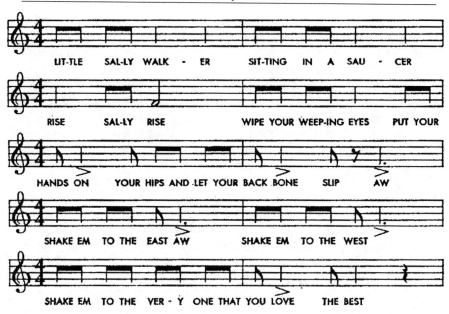

With a hip and a hoe
and a rock and a ro'
With a hip and a hoe
and a rock and a ro'
With a hip and a hoe
and a rock and a ro'
Work out Care'line

At the end of the chant, Caroline chooses someone to take her place, and the circle game continues.

Another standard that the children did in a different version was "Little Sally Walker" (Figure 2).

Testers and researchers often conclude that these children are unable to discriminate sounds because they cannot rhyme words. Then how do they create and pass on jump-rope chants like the one in Figure 3? I have collected many, many more verses to this song.

Many games and songs are concerned with school-oriented tasks. Children have songs and games that categorize items. Scissors, Paper, and Stone is one such game. To be successful in that game, children must understand the hierarchical order that scissors can cut paper, paper can cover stone, and stone can break scissors.

Children have spelling games and rhymes, and use alphabet letter-sound correspondences:

Figure 3.
"Oh Mary Mack"

(MUSIC REPEATS SAME THROUGHOUT)

Verse 2:
I like coffee, coffee, coffee
And I like tea, tea, tea
And all the boys, boys, boys
They all like me, me, me.

Verse 3:
Asked my mama, mama, mama
For fifteen cents, cents, cents
To see the 'lphant, 'lphant, 'lphant
Jump the fence, fence, fence.

Verse 4:
He jumped so high, high, high
He touched the sky, sky, sky
And never came back, back, back
Till the fourth of July, ly, ly.

A my name is Amos
My wife's name is Amanda
We come from Alabama
And we bring back Artichokes

For choosing up sides or deciding who is It, the children count off:

First Child:
My mother and your mother were hanging out clothes
My mother punched your mother right in the nose.
What was the color of her blood?
Second Child:
Pink [or any color].
First Child:
P–I–N–K spells pink, and you are out.

The chant repeats with the "second child" calling any color until all the children are eliminated, and the choosing is completed. Another more complicated alphabet song appears in Figure 4.

Doing descriptive research of cultural patterns to get a more accurate picture of children's strengths is not simple. It is easy to impose

Figure 4.
Alphabet Song

our own expectations on every situation, no matter how aware we are. The children generally want to please us. Often they do not think highly of their own cultural forms and therefore go along with us. I did not collect one delightful folk song from the children for almost two months because I kept presenting my version of the folk song. I kept saying, "Sing 'Hush Little Baby.'" The children would look at each other hesitatingly, and I would say, "I'll start it for you," and proceeded to. Finally one day, when a group was on the playground and I was not involved, I collected *their* song (Figure 5).

Figure 5.
"Ham Bone"

If that mockin' bird don't sing
Papa gonna buy you a diamond ring
If the diamond ring don't shine
Papa gonna buy you a bottle of wine
If that bottle of wine get broke
Papa gonna buy you a billy goat
If that billy goat run away
Papa gonna buy you a Chevrolet
If that Chevrolet don't run
Papa gonna buy you a b.b. gun
If that b.b. gun don't shoot
Papa gonna buy you a baseball suit
If that baseball suit don't fit
Papa gonna say
Aw shoot! I quit.

In our desire to help the poor in our country, we may be destroying not only the culture of a people, but also part of the foundation of modern American culture. Author Ralph Ellison has said it most eloquently:

> If you can show me how I can cling to that which is real to me, while teaching me a way into a larger society, then I will drop my defense and my hostility, but I will sing your praises and I will help you make the desert bear fruit. (Quoted in Riessman 1967, p. 47).

References

Drake, Charles C. 1964. Reading, riting and rhythm. *Reading Teacher, 18,* 202–5.

Riessman, Frank. 1967. *Blueprint for the disadvantaged.* New York: Anti-Defamation League of B'nai Brith.

Rosenthal, Robert & Jacobson, Lenore F. 1968, April. Teacher expectations for the disadvantaged. *Scientific American,* 19–23.

One Among Many: A Multicultural, Multilingual Perspective

Multicultural education is as important for teachers and other adults in our society as it is for the students in our classrooms. In fact, I want to argue that unless teachers are actively involved in continually learning about multiculturalism, their students' knowledge and experiences will be seriously limited.

Thoughtfully organized whole language curriculum is immersed within a multicultural perspective because it takes seriously the language and culture of the learner. Both whole language and multicultural education call for a view of students as capable learners. Concern for multicultural education provides opportunities and experiences to view with understanding the various perspectives and beliefs expressed by our students, their parents, and their communities and helps teachers begin to appreciate that within every community there is a culture that can inform the student and the school (Moll et al. 1990). Within a multicultural framework, we respect each other, recognize our similarities, debate our multiple perspectives, accept and celebrate our differences, and are constantly involved in exploring the strengths and influences that all the members of our world community contribute to our own growth and well-being.

Originally published in *Under the Whole Language Umbrella: Many Cultures, Many Voices,* edited by Alan D. Flurkey & Richard J. Meyer (Urbana, IL & Bloomington, IN: National Council of Teachers of English and Whole Language Umbrella, 1994), pp. 267–77. Copyright 1994 by the National Council of Teachers of English and the Whole Language Umbrella. Reprinted with permission.

Multicultural education is equally important for all groups of students and their teachers, whether they are part of the dominant cultural group or members of various parallel cultural groups within the society. (I borrow the term *parallel culture groups* from my colleague Rudine Sims Bishop since I feel the term *minority* is a misnomer.) Each cultural group, regardless of its position in society, has a tendency to be ethnocentric in its orientation. As we find ways to understand each other, every group benefits.

In the past year, I have had a number of experiences that have heightened for me the importance of and need for multicultural education for all of us—adults and children. There have been repeated editorials in daily newspapers raising specters of disaster for American schools because there are school districts, universities, and colleges that are finding ways to provide a broader base and deeper understanding of history and culture than the one that has been typically available to students, especially through standardized textbooks. These editorials seem to deny multiple perspectives concerned with ways of knowing, believing, and valuing.

George Will was one such journalist who sounded an alarm, speaking against "compensatory history that preaches the virtues of the oppressed by exaggerating their achievements." In a 1991 column entitled "Multicultural History Becomes a Political Tool," Will indicated that such a view suggests that "there's always an Irishman at the bottom of it doing the real work." He means that in such presentations of history, ethnic groups exaggerate their achievements in the grand scheme of things. He suggests that this kind of teaching is politically motivated without acknowledging that teaching from only a European/Western tradition is equally politically motivated.

Another experience occurred at a whole language conference that I attended in Massachusetts. Of the over two hundred people there, two participants complained that there was "too much multicultural content" at the conference; "too much about the Holocaust and various minority groups"; and "not enough content for middle-class white kids."

And a continual experience that I have is related to the look of surprise that I get from people when I mention how much I loved living in Detroit, Michigan. I spent my years in Detroit learning from friends and colleagues from different racial and ethnic groups. Those fourteen years have had a lasting influence on my professional life as well as my personal life.

These experiences and others like them make it obvious that we have a long way to go and much work to do to free ourselves from biases and prejudices. Myths about others are often established by the

educational system, even in professional literature and in the classrooms of universities and colleges. Because of the need for all of us to
understand the nature of prejudice, which I believe stands in the way
of strong multicultural education, I want to discuss multicultural education not only from the point of view of what it means for curriculum in the classroom but what it means for each and every one of us
concerned with whole language.

Multiculturalism: A Curriculum for Problem Solving and Democracy

James A. Banks of the University of Washington has written widely
on multicultural education (Banks 1988; Banks & Banks 1993) and
is thoughtfully critical of what he calls the contributions and ethnic-
additive approaches to multicultural curriculum. These approaches
add ethnic heroes, holidays, or customs to the ongoing curriculum by
simply adding a book, a unit, or a course without examining how
what is being studied impacts major issues and movements in society.
Banks suggests that instead it is necessary to understand the "nature,
development and complexity" of society by examining how different
perspectives, frames of reference, and content from the various groups
interrelate and impact the world as we know it. In addition, once we
discover that there are problems occurring because of these complexities, then we need to become actively involved with our students in
solving the problems as members of a democratic society. It is not
enough just to *know*—we must act on that knowledge. That is the nature of a democracy. Our programs must move our students to action.
I believe that through meaningful activity or experiences, more powerful and long-lasting learning occurs.

Using Literature to Extend Multicultural Experiences

I want to share some of the things I have read that have helped me consider different perspectives, frames of reference, and content. Reading
about others and understanding their perspectives allows us to expand
and enrich our world. My purpose is that these ideas may not only impact your ideas about multiculturalism but also may point to ways in
which such expansions will impact the classroom. I am concerned that
teachers who do not continually add to their own knowledge about the
worlds of others cannot develop a multicultural curriculum that will seriously affect the thinking and actions of their students. Without taking

multicultural issues seriously, we may add nice units about others to the curriculum, but these will not provide the transformations necessary to recognize the complexities of our world and to explore the ways of participating in the problem solving necessary to make the significant changes that will impact all of our citizens.

It has been through these readings that I constantly keep myself sensitive to issues of people who have different views of the world than I do, who see the world in very different terms because they have less money than I do, who speak a different language than I do, or who come from a family that believes very differently than I do. It is too easy for humans to see the world from just their own point of view. The passage from Ralph Ellison quoted in the previous article suggests to me that if I as a teacher can constantly reconsider these issues of difference, then I can take what I believe and what I know and share them with my students. I will also be in a position to recognize the ways in which our lives are similar as well as different. If my college students see that the way I act (not just what I say) reflects a multicultural view and my acceptance and respect for every one of my students regardless of age, race, creed, national origin, language, gender, or sexual orientation, then they will be comfortable and able to reach out and understand my world, and the world of their students as well.

The more we read and the more we try to discover the backgrounds of the students whom we teach, the more opportunities we will have to dispel the myths that strongly influence the way in which we teach.

Looking Historically

By examining historical documents, it is possible to gain glimpses into the ways in which myths about various individuals and groups are developed and maintained. I have always been amused by an article written in 1905 about Jewish immigrant children (Fortune 1905/ 1975). It is interesting to note the misconceptions and overgeneralizations that this middle-class, well-educated teacher has about the new Jewish arrivals in New York schools. There are teachers and other authors writing about the children of the poor today who lack the sensitivity and insight of the African American author Jessie Fortune. Although she writes eloquently about the plight of Jewish immigrant children, she perpetuates the myth about Jews and money:

> Unlike the best Hollander, the Jew does not seem to take naturally to cleansing or scrubbing; his sole aim seems to be earning money, and all household duties are subservient to this purpose, so that as often

as not the dining room, parlor and sitting room serve as a tailor shop or work shop. . . . They are interesting children to know. Some of them are very beautiful, physically and temperamentally, and some are quite the reverse. . . . One grows to have an interest in their development which one would never imagine feeling when one first views the swarms of them playing around the streets. (pp. 6–7)

Another historical examination that can be enlightening for our own knowledge and for our students' relates to major anniversaries and celebrations. In 1992 we observed the five-hundred-year anniversary of Columbus's trip to the Americas, which led to many accounts in the popular press that were useful in the classroom. Many groups legitimately raised questions about who really discovered America and when, and about the nature of Columbus's contributions to the New World and the Old World. I do not want to deny Columbus his due, but a feature article in *U.S. News and World Report* entitled "America before Columbus" (1991) suggests an interesting way to explore the issue of the Americas and who lived here during which periods of time. It provides a broadened framework from which to explore the contributions of Columbus by presenting not just the impact of the Old World on the New but also the contributions made to the Old World from the New. A publication for teachers called *Rethinking Columbus* (Bigelow et al. 1991) focuses on helping readers examine the sources of readily accepted beliefs about Columbus, many of which are critiqued from a variety of points of view. By using these resources, students and teachers broaden their views about the variety of concerns related to the development of the Americas.

In the past there have been fairly few children's picture books concerned with life in the Americas before Columbus, but the five-hundred-year anniversary of Columbus's sailing has sparked the publication of numerous books documenting this period from a wide range of perspectives. Teachers and their students may write their own accounts as they research this period.

Biographical Accounts

Many of our students come to school with backgrounds that are very different from North American culture and language. Eva Hoffman's *Lost in Translation: A Life in a New Language* (1989) helped me understand the powerful transitions that such people are called on to make. Hoffman emigrated with her family to Vancouver, British Columbia, from Poland in 1959 and felt as if she had moved from paradise to exile as she exchanged cultures and languages. She recounts the intensity of her innermost emotional and intellectual responses to these major changes in her life. Hoffman relocated again to attend college in Houston, Texas, and then moved into the intellectual literary world of New York City, where she is now an editor for the *New York Times Book Review*. This is a poignant personal narrative for those concerned with discovering how anyone who crosses over from one culture to another and from one language to another feels emotionally and intellectually. It helps to sensitize us to our students and to their parents, whether they come from overseas to this part of the world, from a reservation to an urban metropolis, or from a big city to the mountains of Colorado. Those who identify with Eva Hoffman must take into account what would happen to any of us as we move from culture to culture, from language to language, from society to society. We take our old selves with us and must make peace between the two or more worlds that are coming together for us. Hoffman uses language in a most powerful and sensitive way to reveal to us the impact that the complexities of being bilingual has on understanding both our old and new worlds.

This is described poignantly as she recounts the response to her own and her sister's Polish names by the school teacher who

> has seen too many . . . come and go to get sentimental about a name. Mine—"Ewa"—is easy to change into its near equivalent in English, "Eva." My sister's name—"Alina"—poses more of a problem, but after a moment's thought . . . the teacher decides that Elaine is close enough. My sister and I hang our heads wordlessly under this careless baptism. (p. 105)

Hoffman also helps to awaken her readers to what happens to any bilingual learners when they come to see the differences in their perceptions and conceptualizations in one language and the other:

> "River" in Polish was a vital sound, energized with the essence of riverhood, of my rivers, of my being immersed in rivers. "River" in English is cold—a word without an aura. It has no accumulated associations for me, and it does not give off the radiating haze of connotation. It does not evoke. (p. 107)

Multiple Languages, Genres, and Forms

Perhaps one way to get us all to think simultaneously of the differences and the similarities of language and literacy in the world is to bring into our classrooms languages that we do not understand. We need to become exposed to the multilingual nature of the world as well as to multiculturalism.

Classrooms should include resources that appear in many different languages. Picture storybooks in such languages as Japanese, Spanish, Hebrew, French, and Vietnamese, among others, should line our bookshelves. With our students, we can explore the differences and similarities of the multiple types of written languages and illustrations that are published in the world. We can examine versions of the same books that appear in different languages and can compare them in a variety of ways. We can invite speakers of those languages to read aloud to our classes. Children can follow along if the books are familiar to them; if the children are not familiar with the material, translations of words or actions can be provided.

Examining Our Own Biases

I believe another multicultural concern that can be affected by literature is recalling and understanding the injustices inflicted on one group of people by another. What are the sociocultural and political conditions that allow one group of people to reduce others to nonentities? In my own Jewish tradition, we often recite on the Passover holiday, "Remember that you were once slaves in Egypt and teach this diligently to your children," so that we can be vigilant about those who forget the lessons of various tyrannies committed over the years. The last ten years have seen a growing number of books written for children about the Holocaust caused by Hitler and the Nazis. *Rose Blanche* by Roberto Innocenti (1985) is a picture storybook that captures this horrible time in a way that encourages even young children to talk about and wonder about what happened. But we also need to be concerned about the treatment in the United States of various parallel groups over the years. We can institute time for the discussion of current events in our classrooms and can use magazines and newspapers extensively, as well as books, to explore these controversies.

Melor Sturua, a political journalist for *Izvestia* for over forty years who is now working on his autobiography at the University of Minnesota, quotes Chekhov by saying that all his life "he squeezed the slave out of himself drop by drop" (1991). Sturua uses this metaphor to explain the influence of Stalin over the Soviets. I would like to use the metaphor to help us all to recognize the attitudes and values that we need to squeeze out of ourselves drop by drop in order to establish a classroom community in which multiculturalism will have a chance to flourish and have a real impact on the lives of our students.

In 1991 Ron Somers, a sportswriter for the *Arizona Daily Star*, reviewed a new publication called *I Had a Hammer: The Hank Aaron Sto-*

ry, by Hank Aaron and Lonnie Wheeler (HarperCollins, 1991). Somers quotes Aaron, who began to receive the vilest hate mail when he was closing in on Babe Ruth's home-run record: "The Ruth chase should have been the greatest period of my life, and it was the worst. I couldn't believe there was so much hatred in people. It's something I'm still trying to get over, and maybe I never will. I know I'll never forget it, and the fact is, I don't want to." The review ends: "That's the compelling theme of the book. [Hank Aaron] appears to transcend racism by becoming a sports hero. Yet he is forever haunted by the hatred he faced just because he had black skin and could hit a ball over a fence."

In addition to the issue of racism here, the language used is another concern that I would explore with students. The reproduction of one of the hate letters in the newspaper article reads: "Hey nigger boy, We at the KKK Staten Island Division want you to know that no number of guards can keep you dirty [expletive] nigger [expletive] alive" (quoted in Somers 1991). What is interesting is that the expletives that are not printed are probably words that my students and I use without much thought, but the word *nigger* is one that I always hesitate saying, even in settings such as this one where it serves an important purpose. Yet in the newspaper, common swear words are omitted and a term of great derision is allowed to stand.

A biography called *Sorrow's Kitchen* that was written for adolescents by Mary E. Lyons (1990) has helped me gain access to a range of concerns about racism, feminism, and dialect variation. In this unusual and powerful biography, Lyons not only tells the history of a great writer and anthropologist, Zora Neale Hurston, but embeds the stories and folklore written by Hurston within the chronology of the biography.

This book enlightens the reader about African American writers during the 1920s. It explores why a woman who writes passionately about her southern roots, language, and experiences was rejected by other African American authors, mainly males. Hurston was part of the Harlem Renaissance in the 1920s, which Lyons describes: "Harlem became a cultural magnet that attracted unknown musicians and artists. . . . Here they were free to develop their artistry and become part of the 'golden legend' of Harlem" (p. 34). Harlem attracted poets and novelists who, in a ten-year period, wrote some of the most memorable literary works of this century.

Hurston, who went to Howard and Columbia Universities, had poor and rural southern roots. Even at Howard, a prestigious African American institution, she was different—a woman from the rural South, which allowed her to create "unforgettable folk characters and speech." However, many African American writers, such as W. E. B. Du Bois, Ralph Ellison, and Richard Wright, were unhappy when blacks were portrayed "as common folks working in bean fields" (p. 97). To them, racial stereotype included folklore and writing in dialect. In 1973, author Alice Walker rediscovered Hurston as an important literary figure.

Hurston's books, some fictional with the flavor of folktales and others anthropological research accounts, provide a rich description of the culture, language, beliefs, and religious orientations of rural southern African Americans at the beginning of this century. Mary Lyons brings this significant figure to adolescents and their teachers.

Multicultural education should be the central theme in social studies and literacy education. It allows our studies of history, geography, political science, government, archeology, and anthropology, among others, to include wide ranges of perspectives. It suggests that in order for students to become active, democratic adult citizens, they must be able to understand and take part in the controversies that represent a diversity of perspectives.

Call to Action

One book that documents the notion that problem solving concerning multicultural issues includes action is a Venezuelan book titled *La Calle Es Libre* [*The Streets Are Free*] (Kurusa 1981). This book helps teachers and students realize that the solutions to many problems rest in the hands of each and every member of the society. It clearly explores the need that people have to act in concert with others in order to solve their own problems.

The children in this book live in a poverty area of a big city. They have no place to play in their community of crowded streets and houses. With the help of a librarian and an aggressive newspaper reporter, the children confront city officials and organize their parents. After going through a series of problematic events, they eventually are able to have their own *parque*. They invite all to their free park with a sign on the fence that reads:

> El parque es libre [The park is free]
> Pasen todos [Everyone come on in]
> Muy felices [very happily].

All students, including those from the middle class, need to explore what contributions come from the many and varied groups with whom they share this world. They need to experience what collaboration and interdependence can accomplish. As schools and teachers organize for a powerful multicultural curriculum involving various parallel cultural groups, it is necessary to explore the role of power, what happens to those who face a sense of powerlessness, and the ways in which power is shared in a democracy.

Literature is a place to start such understanding and a place to which the teacher and the students return time and time again for new insights and understanding. They can assume responsibility collaboratively to respond to issues that rise out of the literature. Students and teachers may find that they need to rewrite the text in new ways to more accurately reflect the realities of the present or to discover unusual new texts.

But we cannot build a strong multicultural curriculum until we are committed to understanding the many lessons available to us from the many groups that we face in our classrooms. We need to see each of our students as a representative of his or her own cultural life. We need to be willing to rejoice in the cultures represented in our classrooms and to learn from them so that our students will in turn find reason to learn from us. It is really in the hands of each and every one of us to take responsibility to actively and democratically build a multicultural curriculum.

References

America before Columbus. 1991, July 8. *U.S. News & World Report,* p. 22.

Banks, James A. 1988. *Multiethnic education: Theory and practice* (2nd ed.). Boston: Allyn & Bacon.

Banks, James & Banks, Cherry A. (Eds.). 1993. *Multicultural education: Issues and perspectives* (2nd Ed.). Boston: Allyn & Bacon.

Bigelow, Bill, Miner B. & Peterson, B. (Eds.). 1991. *Rethinking Columbus: Teaching about the 500th anniversary of Columbus's arrival in America.* Milwaukee: Rethinking Schools.

Fortune, Jessie. 1975. Among the children of the East Side Jews. *Jewish Currents, 29,* 4–7. (Originally published 1905)

Hoffman, Eva. 1989. *Lost in translation: A life in a new language.* New York: Dutton.

Innocenti, Roberto. 1985. *Rose Blanche.* New York: Tabori & Chang.

Kurusa. 1986. *La calle es libre.* Caracas: Ediciones Ekare Banco del Libro.

Lyons, Mary. 1990. *Sorrow's kitchen: The life and folklore of Zora Neale Hurston.* New York: Scribner's.

Moll, Luis C., Velez-Ibanez, C., Greenberg, J. & Whitmore, K. 1990. *Community knowledge and classroom practice* (Final Report No. 300 87-0131, Office of Bilingual Education and Minority Language Affairs). Tucson: College of Education, University of Arizona.

Somers, R. 1991, July 28. [Review of the book *I Had a Hammer: The Hank Aaron Story*]. *Arizona Daily Star*, p. 10E.

Sturua, Melor G. 1991, July 28. How a tyrant made us believe in him. *Parade*, p. 4.

Will, George. 1991, July 18. Multicultural history becomes a political tool. *Arizona Daily Star*, p. 13A.

Part Two

Miscue Analysis, Reading Strategies, and Comprehension (1972–1994)

I remember late in the 1960s being part of the data collection and analysis team at the Reading Miscue Research Center at Wayne State University in Detroit, Michigan. During our meetings, we came to realize the power of what we were learning about the reading process and the impact this knowledge would have on reading instruction. All of us had been classroom teachers and often discussed what we would have done differently if we had known as teachers what we were now learning as reading researchers. We believed that if teachers could develop their own insights about the reading process from their own immersion in miscue analysis, this would inform their teaching in ways that would benefit their students. We planned presentations at professional conferences, organized workshops for schools and school districts, developed syllabi for university courses, and started writing about what we were discovering. Not only were some of the articles in this volume conceived at that time, but books such as the *Reading Miscue Inventory Manual* (Goodman & Burke 1972) and *Reading Strategies: Focus on Comprehension* (Goodman & Burke 1980) also came to life.

Every reader with whom we worked became a case study. Although we wrote about what we were learning, we should have published more about each case and about the implications of what we were learning for reading instruction. I didn't realize in those early days the impact of professional articles on teacher audiences. Now I encourage all the doctoral students and classroom teachers with whom I work to write about what they do and what informs their work. Perhaps if we had written more about the early miscue analysis research, the wider public would be more aware of the relationship miscue analysis has to our understanding of how people read.

I hope that throughout my writing, the respect I have for teachers and for their professional capabilities to make curricular decisions is evident. I believe that only the teacher in transaction with learners can ultimately make a difference in education. I am often in awe of the ability of teachers to assimilate ideas about miscue analysis in their daily work with the students in their classrooms. That has become a highlight in my emerging work related to retrospective miscue analysis (Goodman & Marek 1996). My interest in helping teachers understand the reading process through miscue analysis has expanded to involve readers in understanding their own reading by retrospectively reflecting on what their miscues and the strategies they use mean about themselves as readers.

Miscue analysis research is where I started my writing career, and I have continued to conduct research and publish in this area throughout my career. I teach courses in miscue analysis, conduct workshops, and inform my beliefs about pedagogy based on what I continue to learn from readers about the reading process and from teachers who use knowledge gained from miscue analysis to inform their teaching.

Miscue analysis has helped me understand the significance of experimentation: playing around with ideas about learning. All learning processes involve taking risks, erring in order to explore and wonder. I no longer consider a miscue something that simply happens in reading. It is the essence of all learning. It needs to be respected, nurtured, and understood.

References

Goodman, Yetta M. & Burke, Carolyn L. 1972. *Reading Miscue Inventory manual: Procedures for diagnosis and evaluation*. New York: Macmillan.

Goodman, Yetta M. & Burke, Carolyn. 1980. *Reading strategies: Focus on comprehension*. New York: Holt, Rinehart & Winston.

Goodman, Yetta M. & Marek, Ann. 1996. *Retrospective miscue analysis: Revaluing readers and reading*. Katonah, NY: Richard C. Owen.

Qualitative Reading Miscue Analysis for Teacher Training

For years, teachers of reading have been trained to teach children the physical components of reading print. The only argument about method concerned whether the input had to be words as a unit or words broken into their constituent parts. Regardless, the view was to teach youngsters either how to recognize words or how to sound out letters or groups of letters. To be sure, there was concern with meaning, contextual clues, and so on, but the lack of understanding that reading is a language process allowed teachers to emphasize word attack skills, either *look-say* or *phonics.* Children had to discover on their own the interrelationships of the language aspects that formed the communicative utterance they needed to grasp in order to read.

The use of principles and methodology from various social science disciplines has helped us to question many of the notions we used to have. Linguists, anthropologists, psychologists, sociologists, and other social scientists have learned that it is necessary to describe behavior in order to attempt to understand behavior, categorize it, and make hypotheses that are accepted or rejected through further research.

In the reading field up to now, we have stated assumptions, placed a value judgment on them, and then described and prescribed based on the value judgment. We must help teachers move away from this unscientific way of viewing reading and readers to a more scientific approach.

Originally published in *Language and Learning to Read: What Teachers Should Know About Language,* edited by Richard E. Hodges & E. Hugh Rudorf (Boston: Houghton Mifflin, 1972), pp. 160–65. Copyright 1972 by Houghton Mifflin Company. Reprinted with permission.

The Teacher as Reading Researcher

Teachers of reading have available to them the most basic source of reading research data—the child as he reads. The best way to become aware of the reading process is to watch and listen to children reading orally. Their miscues, which have usually been thought of as reading mistakes, are extremely revealing. Instead of attacking the miscues children make when they read as something that must be eradicated, teachers of reading must learn to describe overt reading behavior and then to understand this behavior by asking such questions as:

1. Why do readers make miscues?
2. What categories or patterns do the miscues make?
3. What is the significance of the miscues?

Teachers of reading and reading specialists can discover many aspects of reading if they examine the reading process through *qualitative miscue analysis*.

Miscue Analysis: The Technique

In order to provide data for qualitative miscue analysis, the reader is presented with something interesting to read that is entirely new to him. The selection of reading material is important and must be thought out carefully. It should be neither too easy nor too difficult for the reader. The reader is then asked to read the selection, and the reading is audiotaped. At the time of audiotaping, the teacher or researcher sits with a copy of the reading material and marks each miscue. The reader receives no help from the researcher, since important evidence is gained as readers discover ways to solve their own reading problems.

A miscue is an observed oral response that the researcher hears that does not conform to what is expected. The reader is asked to read orally since this is the only way miscues can be identified. After the miscues have been marked and subsequently rechecked by listening to the tape, each miscue is qualitatively analyzed. This is done by asking a series of questions related to psycholinguistic principles.

Miscue Analysis: Meaning

The first question might deal with how much the meaning of the text has been changed by the miscue. If the text meaning has been changed a great deal, the miscue is placed on a code sheet for further analysis, but in the case of miscues like the following we may prefer another course:

Text: "Our Kitten!" the Jones children said.

Reader: "Our kitten!" the Jones kids said.

Text: In a little while he was asleep.

Reader: In a little while he was sleeping.

Text: The three brothers went home.

Reader: The three brother went home.

There has been no change of meaning in the preceding examples. Since the major purpose in the teaching of reading is for meaning to be extracted from the printed page, there need be no concern with these miscues and such behavior should not be considered as weakness. Such miscues may, in fact, point to the strengths readers have as they move toward the ability of going directly from print to meaning. In the oral encoding, the reader in the examples has used an alternative surface structure. Most dialect miscues belong in this category and would suggest that reading is not the place to be concerned with changing a child's dialect. The ability to read in one's own dialect is a strength. The reader translates the language of the text into his own language for greater understanding. Correcting dialect while a child reads tends to confuse him and interferes with his development of reading proficiency. Examining the degree to which the miscue changes the meaning of the text often gives a good deal of insight into how important meaning is to the reader. Also, the experiential background of a child is often revealed through his miscues.

Miscue Analysis: Grammar

After the miscues that do not change the meaning of the text are set aside, then the remainder of the miscues may be put through another group of questions. When miscues do change the meaning of the text to some degree, the next questions deal with the acceptability of the passage that resulted from the miscue, keeping in mind the child's language and experiential background. Children bring their understanding of grammar and meaning to the reading task, and a large percentage of their miscues reflect this understanding. Children's miscues often produce grammatically acceptable sentences even when they are not acceptable in terms of meaning.

Text: showing calmness and courage

Reader: showing climeness and congress

The reader in the preceding example came up with two words that semantically could not fit the passage. Yet, *climeness* has a morphemic ending that corresponds to *calmness*; and both *climeness* and *congress* function as nouns, as do the words they replaced—*calmness* and *courage*. Even beginning readers produce miscues that are the same functional part of speech as the expected response. This phenomenon increases as children become more proficient readers.

The grammatical system of a reader's language has great influence on the reading process. All readers, even at beginning stages, bring this strength with them to the reading task.

Text: I opened the dictionary and picked out a word that sounded good.

Reader: I opened a dictionary to pick out the word that sounded good.

Text: I mean I really yelled it.

Reader: I mean I'll really yell it out.

Value judgments will come into play in the examination of a child's miscues. Do the above examples make enough of a difference to the text to be concerned about? Is the subtle difference between *a* and *the* important enough to call attention to it? Is it very important to the whole story that at this particular point in time the reader put the second of the above examples into the future tense? Obviously it is necessary to know more about the story, which means that this analysis cannot be done by looking at miscues apart from the context of the reading material. It may also suggest that reading cannot be taught apart from the context of reading materials.

When miscues result in passages that are fully acceptable within the child's language and experiential background and do not cause too great a change in the meaning of the text material, these miscues may also be put aside as ones that are not important enough to be concerned with. Again, strengths are revealed in the reader rather than weaknesses.

Miscue Analysis: Correction Strategies

When miscues that do change the text to a great extent or that do not produce acceptable passages are examined, an additional question must be asked: Does the reader make any attempt to correct these particular miscues? The self-correction strategy is observed through the phenomenon of regressing, of looking back over text previously read. This is a strength that the reader learns as he becomes more proficient. Virtually every regression a reader makes is for the purpose of grasping better understanding of the reading material. Often correction strategies give insight into how much the reader is concerned with meaning or comprehension, as well as evidence that the child applies his sophisticated knowledge of the grammatical system to reading. When proficient readers use correction strategies, they are likely to correct miscues that result in semantically unacceptable passages but even more likely to correct syntactically unacceptable miscues.

Children often correct during subsequent tries at the same word. Examining the different attempts at one try or different attempts at different tries can give insights into the reader's use of phonics skills as well as his priorities in the reading task. Sometimes readers abandon a word that has close phonemic similarity to the expected response to move to a word that makes sense in the passage. This ability is a strength in reading.

Concepts of words or phrases are often developed through the reading of a story. In one story used in our research, the basic concept of the story was related to the fact that a "typical baby" turns into a baby who isn't so typical. Most of the readers had never heard or seen the word *typical* before. It was not pronounced correctly—most readers said *topical* or *typeical* for *typical*. Yet, at the end of the story, most of the children could explain that the baby was an ordinary baby or a normal baby or a usual baby.

Those miscues that are corrected by the reader either immediately or at subsequent tries can be set aside. Again, the child indicates an additional strength—his self-correction strategy. This will serve him in good stead in his silent reading.

Other Reasons for Miscues

The next questions deal with specific aspects of the reading process. Miscues are sometimes caused by something that the child sees peripherally and that he draws into his reading, either inserting the word or phrase or substituting it. This sometimes gives insight into the visual range the reader perceives as he reads. Young readers and less proficient readers sometimes associate words with an incorrect printed representation. For example, a child might read *happy birthday* every time the word *happy* appears in print. *Then* and *when, said* and *is,* are some common habitual associations. These are problems that persist for some children over a long period of time. Special material may have to be written for an individual youngster to help her differentiate words like these from each other. Drilling on these out of context only tends to reinforce the association. Questions dealing with how the reader handles peripheral and habitual association miscues will give insights into a child's reading ability.

The last questions deal with the relationship of the miscue to the printed text in terms of the graphic system and the sound system. All readers pay attention to the graphic shape of what they read, and miscues most often look like the words or phrases they replace. Knowledge of sound-letter correspondence is not highly sophisticated in early reading. Qualitative miscue analysis gives the teacher the opportunity to decide how close to the printed text the miscue is phonemically. *Men* for *man* is a much closer miscue than *monkey* for *man*. We need to find ways in the teaching of reading to help beginning readers zero in on phonemic similarity and not have a model of perfection from the earliest stages. Children who overuse phonic and graphic clues often do this at the expense of comprehension.

Conclusions

Preservice and inservice teachers often become enthusiastic about the use of qualitative miscue analysis as they begin to make all types of discoveries about reading. Such analysis:

1. Produces greater insight into the process of reading and the acquisition of reading proficiency.
2. Recognizes the strengths and weaknesses of the individual reader.
3. Helps readers use the reading process with greater awareness.
4. Focuses on the important and significant aspects of the reading process.

Only when preservice or inservice teachers gain insight into the reading process and are aware of the interrelatedness of its various aspects that qualitative miscue analysis provides can they begin to diagnose and plan programs for individuals within their classes.

I Never Read Such a Long Story Before

He came into the room. It was packed; to Frankie it seemed to be wall-to-wall teachers. He wondered if any of his own teachers were there, but he was too anxious to look around and study every face. There was a big man way over in the corner. He wondered if that was Mr. Bender, his English teacher. He didn't get along too well with Mr. Bender. Mr. Bender was always upset if you were even a little bit tardy.

He wondered what he was doing in this room. How could he help these teachers learn about reading? He didn't read too good himself. But Mr. Castillo had asked him if he would read a story for a bunch of teachers who were trying to learn about how kids read. Well, he knew he read lousy. He didn't read much anyway except for magazines at the drug store. But Mr. Castillo had said he could be a big help. He would do anything for Mr. Castillo. Mr. Castillo was the junior high counselor. He had known him since seventh grade. Mr. Castillo was always helping him get back into class. He liked the buzz group Mr. Castillo held two times a week. He never missed that if he could help it. They talked about important things like why they had problems with teachers, about girls, problems with parents, even being Mexican. He only missed the buzz group when he had to take Mama to the hospital. She went to that shrink every week. He wondered if the shrink spoke Spanish. How would the shrink understand Mama without knowing Spanish?

He got to the table. There was the lady Mr. Castillo had told him about. She was going to help the teachers learn about reading.

Originally published in *English Journal* 63 (1974), 65–71. Copyright 1974 by the National Council of Teachers of English. Reprinted with permission.

"Hi!" she said to him. "My name is Yetta Goodman."

He brushed his long straight black hair from his eyes and nodded a greeting.

"You're Francisco?" the lady asked.

"Yes" he answered, "my name is Francisco, but most people call me Frankie."

"What would you prefer I call you?" the lady asked.

"Frankie," he responded.

Frankie was an eighth grader in a Southern California junior high school. He lived alone with his mother. She was an outpatient at a psychiatric clinic; she spoke Spanish most of the time. Frankie's cumulative folder indicated that he did not do well in written language, either composition or spelling. His grade-level reading test score a month earlier had been 5.3.

His profile indicated that he was the kind of young man who would help the teachers of this workshop begin to focus on the reading process. Since I knew the student would be reading before a large group of teachers, I also asked Mr. Castillo for an outgoing student, one with good self-confidence. I selected a story, "Anita's Gift" (Goodman & Burke 1973), from a literature series for junior high students because there was some Spanish language in the story. In addition, although the story dealt with a Puerto Rican rather than a Mexican American family, I hoped that the reader would be able to relate to the young man in the story, who is assuming responsibility and solving problems for the family.

I started the taping session immediately, expecting that Frankie might be somewhat nervous.

"Frankie," I said, "All the teachers are here because we want to find out how people read when no one helps them. I'm going to ask you to read out loud, and I'll be taping your reading so we can listen to it after you've returned to your classes. When you finish your reading, I'll ask you to tell me everything you remember about the story. Remember that I won't help you. If you come to a problem as you read, work it out the best you can."

The tape recorder was started and Frankie began to read.

Reading Miscue Analysis

So began a workshop in miscue analysis to help secondary teachers understand more about the reading process. Miscue analysis helps the reading teacher examine the reading process almost as a scientist might look through a microscope in order to examine biological phenomena.

Evaluating students' miscues when they read orally gives the teacher the opportunity to discover why students make miscues as they read and to infer something about their ability from the quality of the miscues they make.

A miscue is any unexpected response that is heard during oral reading. For example, if the text says, *Where did those come from?* and a reader reads, *Where did these come from?* the spoken word *these* is a miscue for the text word *those*. Through miscues, teachers can see if readers are using language knowledge. In evaluating *these* as a miscue for *those*, it is obvious that the two words have a very high degree of graphic similarity (they both look very much alike) as well as a great deal of sound similarity. In addition, both words function the same way grammatically in the sentence in which they occur. This miscue produced what is essentially an "acceptable" sentence, since it only minimally changed the meaning of the story in which it occurred (Goodman & Burke 1972). In miscue analysis, every miscue that a student produces is analyzed using questions that provide information relating to the graphophonic, syntactic, and semantic systems of language.

In this article I will use selections from Frankie's reading to provide evidence about the amount of language information he brings to his reading. At the same time, I will suggest means by which proficient secondary students use language in reading and I will finally make suggestions for classroom teachers.

To learn about Frankie's pattern of reading strategies, I evaluated the first fifty consecutive miscues he made during his reading of the story "Anita's Gift."

This evaluation provides a pattern of reading miscues. I asked the student to read something orally that he had never seen.[1] Figure 1 is a section of "Anita's Gift" showing how Frankie's miscues were marked on a copy of the story. Frankie read directly from the printed text.

Quantity of Miscues

"Anita's Gift" is a story of approximately 1,550 words. In the total story Frankie made 7.8 miscues per hundred words (not including re-

---

[1] Oral reading provides the opportunity to examine miscues, but it does pose limitations, since the reader's understanding may be greater through silent reading. However, by giving the student a total story, article, or self-contained chapter to read, a continuous language context is available in which the reader can become involved, thus providing a picture of what reading would look like when the student reads independently. Students are never aided during their reading, because the purpose is to discover what strategies readers use when they do not have a teacher or other outside resources available to help them.

Figure 1.
Frankie's Reading of "Anita's Gift"

There was no jumping around this morning and no whistling.
He
They walked in silence, and each step seem⟨ed⟩ⓓ to Pablo to be

bringing them near something serious and he wished they were

running the other way.

At last they reached the florist⟨'s⟩ⓓ corner. The door of the

shop was open. A gray-haired man was ⟨setting⟩ⓒ *sitting* cans of flowers on
                                                                    ⓒ *They*
the sidewalk, *There* where Anita said they had been yesterday. The two
                                                      ⓒ *and they*   *they*
stood behind him ⟩ as he pushed the can⟨s⟩ this way ⟨and⟩ that and
                                                                              ⓒ *seem.*
arranged blossoms in several of the cans. Would he never ⟩ see
Then
them?

(Substitutions are marked over the word; omissions are

circled; insertions are indicated with a ∧, corrections

are shown by underlining the portion repeated and the

mark ⓒ , ⓓ indicates a dialect-influenced miscue.)

peated identical miscues).[2] Numbers of miscues can vary from one
group of a hundred words in a story to the next group of a hundred
words. Frankie's miscues within every hundred words in the story
ranged from three to fourteen. Table 1 shows Frankie's miscues per
hundred words calculated for each four hundred words of the story.
In the last section of the story Frankie made almost nine miscues per

[2] Many reading evaluations suggest that the number of miscues made per hundred
words can provide information about the ease or difficulty of a passage. My own research does not support such an assumption (Goodman 1972).

Table 1. Frankie's Miscues per Hundred Words

	Number of Miscues	Miscues per Hundred Words
First 400 words	25	6.3
Second 400 words	35	8.8
Third 400 words	29	7.3
Fourth 400 words	31	8.9
TOTAL	120	7.8

hundred words, while in the first quarter of the story his miscues were about six miscues per hundred words.

Implications for Instruction. Frequency of miscues in and of itself is not an especially useful measure. Teachers should not be too quick to judge or evaluate a student's reading ability based on numbers of miscues. Students who are very adept at silent reading have learned to read quickly and often produce many miscues that show sophisticated language transformations. The grammatical structure, style of writing, and concept load of any particular part of a story all are involved in the complex reasons that cause readers to produce miscues and that cause miscue numbers to vary from one part of a story to another.[3]

Using oral reading for evaluative purposes, however, can provide insight into which miscues do or do not interfere with the reader's ability to reconstruct the author's meaning. By looking at the *pattern* of miscues through such a screen, the teacher can begin to understand not only the reading process but the degree to which the student is proficiently comprehending.

Graphic and Sound Similarity

Through miscue analysis, we can evaluate the use readers make of the graphic and sound systems of language. The questions asked to evaluate these two aspects of language in reading are: To what degree do

---

[3] Interpretative or dramatic reading may call for carefully acted out oral reading; however, this is a specialized kind of reading and is never used by most readers. Flawless surface reading focuses on careful pronunciation and away from the major priority of reading—the reader's search for meaning.

the two words (the text word and the miscue) look alike? and To what degree do the two words sound alike?

In Frankie's case, 81 percent of the expected and observed responses of word substitutions looked very much alike. Such substitutions included:

TEXT	MISCUE
then	when
the	he
voice	voices
they	then
the	their
though	thought

Ten percent of his substitution miscues showed no graphic similarity at all. Every one of these words, however, was either the same part of speech as the text word or produced grammatically acceptable sentences. These included:

TEXT	MISCUE
of	at
a	the
and	that

High sound similarity between the text word and miscue was 57 percent while 20 percent of the miscues had no sound similarity. Miscues with no sound similarity included many of the same miscues that had no graphic similarity, but also included words that had high graphic similarity but no sound similarity such as the substitution of *the* for *he* and *thought* for *though*. In all miscue analysis studies, virtually all readers, regardless of ability, more frequently produce miscues that look like the text word than ones that sound like the text word. In other words, readers tend to pay more attention to the graphic system than to the sound system as they read. Proficient readers seldom produce substitution miscues that consistently show high sound and graphic similarity. Often substitution miscues that have very few look-alike or sound-alike qualities are the very best miscues. Examples of such miscues include *baby* for *child, home game* for *home opener, third floor* for *third level.*

Implication for Instruction. Some readers in junior high and high school are more concerned with the way words look than they are with the meaning of what they are reading. This tends to be especially true of readers who have been considered problems for whatever reasons. Much remediation helps students concentrate on the way words look, on sounding-out techniques, or on syllabication rules. It seems that when students concentrate on the graphic system, they become less aware that reading is supposed to make sense. This interferes with their development as proficient readers. Secondary school students would benefit most from reading instruction that helps them concentrate on comprehending what they are reading rather than on careful surface accuracy. It is *not* important for a reader to be able to sound out carefully a word like *contented* that may appear six or seven times in a story. A reader needs to be encouraged to keep reading and decide what the word means from the cumulating context. Any reading instruction that does not emphasize comprehension and the use of context through which to build meaning as the main concern for readers will shortchange the student and will help produce reading problems rather than eliminate them.

Dialect

In the first fifty miscues Frankie produced in "Anita's Gift," four of the miscues were related to his dialect. One of the dialect miscues was the insertion of the modifier *the* prior to a proper name, which is probably an influence from his knowledge of Spanish.

Text: . . . to go down the stairs to Ferris Center.

Frankie: . . . to go down the stairs to *the* Ferris Center.

The other dialect miscues included reduction of consonant clusters in certain environments, particularly the omissions of *ed* and *s* endings. In the miscues that occurred after the initial fifty, Frankie produced eight more dialect-related miscues, which all involved the omission of *ed*, the *s* on plural nouns, or the possessive *s*. In all cases the sentences were read with intonation indicating that Frankie was comprehending what he was reading. His retelling of the story that followed his reading also confirmed a good understanding of the story. The dialect miscues never got in the way of his understanding tense changes or numbers in the story. All the Spanish words in the story like the names *Anita, Mamita, Pablo, Pablito, Don Antonio*, and one Spanish phrase, "y yo tengo, tambien" were read appropriately. Frankie shifted to Spanish phonology whenever he read those words although he had never had any formal teaching in Spanish.

Implication for Instruction. Dialect in and of itself does not seem to present a significant problem for readers (Goodman 1973). It is only when a teacher focuses a reader's attention on producing some standard dialect that may be artificial that the student focuses on surface features in reading and loses concern for comprehending. When a student produces features of his own dialect as he reads, he is providing evidence for the teacher that he is understanding so well that he is translating the written code into his own oral code. Reading instruction should *never* be the time to attempt to change a student's pronunciation.

Use of the Grammatical System

Even ineffective readers' substitution miscues usually retain the same part of speech as the text word that they replace. Seventy percent of Frankie's substitution miscues were the same part of speech as the word they replaced. This indicates that he was making use of the grammatical cueing system. Also, half of the miscues that were not the same part of speech were self-corrected.

Related to substitution of grammatical function is the reader's ability to produce acceptable sentences regardless of miscues. Although Frankie's score for appropriate part of speech indicated that he was predicting grammatical function rather successfully, the miscues did not always produce acceptable sentences. However, it is significant to explore which portion of the story produced the greatest number of unacceptable sentences. For this purpose, the first twenty-five miscues of Frankie's reading, which occurred in the first four hundred words of the story, were scored separately from the second twenty-five miscues. Fifty-six percent of the first group of miscues produced acceptable sentences. Sixteen percent were grammatically but not semantically acceptable and 28 percent showed weaknesses both grammatically and semantically. Sentences with miscues that showed weaknesses included:

Text: Then he saw them.

Frankie: When he saw . . . (no). Then he saw . . . Then he saw them (no wait) . . . Then he saw then.

Text: By this time Anita was clinging to Pablo crying against his sleeve.

Frankie: By the time Anita was climbing into Pablo's . . . clinging into Pablo's crying against his sleeve.

Text: How Pablo wished for Papa to tell them what to do.

Frankie: No Pablo wished for Papa to tell them what to do.

During the reading of the next three hundred words, Frankie made twenty-five additional miscues but this time 92 percent showed both grammatical and semantic acceptability, and the remaining 8 percent were grammatically acceptable although not acceptable semantically. During the second twenty-five miscues, Frankie began to make miscues that resulted in sentences like the following:

Text: The flowers would wither and be thrown out and that would be all there would be to it.

Frankie: The flowers would wither and be thrown out. That would be all there would be to it.

Text: . . . the flower man is a kind man and does not hate Puerto Ricans.

Frankie: . . . the flower man is a kind man that doesn't hate Puerto Ricans.

It is clear by examining the second twenty-five miscues and those even later in the story that Frankie was learning to read by *reading*; he developed control over reading the syntactic structure of the author. He learned to predict and handle the structure well enough that his miscues produced acceptable sentences. The sample of Frankie's reading provided at the beginning of this article occurred in the third quarter of the story. By reading that section over again, including Frankie's miscues, you can see how he was controlling syntactic structure.

Implications for Instruction. Such a dramatic change from the first twenty-five miscues of a story to the second twenty-five miscues is evidence that reading something one has never read before can be an excellent self-teaching device. The ability to develop the necessary strategies to handle the structure of the author as he began to move into the story indicates that the best way for Frankie to learn about variability in language structure is to have available a variety of language materials to read. The content of the materials needs to be within the interest and concept level of the student, but the greater the variety of types of reading materials, the more opportunity students will have to expand their ability to handle varieties of material. Students should be encouraged to read magazines, newspapers, and various types of books. By limiting students to a standard text and a few required stories, teachers are severely limiting the students' opportunities to become flexible readers.

Frankie was able to verbalize for Mr. Castillo a level of awareness of his own limitations. After Frankie had finished his reading before the teachers, Mr. Castillo drove him back to school. On the way, Mr. Castillo said to Frankie, "You did a pretty good job of that." Frankie replied, "No, I really messed it up." Mr. Castillo said, "But you seemed to understand it." "Yes," said Frankie, "but I found it sort of confusing because I'm not used to reading stuff where people always keep interrupting each other. You know," he continued, "that story was interesting and if I could find more things like that I might read them. *I never read such a long story before.*"

Frankie was aware that there was something unusual about the grammatical structure of the story and that he wasn't used to reading materials that had a good deal of dialogue. The experience of reading such materials provided him with the opportunity to learn to read such materials. No direct or formal teaching was necessary. The reader interacting with an author from whom he wishes to gain a message or meaning can learn a lot about the language of the author. Relegating readers to materials with short words and sentences on the basis that this is easy for students may actually get in the way of students' developing the ability to handle various materials. Short, simple sentences can cause older readers confusion because they expect more from written language. It also conditions students to predict a somewhat limited number of sentences and author styles. If the *concept* of the material is within the student's knowledge system and if the reader is *interested* in the subject matter, he can often handle material that seems to be more sophisticated than his test scores might imply. The reverse of this is also true. No matter what reading test scores indicate, if the material is beyond the knowledge and interest of readers, they may not be able to comprehend what they are reading.

Frankie's comment about the length of "Anita's Gift" is a common one made by students who have been considered reading problems after they have read for a miscue analysis. Many students after completing a story have indicated, "Boy, that was really long, but I liked it" or "That's the first time I ever read a whole story by myself" or "I didn't know I could read something so long."

Often because students are having some difficulty with reading, it is assumed that skills materials that concentrate on words, sentences, or sometimes paragraphs will be the easiest for such students to read. All readers should be provided with materials of some length (more than four hundred words). When a story has length it can provide interesting content that may be relevant to the student. Longer written material can also provide the necessary context through which students can build concepts as well as become acquainted with stylistic differences. In a sense, reading longer materials is easier than reading words, sentences, or paragraphs.

Comprehension

The most significant aspect of reading is the comprehension the reader gains. Miscue analysis provides two measures of comprehension. One is a score based on the degree to which the miscues produced by readers change the meaning or intent of the author. After self-correction, 82 percent of Frankie's fifty miscues did *not* change the meaning or intent of the author. This score was substantiated by Frankie's retelling of the story after his reading, the second measure used in miscue analysis.

In an open-ended fashion, Frankie was asked to simply retell what he had read. He did a very adequate job of recalling the events and the characters, but more important, he was able to infer from the story aspects of characterization and theme. His retelling score was 90 out of a possible 100 points.

I asked Frankie why Pablo had to think about something to do (referring to something Frankie had said earlier about the main character). Frankie said, "'Cause he was, well, at that time he was the man in the house." Here he suggested one theme in the story.

In another question-answer sequence Frankie stated two more of the themes in the story.

YG: Was there some problem the story was trying to solve?

Frankie: It just proves that people are kind to other people, not just to their own race.

YG: Was that what the author was trying to say?

Frankie: No, the author meant that you shouldn't *get* anything. The grand-mother said in the story [Anita] shouldn't pick up anything without paying for it.

After Frankie left the room, the teachers and I talked about his comprehension. Most of the teachers were surprised that a reader could make so many miscues and still retain so much of the meaning of the story, but Frankie's own teachers were the most surprised. They all regarded Frankie as a student who was unable to handle most reading tasks. One of them said, "I always considered that he was just a nonreader." Another said, "But he never gives any indication that he reads or understands anything that he reads in class. Maybe it's because I expect that kind of behavior from him."

Implications for Instruction. Generally, miscue analysis has shown that many of the students in junior and senior high school who are diagnosed as being problem readers are able to do a lot better job of reading and thinking than they are given credit for. Students with whom I have worked who have profiles like Frankie's, when given an opportunity to read without interruption a whole story that has some relevance to them, are often able to comprehend and discuss significant issues from the story. Frequently, however, these students are defeated by the belief that they are bad readers. They may refuse to even make simple attempts at reading material unless they are working with someone they trust not to laugh or constantly correct their efforts.

Classroom time should be organized so that more actual reading takes place. Students should have the opportunity to read silently and independently in the classroom setting. If learning to read is a major priority in schools, then it seems logical that opportunity should be provided for students to read. The material to be read should be interesting to the students so that class discussions related to their reading could be as meaningful and interesting as Mr. Castillo's discussions, which Frankie never missed. This might not be too difficult a task if students were involved in the selection of a good deal of their own reading material. Teachers should become better acquainted with books written specifically for teenagers and dealing with their problems. These are becoming greater in number and more available for classroom use (Reid 1972).

In this article, I have attempted to provide some insights into the reading process through analyzing Frankie's reading. I have suggested some implications for teachers based on more than a decade of miscue analysis. I wish to conclude with three suggestions that teachers should keep in mind during the teaching of reading.

1. *Permit your students to read.* No one has learned to swim by practicing the skills of backstrokes, flutter kicks, or treading water while staying on the edge of the swimming pool. Yet, in the teaching of reading we often do just that. Rather than let readers "into the water," we keep them in skills books learning rules about letters, syllables, or definitions of words rather than letting them into the book itself, permitting them to be immersed in the language that comes from the author as the readers try to reconstruct the written message.

2. *Encourage your students to guess or predict.* Readers' guesses or predictions are based on the cumulative information and syntactic structure they have been learning as they have been reading. Therefore, their guesses are more often than not appropriate to the material. Students have to realize that risk taking in reading is appropriate; that using context to decide what words mean is a proficient reading strategy; and that they have the language sense to make appropriate guesses that can fit both the grammatical and semantic sense of what they are reading.

3. *Focus your students' attention on meaning.* Help your students understand that the only reason to read is for themselves. They have to have their own *purpose* to read, and reading *must make sense to them.* If reading does not make sense, they have to find ways of doing something about it. They should be encouraged either to reread or to continue reading to gain meaning. But they must re-

alize that the meaning is not in the teacher, but in the interaction between the reader and author. Students should be encouraged to ask themselves repeatedly, Does this make sense to me? Students should be encouraged to reject and to be intolerant of reading materials that do not make sense. It has always impressed me that when we adults cannot make sense out of what we are reading, like a text on statistics or Chomsky's latest article on transformational-generative grammar, we have the right to say, This is badly written, I really don't want to know that stuff, or It's beyond me, but when students say they can't read something, the student is said to have a reading problem.

The lesson that should be learned from the many Frankies in our schools is that much of what we do in the teaching of reading gets in the way of the student's learning. We can cause problems by underestimating students as well as by looking at reading as a careful, exact process. Kids have a lot going for them. If teachers can turn their hard work toward supporting the language strengths kids already have, providing kids with a feeling of success, finding materials and planning classroom experiences that will turn kids on to reading, then reading will develop with much greater ease than it does now.

References

Goodman, Kenneth S. (Ed.). 1973. *Miscue analysis: Applications to reading instruction.* Urbana, IL: ERIC Clearinghouse on Reading and Communication Skills.

Goodman, Kenneth S. & Buck, Catherine. 1973. Dialect barriers to reading comprehension revisited. *The Reading Teacher, 27,* 6–12.

Goodman, Yetta M. 1972. Reading diagnosis: Qualitative or quantitative? *The Reading Teacher, 26,* 32–37.

Goodman, Yetta M. & Burke, Carolyn L. 1972. *Reading Miscue Inventory manual: Procedures for diagnosis and evaluation.* New York: Macmillan.

Goodman, Yetta M. & Burke, Carolyn. 1973. Anita's gift. In *Reading Miscue Inventory: Readings for taping.* New York: Macmillan.

Reid, Virginia M. (Ed.). 1972. *Reading ladders for human relations* (5th ed.). Washington, D.C.: American Council on Education.

What Beginning English Teachers Need to Know About Reading: Mythologies and Reading

In order to build knowledge and insights about a field as common to all as reading, it is important to explore the commonsense beliefs people have so we may move beyond them. Since all beginning teachers are readers and have had reading instruction during their own schooling, their commonsense beliefs about reading come not only from outdated texts on reading and reading instruction but also from years of being a reader and being exposed to reading instruction.

But many of these commonsense beliefs are counter to what is now understood about the reading process and how people learn it. We'll examine here such myths about reading and suggest what some of the research into the reading process has to say about such beliefs.

Commonsense Belief #1: *Reading is an exact process.*

Generally it is believed that oral reading is or should be error free—that the reader is to reproduce orally exactly what is written in the text. Miscue analysis research has provided a mass of data to cast aside

Originally published in *English Education* 10 (1979), 203–6. Copyright 1979 by the National Council of Teachers of English. Reprinted with permission.

this notion. Only when a reader has chosen to produce a dramatic reading with repeated rehearsal and focus on expressive quality does reading become a perfect performance. Miscues, or responses to the text that are unexpected, have provided evidence that good readers produce miscues or errors that reflect that they comprehend as they read, while the miscues of less proficient readers often reflect a careful analysis of the surface features of the written language.

A related belief is that the reader is supposed to comprehend exactly what is written in the text or what is intended by the author. This denies the dynamics of reading and the significant role of the reader in developing his or her own comprehension. Reading is not passive; on the contrary the reader is active in creating meaning as she or he reaches out to understand the author. Comprehension results from this interaction through a text.

Commonsense Belief #2: *First readers learn to decode, then they learn to comprehend.*

In this view one first learns mechanical skills and then how to use them to comprehend text. Most reading instruction reflects this belief although there is no research that clearly supports it. This is especially an unproductive view for those readers identified as having reading difficulties. Such students are repeatedly given skills activities that focus on word attack, structural analysis, syllabication, phonics, and other abstract knowledge about language even though these students have failed to learn using such activities. Secondary teachers often assume that if students are unable to achieve on tests of these skills, the skills must not have been taught. Evaluation of the records of such students often provides the opposite picture. Such students have almost never been directed toward purposeful or self-selected reading experiences.

Readers learn what reading is when they know what reading does. Learning skills prior to understanding the significance of reading is meaningless. Learning does not take place if the individual does not believe that the experience will be significant. Children prior to coming to school are comprehending written language in their environment—signs, TV advertisements, names of cars and food products, labels. These are the important, significant functions of reading for preschoolers. It is through these experiences and subsequent experiences with understanding the purpose of books, letters, and newspapers that beginners become aware of the significance of reading. Through real reading experiences students become aware of the personal needs that reading serves. Only when reading is significant to the learner will an interest in the importance of the form and abstract units of language develop.

Commonsense Belief #3: *You have to be familiar with all the words and know all the vocabulary before you can read something.*

This view reduces language to strings of words and vocabulary. It suggests that meaning exists apart from language context. However, meaning is built and developed throughout a reader's interaction with the author through the medium of print. Words and vocabulary are developed, refined, and understood because they occur in the context of language that occurs in the context of situations. It is because the reader understands the pragmatics of a situation and has knowledge to bring to reading that a sentence like the first one of the following can be understood:

> The horse was slowly glearing down the road. The road was muddy and filled with holes. As the car came around the bend and the lights shined into the horse's eyes, it reared up and stopped altogether.

It is knowledge about horses and how they behave that provides the information about an unknown term such as *glearing*. Awareness of how other language units such as *slowly, reared up and stopped* relate to *glearing* provides additional information. Knowledge of how written language works suggests that if something is important the author will deal with it again and provide even more information to build an understanding of *glearing*. If nothing more is said about this, then the author has provided, through the cue of omission, information that *glearing* is not significant enough to get more attention. When readers focus on development of meaning through the context of written language, comprehension occurs.

Knowledge about language and reading has exploded in the last few years. It is being integrated with already existing knowledge about reading. As society demands more and more literacy from its citizens, more people take part in the debate about how people read, how people learn to read, and how people should be taught. Self-proclaimed reading experts provide contradictory views. It is certainly difficult for a beginning teacher to make decisions about what is appropriate. There is no substitute for knowledge, and for those interested in knowing about reading, it is important to keep up with the field.

As beginning teachers build their knowledge base about reading, there are some notions to keep in mind. Fortunately people can use knowledge before scientists can explain the process of how such knowledge is used. People have been reading long before any attempt to understand the reading process. In addition to theoretical knowledge about reading, a sensitive teacher can discover much about reading by observing students reading. It is easy to see that when students are interested in something, they find it easier to read. That's a place to start. If a student is focusing on trying to comprehend something significant to himself or herself, reading seems to be easier than when attempts are made to comprehend material that seems not to be very functional to the reader. A sensitive teacher can help students believe they can learn to read and view themselves as readers. If teachers keep three things in mind they can be confident of helping most pupils to better reading:

1. Keep the students' focus on meaning.
2. Encourage students to be confident risk takers as they read.
3. Keep students reading. That means finding a wide range of relevant materials for pupils to choose from.

Retellings of Literature
and the Comprehension Process

What is involved in a reader's comprehension of literature? What happens during the act of reading itself and what occurs at the end of the reading that has impact on a reader's comprehension? In what way do the features of written literature aid or interfere with readers' comprehension? Through miscue analysis (Goodman & Burke 1972), which always includes readers' retellings of what they have read, researchers and teachers can begin to find some answers to these questions. In this essay, I will share what insights I have gained into readers' comprehension processes from retellings of literature and then discuss the significance for instruction.

Two aspects of reading that help us understand comprehension processing have been identified by Kenneth Goodman, the developer of miscue analysis. These aspects are *comprehending,* the process of trying to make sense of a text, and *comprehension,* what the reader has understood the text to mean at any point in time. Retellings after reading provide another opportunity for the reader to continue to construct the text. They extend and enhance the reader's comprehending and comprehension processes while they provide evidence for and insights into understanding these two processes for teachers and researchers.

Comprehending is the process of how the reader integrates reading strategies such as predicting and confirming with language cueing systems: the graphophonic, syntactic, semantic, and pragmatic systems. Comprehending is revealed in the semantic and syntactic acceptability of language structures produced by the reader and reflected

Originally published in *Theory into Practice* 21 (Theme issue on Children's Literature) (1982), 301–7. Copyright 1982 by The Ohio State University. Reprinted with permission.

Figure 1.
First Reader of "Freddie Miller"

```
                                                      that
518   "I'LL GET MOTHER," HE CALLED TO ELIZABETH. HE KNEW ∧ THIS
           be
519   COULD BECOME A SERIOUS MATTER.
         uc  2.sister
             1.mother    cried
520   HIS SISTER'S CRIES GREW LOUDER. "DON'T LEAVE ME ALONE.

521   IT'S DARK IN HERE."
```

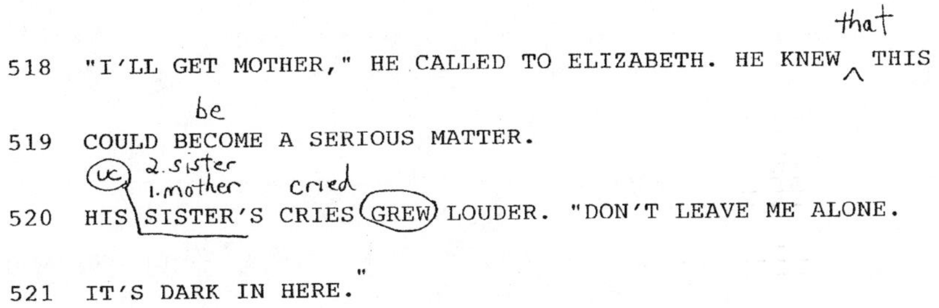

Figure 2.
Second Reader of "Freddie Miller"

```
518   "I'LL GET MOTHER," HE CALLED TO ELIZABETH. HE KNEW   THIS
           some    servant
519   COULD BECOME A SERIOUS MATTER.

520   HIS SISTER'S CRIES GREW LOUDER. "DON'T LEAVE ME ALONE.
      It is
521   IT'S DARK IN HERE."
```

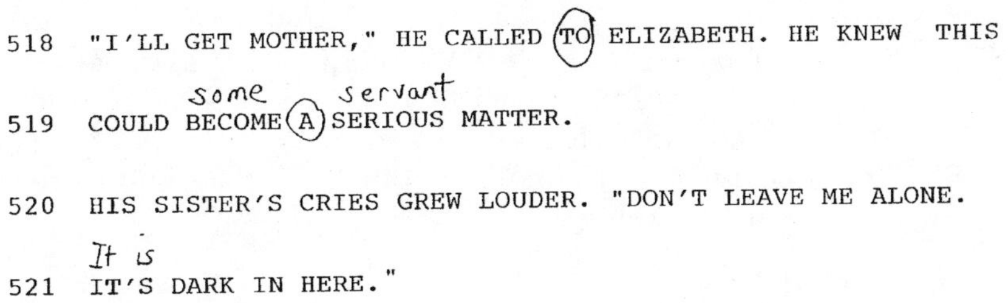

by the quality of miscues that readers produce and their patterns of self-correction. One major difference between good and poor readers is their control over the comprehending process. Proficient readers are able to integrate their uses of strategies and cueing systems to produce a text that generally results in semantically and syntactically acceptable structures.

Figures 1 and 2 illustrate how two fourth graders deal with a passage from the story "Freddie Miller, Scientist," by Lillian Moore (1965). In Figure 1, the reader changes syntactic structures (represented by the writing over the text sentences) but her predicting and confirming strategies help her produce a passage of text that only minimally alters the meaning of the passage. In Figure 2, although this less proficient reader does produce some acceptable structures, when she produces unacceptable structures she makes no attempt to correct. She also seems preoccupied with the form of language as she reads slowly and carefully the full form for the contraction, showing more concern for a careful oral reading than for making sense.

By examining comprehending apart from comprehension we are able to gain insights into the way in which a reader is trying to make sense of the author's text at any moment during the reader's transaction with the text. Also adding to these insights, which are crucial for both teachers and researchers interested in comprehension, is the process of retelling.

The retelling procedure reported here includes an unaided retelling followed by open-ended questions expanding on information the reader has already provided during the unaided retelling. Any procedure that takes place after reading, such as retelling, can never completely represent comprehension; however, the retelling procedure when compared with other procedures least constrains the reader's ability to represent what has been comprehended.

By using quantitative scores cautiously and relating the knowledge gained about the reader's retelling to other aspects of comprehension processing, such as the patterns of semantically and syntactically acceptable structures readers produce in reading aloud, teachers and researchers gain insights about comprehension processing. The following conclusions about predictability, relevance, and conceptual complexity in literature have come from the examination of hundreds of readers' retellings.

Predictability and Relevance

Readers use their background knowledge in order to select and predict the author's message at various linguistic levels. That is, the reader predicts sounds, letters, words, phrases, and clauses, as well as the meaning of the story and how the story is organized.

An overall context is also predicted, probably at the initiation of the reading, which helps guide the predictions at all the other language levels. For example, the reader must decide very early whether a story will be realistic fiction or fantasy. The name of the author, book cover, title, and initial sentences, if the reader chooses to make use of them, provide cues that the reader may use for predicting and generating hypotheses. The more predictable the story is to the reader—the more familiar the language of the text, the actions of the characters, the description of the setting, the sequence of events—the closer the reader's predictions will match the author's expression and the easier the text will be for the reader to comprehend. This degree of familiarity to the reader can be considered the degree of relevance the story has for the reader. Even when the author surprises the reader with unpredictable structures, style, and content, the greater the familiarity the reader has with many aspects of the text, the more quickly and easily the reader can disconfirm inappropriate predictions in order to self-correct.

The degree of relevance of the literature to the reader aids considerably in its predictability. However, relevance to readers is a complex set of relationships.

In one miscue study (Goodman and Goodman 1978), readers used what were termed culturally relevant materials. Each subject in the study read and retold two stories. One was called the "standard" story and had been read by subjects in previous miscue analysis studies. A second story was chosen that more closely represented the cultural background of the varied populations in the study. These were called culturally relevant stories. Many of the subjects were able to retell the standard stories more easily and with greater understanding than the culturally relevant story. As we examined why this might be, the complexity of the concept of relevance for any one reader was explored.

We identified seven aspects of life experience other than ethnicity that need to be considered when exploring issues of relevancy. These are:

1. Sociocultural-economic institutions, including such features as occupations, housing patterns, family relationships, schooling, religion, and so on.
2. Setting.
3. Chronological time.
4. Age and sex of characters.
5. Language variations represented in the text.
6. Theme, moral content, worldview.
7. Readers' experience with certain kinds of texts.

If we examine one of the standard stories that many readers were able to retell better than their culturally relevant story with this list in mind, we can see how this story can be considered relevant even though the ethnicity of the characters in the stories does not match the ethnic background of the readers.

"Freddie Miller, Scientist" is a story about a boy who gets in trouble by trying a number of scientific experiments that fail. Finally, his inventiveness saves his younger sister and he becomes a hero in the eyes of his family.

The family is typical to the point of being stereotypical. Freddie has a younger sister. Mother works in the kitchen. Father works away from home. The story takes place in the home and could occur in the present time. Freddie could be from nine to twelve years old. Our subjects usually think Freddie is their own age. The story has a pattern that is common and frequent in basal readers, although it may not be common to the everyday experience of the reader. The readers also seem to relate to the overall story structure of Freddie's getting into trouble, although always with good motives, ending with a final event through which he achieves respect in the eyes of his family.

One fourth-grade Arabic subject provided an example of the relevance of "Freddie Miller, Scientist" in his retelling.

"[Freddie] want to be a man. . . . Because he make science and things and so his father proud of him and tell him, you're a man."

Hawaiian Pidgin and Hawaiian Samoan subjects had much better retellings of "Freddie Miller, Scientist" than of their culturally relevant story, called "Royal Race," by Robert Eskridge (1966). "Royal Race," set in the Hawaiian Islands, is about two young boys in competitive sport, but the story takes place in olden times when kings still ruled tribal groups. The competitive sport, only for royalty, is a race on sleds down the side of a mountain on a track made of rocks. The sleds are seen only in museums now. The experiences lived by the characters in this story are unrelated to the lives of the Hawaiian Pidgin group, who have as much Asian as Hawaiian cultural background, and even to the Hawaiian Samoan group, considering their modern cultural experiences.

For Navajo subjects, the culturally relevant story was easier to retell than "Freddie Miller, Scientist." *Salt Boy,* by Mary Perrine (1968), presents information on the agricultural life of the Navajos and focuses on some sheepherding and horse-raising customs. The male character yearns to learn how to rope, saves one of his mother's lambs, and has a sensitive relationship with his father. The Navajo fourth graders found this more relevant to their lives than the Freddie Miller story was and did a better job of retelling it.

Although some other factors of text also affect predictability, the more a reader's own life experience is relevant to the experiences expressed in a text, the greater the predictability and the easier it will be to comprehend.

As with many other conclusions about the reading process, there are exceptions that need to be addressed. Reading or listening to a lot of a certain kind of literature in and of itself helps to make it relevant. Therefore, it shouldn't have surprised us that some readers had trouble with culturally relevant stories. Because of a lack of exposure to such stories, some readers don't expect stories to be relevant to their lives.

Sometimes readers had difficulty with the names of people and places related to their own culture. They had limited experience reading about people like themselves and thus did not expect to find familiar proper names, language structures that represent their own native language dialect, or experiences very familiar to their lives outside school. In *Sancho,* by Helen Rushmore (1972), a story about a Mexican woman named Rosita who has a "way with animals known throughout the ranch country," Spanish terms occur once in the story—*tortilla, tamales, frijoles.*

Most of the South Texas bilingual Spanish-English children who read this story did not predict such linguistic terms and read nonwords that sounded like tor-til-la for *tortilla,* and far-see-jolees and fra–jews for *frijoles.* They read *Rosita* as Rosetta or Rossta. One child who produced a nonword for *frijoles* used the information in the story to disconfirm his miscue so that in his retelling he talked about the "frijoles that the lady in the story cooked." In many cases, however, a lack of experience with literature interferes with any kind of story's being predictable.

Conceptual Complexity and Predictability

New concepts and their accompanying labels are not by themselves what cause conceptual complexity. There is an interplay between the knowledge readers have and the degree to which an author explicates and provides appropriate cohesive devices so that readers can develop concepts through their reading.

Readers may assume that certain concepts are unknown or that certain words or phrases are unfamiliar and omit them as they read, or they may try different nonwords or inappropriate real words throughout a text for the same text word and then when referring to the text word in their retelling use still other nonwords or inappropriate real words. This strategy suggests that readers have a handle on *knowing when they don't know.* Readers indicate through miscue analysis and their retellings that they use complex predicting and confirming strategies when they are concerned with unfamiliar words or phrases representing unfamiliar concepts in a text.

Misconceptions and concepts seem to develop in the same way. Readers use their own storehouse of knowledge to relate labels to new concepts and relate these concepts to the information available from the author. Based on this interaction between themselves and the author, readers may develop concepts about things they have never heard of before or about words for which they may have conceptual understanding but no label. There are a number of good examples of this in "Freddie Miller, Scientist."

Many readers tell about Freddie's movements up and down stairs as he experiments and finally as he helps Elizabeth by putting the flashlight he has made through the transom into the closet where Elizabeth is accidentally locked up. Following are excerpts taken from four different pages, in the order they occur in the story, about particular concepts related to *cellar* and *transom*. These are followed by excerpts from the retellings of selected fourth-grade subjects responding to these concepts.

Text Excerpts

Taking the clock to the cellar, Freddie worked hard . . .

Freddie hurried to his cellar worktable.

Just as he got the parts in place, he heard a faint tapping and a voice calling, somewhere above.

When Freddie ran up from the cellar, he heard his sister's voice calling, "Freddie" . . .

Freddie, trying to think, looked up at the small window above the closet door. He had an idea! "Listen, Elizabeth," he called. "I'll fix a light and drop it to you through the transom."

He ran to the cellar and picked up . . .

He tied a string around the end of the ruler and hurried back upstairs. Pulling the kitchen stepladder out into the hall and climbing up on it, he found the transom within easy reach. "Elizabeth," he called. "I'm going to drop this light down to you through the transom. Catch it by the ruler and let me know when you can reach it."

Retelling Excerpts

Spanish-speaking child:
Freddie went downstairs to crell [a nonword produced by the child] . . . then he came out. . . . He pulled the ladder to his sister and then he went up and put the flashlight to the ceiling. Freddie did his work in a cellar.

Navajo child (translated from Navajo):
He says to come upstairs. Elizabeth went upstairs. Then he went back downstairs and made the flashlight. And went back upstairs. Then he gave the flashlight to Elizabeth. . . . I think he broke down a wall and gave it to her.

Appalachian child:
[Freddie] was doing things with his chemistry set in the cellar . . . He

had a string tied to the end of the ruler and he slid it down on . . . I forgot what you call it. I think it's a cellar. He slid it down and I don't know what it does . . . so it could get to Edith. He dragged the ladder out and there was a window up on top of the door that went down to the chute like.

Arabic-speaking child:
And if he came a flashlight, then he put, got it down from . . . forgot that name. And then he went down in the basement, I think, to the table, and he tried another big experiment. I think where he put it was the top . . . on the top of the door and it was glass and it opens and closes.

All readers use information from the text for their retellings. What causes the differences between readers' retellings is the set of schemata and experiences that readers bring to their reading. A reader who has had experiences with closets, transoms, cellars, and life in a more-than-one-story house will be able to assimilate the information provided by a story like "Freddie Miller, Scientist" differently than those who have had limited experiences with closets, cellars, or transoms. This will be true whether they have heard of the particular word or not. Readers who know basements can say to themselves as they read *cellar* (whether or not they pronounce the label appropriately), Oh, that's some kind of basement. If they know basement as one kind of subterranean floor in a building and cellar as a place where winter vegetables are stored, such as the Appalachian subject, they may need to make some modifications in order to predict how Freddie could be doing his experiments in a cellar.

On the other hand, the student who has had little personal experiences with any kind of subterranean floor and who has no idea of its purpose will have great problems trying to understand how Freddie helped Elizabeth. Those who know closets as little open cubicles in which a person can hang up clothes, such as the boarding school Navajo subject, are going to be confused about how Elizabeth got locked in a closet in the first place and how Freddie got the light to her. The cues in the story help those who already know about cellars, transoms, and closets to predict and understand what happened. To those who have had little or no experience with such places in a home or school, the cues can suggest what happened but provide a confusing picture of aspects of the story.

Retellings provide a large amount of data for researchers to gain insight into a reader's comprehension processes, but this should not make us lose sight of the applications for instruction that retellings can serve.

Retellings as Presenting

This is my letter to the World
That never wrote to Me—
The simple News that Nature told—
with tender Majesty

       —Emily Dickinson

Retelling a story is an opportunity for a reader to present his or her ideas to the world and to have an additional opportunity to rehearse the story again and to integrate it, modify it, and add to its comprehension.

In *Language and Thinking in School*, Smith, Goodman, and Meredith (1976) talk about education as "coming to know through the symbolic transformation and representation of experience." This process involves three phases of mental activity: perceiving, ideating, and presenting. The comprehending process of reading encompasses the first two phases: perceiving new data in the environment and ideating upon these perceptions, which includes conceptualizing and generalizing. The third phase, presenting ideation to oneself and others, occurs during retelling; retellings are one type of presentational form. Presenting one's concepts and generalizations to others allows the presenter to hear reflection from others and build shared meanings. The presenter tests his or her view of reality against the notion of others. The opportunity to present a piece of literature just read to others or to talk about it with others can occur in a variety of settings.

The reader may engage in a silent monologue, living through the story experiences through language or mental imagery. For instruction, this would mean providing time for reflection as part of reading experiences. Or it may mean finding ways for the reader to share the story with others.

In adapting retelling procedures to the classroom, the teacher needs to provide opportunities for readers to relate, rethink, and continue to make sense of the story—to continue comprehending. At the same time, comprehension also will be facilitated.

Anyone who has been in educational settings knows about negative experiences that readers can have when presentational forms are overly controlled by the teacher, such as traditional book reports and short-answer and other closed question formats. However, in their zeal to protect children from ineffective and negative educational practices, teachers may have minimized the significance of providing opportunities for presenting to occur during the process of coming to know literature. We should think about how eagerly children discuss a movie or TV drama or sports events they have seen.

I believe that retellings, adapted from miscue analysis into instructional strategies, will significantly expand both comprehending and comprehension. Given opportunity to present, the reader can try out ideas, suggest events, regroup, self-correct, and keep presenting. Retellings can be done individually or in small groups, either orally or in written form.

For the reader, an open-ended retelling brings together ideas. There are many examples in our data that show that readers who don't know a label for something are able in the retelling to use the word itself or are at least able to relate the event or a definition similar to it, constructing new and expanded meanings.

There are times when readers may attempt to cut off comprehension, saying "That's all I remember." However, with supportive probing during retelling, readers continue to organize and think through what they have read.

Many years ago when I taught children's literature to preservice teachers, I asked students to read Shel Silverstein's *The Giving Tree* (1964), the story of a long-term relationship between a boy and a tree. I collected a wide range of interpretations in almost every class. One woman said she was so impressed with the book's message of love, unselfishness, and giving that she and her future husband had decided they would exchange lines from the book during their wedding ceremony.

Another student countered that he hated the book because it showed such obvious selfishness and because the author condones the behavior of a boy who continues to take and take, never giving anything in return.

One student said she liked the conservationist message in the story, because all of the tree was used for practical purposes. Nothing was wasted.

"But," replied another student, "it was used for only one person's selfish purposes." Therefore, according to her, it was an anticonservationist view of the world. The young man even carved his initials in the tree—what could more greatly prove a lack of respect for nature?

Another student believed the story represented the control of a child's behavior by a domineering stereotyped Jewish mother who always brought her son back to her by giving so much of herself that he had to return because of his feelings of guilt and dependence. As evidence to support his interpretation, the student cited the name of the author, who "must be Jewish."

At this a feminist student declared "this is the most sexist book I've ever read. The author calls the tree 'she' throughout. He treats her like dirt, always coming back to her and demanding more from her. And she continues to give without complaint. And finally, to show his true contempt for women, he sits his ass right down on top of her."

As I used this book for a number of years, I noticed two things. First, the varied interpretations. Second, the modification and adaptation of the readers' interpretations as we all reacted and interacted, sharing our meanings of the text. Without the discussion each of us would have projected our own values and created a personal, but narrow, view of the text.

I believe any individual interpretation of literature is unique, varying greatly from others', and only through the sharing of interpretations of their personal searches for the meanings of stories can readers build a shared meaning. There has been little research on the impact of the group in determining interpretation of literature, because research on comprehension has tended to match an individual reader's retellings with the researcher's or teacher's view of the author's text. Bartlett's study (1932) on remembering is very much concerned with the impact of the social group, but this has been generally overlooked. Bartlett believed that "the manner and the matter of recalls are often predominantly determined by social influences" (p. 244).

We need to analyze readers' interpretations more respectfully and carefully. If my hunch is true about the significance of shared meanings and their relationship to individual interpretations of literature, then retellings and discussion take on added importance. Preservice and inservice teachers need to develop ways to lead discussions and develop questioning techniques that legitimize the uniqueness of an individual's interpretation of literature but at the same time show respect for the opinion of others in order to build the shared meanings of the social community. We must always be consciously aware of the intricate personal and social influences on readers of literature as they come to know.

References

Bartlett, Frederic C. 1932. *Remembering: A study in experimental and social psychology.* Cambridge: Cambridge University Press.

Eskridge, Robert. 1966. Royal race. In Albert J. Harris et al., *The magic word* (Book 4)(pp. 356–64). New York: Macmillan.

Goodman, Kenneth S. & Goodman, Yetta. 1978. *Reading of American children whose language is a stable rural dialect of English or a language other than English* (Research Report No. NIE–C–00–3–0087, U.S. Department of Health, Education and Welfare). Tucson: Program in Language and Literacy, University of Arizona.

Goodman, Yetta M. & Burke, Carolyn L. 1972. *Reading Miscue Inventory manual: Procedures for diagnosis and evaluation.* New York: Macmillan.

Moore, Lilian. 1965. Freddie Miller, scientist. In Emmet A. Betts & Carolyn M. Welch, *Adventures here and there* (pp. 61–68). New York: American Book Co.

Perrine, Mary. 1968. *Salt boy.* Boston: Houghton Mifflin.

Rushmore, Helen. 1972. *Sancho, the homesick steer.* Champaign, IL: Garrard.

Silverstein, Shel. 1964. *The giving tree.* New York: Harper & Row.

Smith, E. Brooks, Goodman, Kenneth S. & Meredith, Robert. 1970. *Language and thinking in the elementary school.* New York: Holt, Rinehart & Winston.

Smith, E. Brooks, Goodman, Kenneth S. & Meredith, Robert. 1976. *Language and thinking in school* (2nd ed.). New York: Holt, Rinehart & Winston.

Retrospective Miscue Analysis: History, Procedures, and Prospects

For more than twenty years, miscue analysis has been a powerful heuristic tool for teachers and researchers. As Kenneth Goodman predicted years ago, miscue analysis has become a window on the reading process (Goodman 1973), helping theorists and researchers build and expand on a psychosociolinguistic model of reading (Goodman 1984). The following major conclusions have emerged from many studies using miscue analysis (Marek & Goodman 1985):

1. There is an active construction of meaning that occurs during reading.

2. Miscues are an important part of the reading process. They inform researchers and teachers about reading development and about how readers interpret text; further, they reveal readers' points of view, background knowledge, and experiences.

3. In constructing meaning, readers use strategies such as predicting, confirming, and inferencing. They also use the graphophonic, syntactic, semantic, and pragmatic cueing systems in language.

4. There is a single reading process. All readers, regardless of ability, use reading strategies and the language cueing systems in similar ways to construct meaning.

5. Differences in readers' experiences, culture, and language influence their construction of meaning.

Originally published as Occasional Paper No. 19, 1989. Tucson: University of Arizona, Program in Language and Literacy. Copyright 1989 by Yetta M. Goodman.

Miscue analysis provides a base upon which teachers and researchers construct theories about how reading works, discover how students read, and explore readers' knowledge about language. Using this information, teachers can support students in the development of effective and efficient reading strategies (Long 1984).

But miscue analysis can also be used by students to gain insights into themselves as readers. In this article, I will discuss ways to involve readers, especially those who have had difficulty, in using miscue analysis to help them revalue their abilities as readers and at the same time come to new understanding about the reading process. I will also suggest ways for researchers to learn more about the reading process by "eavesdropping" on readers as they examine their own reading behavior.

Since the procedure involves readers listening to and talking about the miscues they made during a previous oral reading, it is called "retrospective miscue analysis" (RMA). Ann Marek has explored one way to use retrospective miscue analysis in her work with adult readers. The report of her research (Marek 1987), along with this discussion on the background and procedures for retrospective miscue analysis, provides a backdrop to encourage many forays into the minds of readers as they participate with teachers and researchers in examining and revaluing the reading process.

RMA as an instructional tool is very dynamic, and teachers and researchers will no doubt make many adaptations to the procedures described here. One basic requirement, however, in using and adapting RMA is that teachers and researchers understand the theoretical issues underlying miscue analysis (Goodman 1982) and be knowledgeable about conducting miscue analysis (Goodman, Watson & Burke 1987). They will then be in a position to articulate theoretically grounded rationales for making modifications that they believe will enhance the use of retrospective miscue analysis.

Functions and Purposes of Retrospective Miscue Analysis

Retrospective miscue analysis is a tool that allows readers to become more aware of their own use of reading strategies and to appreciate their knowledge of the linguistic systems they control as they respond to written texts. It provides readers with the opportunity to know themselves as readers, to observe and evaluate their transactions with texts, and to revalue their strengths as learners and language users (Rosenblatt 1978).

Retrospective miscue analysis serves two major purposes. First, it can be used as an instructional tool to help readers build insights into themselves as readers and into the reading process in general. As an instructional tool it provides opportunities for self-evaluation for the student and evaluative information for the teacher that may be used to plan a reading program. Second, it can be used as a research tool to reveal information about the ways in which readers respond to their own miscues as they read and the degree to which a conscious awareness of the role of miscues influences reading development.

RMA General Procedures

General procedures for conducting retrospective miscue analysis sessions are presented below. The discussion of each procedure includes suggestions for possible adaptations for instructional and research purposes. The general procedures include descriptions of:

- The Reading Miscue Inventory (RMI) reading session.
- Preparations for the RMA session.
- Physical arrangements for the RMA session.
- RMA participants and interactions during the RMA session.
- Miscue selection.
- Discussion of and response to miscues.
- Follow-up on the RMA session.

The RMI Reading Session

The first step involves the tape-recording of an oral reading of a whole story or article, followed by a retelling using the steps of miscue analysis as presented in the Reading Miscue Inventory (Goodman, Watson & Burke 1987). The reader is given a selection to read that is considered within the language and conceptual knowledge of the reader but that is unfamiliar and somewhat challenging. The reader reads the text without any aid from the teacher or researcher. The teacher/researcher marks the miscues on a typescript that is a replica of the actual reading material. Following the oral reading, the reader makes a presentation of the reading material, usually through an oral retelling. After the unaided retelling, the teacher/researcher expands on the retelling by asking the reader open-ended questions. The reading and retelling are tape-recorded.

For Instructional Purposes. As students become familiar with the procedures, it may be possible to organize the RMI sessions so that two students working together conduct the RMI session. Different genres and presentational formats may be used to gain information about the readers' responses to different contexts.

It might be useful to use the Reading Interview (Goodman, Watson & Burke 1987) to gain information about students' reading histories and their perceptions about themselves as readers and about the reading process. A range of reading material may be available at the reading session to allow the student to participate in the selection of material.

For Research Purposes. The selection of materials, the types of readers, the retelling/presentational forms, and the retelling probes are all adaptable depending on the researcher's questions about readers and the reading process. The important issue is that the rationale for each adaptation is grounded in miscue analysis theory.

Preparations for the RMA Session

The teacher/researcher listens again to the RMI reading and retelling episode, verifies the miscues marked on the typescript of the story, and either makes a transcript of the retelling or notes aspects of the retelling that might shed light on the miscues and the reader's comprehension. The miscues are coded using one of the miscue analysis procedures (Goodman, Watson & Burke 1987) to discover a profile of the reader's use of strategies and language cueing systems. It is important to be well acquainted with all aspects of the reader's RMI. The teacher/researcher then makes a plan regarding the direction that the RMA session will take and arranges a time for the RMA session with the reader. For example, for some purposes the student may be involved in listening for the miscues and selecting the miscues to be examined, while for other purposes the reader will only hear the miscues that the teacher/researcher selected.

For Instructional Purposes. In deciding the direction the RMA will take, teachers may wish to focus a reader's attention on particular kinds of miscues, such as omissions that result in semantically and syntactically acceptable sentences. In this way, the RMA session becomes a strategy lesson like those described by Goodman and Burke (1980). (See "Miscue Selection" below for further discussion.) Other times, the teacher may observe while two students work together to decide which miscues they want to discuss and when they want to stop the tape recording.

For Research Purposes. Deciding when to schedule the first and subsequent RMA sessions will depend on various factors, including the time and availability of both the researchers and the readers. Younger children probably should not participate in an RMA session on the same day that the RMI takes place. There should be a break between the RMI and RMA sessions if they are both conducted on the same day. Research is needed to examine the ways in which the time between the RMI and RMA sessions affects readers' responses.

Physical Arrangements for the RMA Session

Two tape recorders are set up. The original reading material is on hand, as are two copies (or more depending on the number of participants) of the typescripts of the reading material. One typescript of the text is unmarked; the other is marked with the reader's miscues. One tape recorder is used to replay the original reading session in order to listen to and discuss particular miscues. The second tape recorder is left on to tape record and preserve the discussions during the RMA session.

It is important to have all the materials available from the beginning, including pencils and paper for note taking. Tables and chairs should be arranged so that participants are seated comfortably throughout the session. If possible, a quiet and separate room for the session will aid in obtaining a good tape recording. It is important to establish honestly with students what the purpose of the procedure is, how long the session will last, how many sessions there will be, and what the student can expect during the session.

For Instructional Purposes. An overview of the session or sessions will be helpful for instructional purposes. Students like to know how things will proceed. A printed guide for the session or series of sessions, including the RMA questions, should be available. Any other general procedures might also be presented to the students in the form of a printed guide. In some situations the RMA session may be a classroom experience, and the physical arrangements need to be adapted to such a format.

For Research Purposes. Even though research questions may change during the course of the research, the questions need to be well articulated in order to make appropriate preparations for the RMA sessions and also to involve students and teachers, when appropriate, in understanding the direction of the research.

RMA Participants and Interactions
During the RMA Session

The participants in the RMA session, usually a reader and a teacher/ researcher, turn on the first tape recorder and listen to the original reading, following along with a typescript of the original text. The typescript may or may not have miscues marked, depending on the direction the session will take. There are times when both a teacher and a researcher may be present, or when two or more students are involved in collaborative learning using RMA.

For Instructional Purposes. The power of students working together cannot be underestimated. Two or three students can work together with the teacher in the beginning so that the teacher can demonstrate the possible direction an RMA session might take. Eventually, the students themselves may run the RMA sessions without a teacher present. Conferences should be held regularly with the students to monitor what they are gaining from the experience. Teachers should also sit in on RMA sessions periodically to see that the experience is a dynamic one and not becoming a boring routine. Some teachers may hold an RMA session with a whole class on occasion. It would be necessary to gain a student's permission to be used as an example in such a setting.

For Research Purposes. The role of collaborative learning during RMA sessions can become a focus for research. The ways in which other readers are involved in selecting the miscues to be attended to, the order in which other readers are included in the discussion and in answering the RMA questions, and whether the other readers in the session should have read the material ahead of time are all issues that can be explored. These variations may be held constant from one session to another, or they may change depending on the research questions and on reader differences such as age or reading proficiency.

Miscue Selection

The reader is told to stop the tape recorder whenever he or she hears something unexpected in the reading. As mentioned earlier, there may be occasions when the teacher/researcher chooses in advance the miscues to which the RMA group will attend. It is important for all users of miscue analysis to keep in mind that miscues are unexpected responses. All listeners, researchers, teachers, and students have different views about what to expect as people read. These differences are greater among novices who haven't thought much about the reading process.

For Instructional Purposes. The teacher should decide whether the reader will stop the tape recorder upon hearing a miscue or whether the teacher will select the miscues in order to focus on particular types of miscues. The students' attitudes about themselves as readers may be important in making such a decision. It may be helpful in the revaluing process to select particularly high quality miscues in early RMA sessions so that students can begin to value miscues as part of the reading process.

For Research Purposes. Allowing readers to be in control of selecting miscues by stopping the tape recorder whenever a miscue is heard may give researchers an opportunity to explore the different kinds of miscues selected by different kinds of readers. The responses readers make during RMA sessions provide an abundance of metalinguistic and metacognitive statements. The analysis of such statements will add a good deal to our understanding of metalinguistic and metacognitive strategies.

Discussion of and Response to Miscues

Each time the tape recorder is turned off in order to discuss a miscue, the reader is encouraged to explore with the teacher/researcher what occurred and why. Certain questions based on the ones used in RMI coding procedures are then asked of the reader about each miscue. This process of identifying and discussing miscues continues throughout the RMA session.

Following are suggested questions that may be used to guide the discussion about each miscue. Not all of them will necessarily be used during each session—some may prove to be more useful than others. The first group of questions focuses on the reader's response to the miscue in general:

1. Why did you stop the tape recorder?
2. Listen and let's see if we hear the same thing again.
3. Why do you think you did that? Is that a good thing to do while you are reading? Do you think all readers do that?

The teacher-researcher keeps in mind the reader's response to these initial questions as the questions shift to a more specific focus on reading strategies and uses of the language cueing systems:

1. What does what you read mean?
2. Do you think this section made sense as you read it?
3. Does what you've read sound like language?
4. Did you correct what you read? Why did you correct it? Should you have corrected it?
5. Did what you read look like what is in the text? Did it sound like what is in the text?

It may be necessary to have the reader reread the section, and if students do not understand the questions, the teacher/researcher needs to rephrase them. Questions are asked in order to help students focus on the reading process. Often if the answer to the question *Does this make sense?* is yes, the discussion revolves around the positive nature of high-quality miscues and subsequent questions are not asked. The question that focuses on sound and graphic similarity is used to demonstrate occasions when students rely more on graphophonic information (Yes, it looks and sounds like what is in the text) than on semantic or syntactic information (No, it doesn't make sense or sound like language). Some students need to be helped to realize that an over-reliance on graphophonic information rather than on meaning is a less productive strategy. This is especially true for students who have been exposed repeatedly to skills-based instruction.

These questions may be modified as necessary. It is important, of course, that the theory that underlies these procedures and the questions be kept intact as adaptations are made.

Following the RMA session, the reader reads another selection, the teacher/researcher analyzes the reading using the RMI, and the selection is used during the next RMA session.

For Instructional Purposes. Teachers will want to experiment with the kinds of questions to use with students. Depending on the age of the students and the intensity of the sessions, questions may vary. Decisions about whether questions will vary or remain standard from one setting to another are all issues to be explored. If students are encouraged to question each other in collaborative sessions, questions may be standardized and printed. The roles of the Reading Interview and the retelling or other presentational forms during the question-and-discussion period are all possible aspects to be explored.

For Research Purposes. There are many aspects of the discussion and responses that invite researcher analysis. The researcher may want to explore only certain segments of the RMA session. In some cases, the researcher and the teacher may be one and the same. In other cases, the researcher will be a participant-observer, while in still other situations, the researcher may be analyzing data away from the actual site of the research.

Follow-Up on the RMA Session

The tape recording of the RMA session is transcribed, and plans are made for further sessions.

For Instructional Purposes. The follow-up is the planning of another RMA session. In the same way that teachers plan any lesson carefully, the planning of each RMA follow-up session needs to take into consideration the miscues the reader has made and the goals for the instructional program. In subsequent sessions, students can be encouraged to bring their own reading to the RMA session unless the teacher prefers to use a core of reading materials in order to have typescripts for miscue markings available in advance. Photocopies of the page from the reading material can sometimes be used for a typescript when the reader has selected his or her own material.

For Research Purposes. Follow-up activities will depend on whether the RMA procedure is a one–time experience for the reader or whether there are to be subsequent RMA sessions. Some research questions may be answered in only one RMA session, while others may require a series of sessions.

Further Considerations

Teachers and researchers who have used miscue analysis, especially for readers at risk, are very aware of the negative attitudes that readers often have about themselves as readers. It is not uncommon to hear such readers declare that they are poor readers because they omit words, make mistakes, don't remember everything they read, don't know every word, don't look up new words in the dictionary, read too fast, read too slow, substitute words, or rearrange sentences as they read. It becomes obvious that if these readers could become consciously aware that such behaviors are expected in reading, and that *all* readers use these strategies as they read, then they might re-value themselves as readers and the process of reading as well. Using RMA for instructional purposes is designed to do just that.

Sometimes the teacher may be using RMA for evaluating student growth or for discovering insights into the developmental nature of reading. In such cases, the teacher may have purposes for the RMA that are similar to the researcher's purposes. As the teacher and students become more familiar with RMA, their own purposes may change over time, and this will affect the way the RMA procedures are used.

The age of the student will also affect some aspects of RMA. Even working with adults, Ann Marek found some questions were more easily understood than others, and she made adaptations accordingly. As students and teachers become more sophisticated in using RMA, new questions may be generated to highlight their growing understanding about the reading process.

For Further Reading

This section is not intended to provide a review of RMA literature; rather, it provides a list of references for those who wish to read more about the procedure. Each of the studies or descriptions of RMA reports success in its use, although questions have been raised for further investigation. Many of these questions were mentioned as I discussed the possible adaptations for instruction and research.

Retrospective miscue analysis was developed by a Canadian secondary school remedial reading teacher, Chris Worsnop. Originally, he intended to explore the procedure with research studies, and although there is little description of his work in published literature, his unpublished manuscripts have inspired many of the studies and instructional procedures that have been completed. Worsnop used RMA working one-on-one with his students and later with students working collaboratively.

Dorothy Watson (1978) explored a procedure that gets at some of the same issues that are raised by RMA. She believed that it would be helpful to encourage readers to select their own miscues in a group setting, and developed an instructional procedure called *reader-selected miscues*. During a period of silent reading, the reader notes with a bookmark where there is a problem in understanding the author's message. At the end of the reading period, he or she lists the sentences including the embedded problem on the bookmark and hands it to the teacher. The teacher, either alone or working with the student, categorizes the miscues, and instructional strategies are developed in response to the types of miscues. Reader-selected miscues have also been studied by Hoge (1982, 1983).

Believing that RMA procedures can provide students, teachers, and researchers with greater insights into their own reading and the reading process, I have encouraged a group of graduate students, teachers, and researchers to explore retrospective miscue analysis procedures. Raisner (1977/1978), Coles (1981), and Weatherill (1983, forthcoming) have used RMA in research studies: Raisner with college students, Coles with junior high students, and Weatherill with upper elementary school students. Secondary school teachers such as Miller and Woodley (1983), Stephenson (1980), and Costello (1985) have used RMA with their own secondary school students.

All of these teachers and researchers concluded that they, along with the readers they worked with, learned a great deal about the reading process using RMA. In each situation, the students gained confidence in their reading, and in most cases showed growth in reading development. The researchers also concluded that the potential of RMA as a research and instructional tool has yet to be fully explored. I hope that any teacher or researcher who makes use of these ideas will write to me to share his or her progress.

References

Coles, Richard E. 1981. The reading strategies of selected junior high school students in the content area (Doctoral dissertation, University of Arizona, 1981). *Dissertation Abstracts International, 42,* 1072A.

Costello, Sarah. 1985. *Retrospective miscue analysis: One teacher's approach.* Unpublished manuscript, University of Arizona, Tucson.

Goodman, Kenneth S. 1973. Miscues: Windows on the reading process. In Kenneth S. Goodman (Ed.), *Miscue analysis: Applications to reading instruction* (pp. 3–14). Urbana, IL: ERIC Clearinghouse on Reading and Communication Skills.

Goodman, Kenneth S. 1982. *Language and literacy: The selected writings of Kenneth S. Goodman* (Vol. 1). Boston: Routledge & Kegan Paul.

Goodman, Kenneth S. 1984. Unity in reading. In Alan C. Purves & Olive Niles (Eds.), *Becoming readers in a complex society* (83rd Yearbook of the National Society for the Study of Education, Part I) (pp. 79–114). Chicago: University of Chicago.

Goodman, Yetta M. & Burke, Carolyn. 1980. *Reading strategies: Focus on comprehension.* New York: Holt, Rinehart & Winston.

Goodman, Yetta M., Watson, Dorothy J. & Burke, Carolyn L. 1987. *Reading miscue inventory: Alternative procedures.* New York: Richard C. Owen.

Hoge, G. Sharon. 1982. A study of reading comprehension monitoring using reader-selected miscues with selected tenth-, eleventh-, and twelfth-grade students (Doctoral dissertation, University of Missouri-Columbia, 1982). *Dissertation Abstracts International, 44,* 0447A.

Hoge, Sharon. 1983. A comprehension-centered reading program using reader selected miscues. *Journal of Reading, 27,* 52–55.

Long, Patricia 1984. *The effectiveness of reading miscue instruments* (Occasional Paper No. 13). Tucson: Program in Language and Literacy, College of Education, University of Arizona. (ERIC Document Reproduction Service Document ED 277 980)

Marek, Ann. 1987. Retrospective miscue analysis as an instructional strategy with adult readers (Doctoral dissertation, Universtiy of Arizona, 1987). *Dissertation Abstracts International, 48,* 3084A.

Marek, Ann M. & Goodman, Kenneth S. 1985. *Annotated miscue analysis bibliography.* (Occasional Paper No. 16). Tucson: Program in Language and Literacy, College of Education, University of Arizona. (ERIC Document Reproduction Service Document ED 275 998)

Miller, Lynn D. & Woodley, John W. 1983. Retrospective miscue analysis: Procedures for research and instruction. *Research on Reading in the Secondary Schools* (Tucson: University of Arizona), *10–11,* 53–67.

Raisner, Barbara C. 1978. Reading strategies employed by nonproficient adult college students as observed through miscue analysis and retrospection (Doctoral dissertation, Hofstra University, 1977). *Dissertation Abstracts International, 38,* 5207A.

Rosenblatt, Louise. 1978. *The reader, the text, the poem: The transactional theory of the literary work.* Carbondale, IL: Southern Illinois University Press.

Stephenson, M. 1980. *Using principles of miscue analysis as remediation for high school students.* Unpublished manuscript, University of Arizona, Tucson.

Watson, Dorothy J. 1978. Reader-selected miscues: Getting more from sustained silent reading. *English Education, 10,* 75–85.

Weatherill, David. 1983. Lucas: A reader and his reading. *Reading Education, 82,* 52–59.

Weatherill, David. Forthcoming. The reading strategies of average upper-elementary students observed through retrospective miscue analysis. Doctoral dissertation, University of Arizona.

To Err Is Human:
Learning About Language
Processes by Analyzing Miscues

(with Kenneth S. Goodman)

Everything people do, they do imperfectly. This is not a flaw but an asset. If we always performed perfectly, we could not maintain the tentativeness and flexibility that characterize human learning and the ways we interact with our environment and with one another. This model of imperfection does not cause us as researchers to worry about why people fall short of perfection; rather, we are concerned with why people do what they do and with what we can learn about language processes from observing such phenomena.

The power of language users to fill knowledge gaps with missing elements, to infer unstated meanings and underlying structures, and to deal with novel experiences, novel thoughts, and novel emotions derives from the ability to predict, to guess, to make choices, to take risks, to go beyond observable data. We must have the capability of being wrong lest the limits on our functioning be too narrowly constrained. Unlike the computer, people do not exhibit specifically programmed, totally dependable responses time after time. We are tentative, we act impulsively, we make mistakes, and we tolerate our own deviations and the mistakes of others.

This article, reprinted with permission from *Theoretical Models and Processes of Reading*, edited by Robert B. Ruddell, Martha R. Ruddell & Harry Singer (Newark, DE: International Reading Association, 1994), pp. 104–23, is based on and updated from work published as "Learning About Psycholinguistic Processes by Analyzing Oral Reading" (*Harvard Educational Review* 47 [1977], 317–33), and "To Err Is Human" (*New York University Education Quarterly* 12[1981], 14–19).

If you doubt that perfection in human behavior is the exception rather than the norm, consider how intensely a performer of any kind—athlete, actor, musician, writer, reader—must practice to achieve anything approaching error-free performance. If you doubt our view of how people deal with mistakes, think about the proofreader who skips over errors in a text or the Native Americans who deliberately insert flaws in handicrafts to remind themselves that the crafts are the work of human hands.

Miscues: Unexpected Responses

For more than twenty-five years we have studied the reading process by analyzing the miscues (unexpected responses) of children and adults orally reading written texts. Ken Goodman coined this use of the word *miscue* because of the negative connotation and history of the term *error*. The term *miscue* reveals that miscues are unexpected responses cued by readers' linguistic or conceptual cognitive structures.

We started with the assumption that everything that happens during reading is caused, that a person's unexpected responses are produced in the same way and from the same knowledge, experience, and intellectual processes as expected responses. Reading aloud involves continuous oral response by the reader, which allows for comparisons between expected and observed responses. Such comparisons reveal the reader's knowledge, experience, and intellectual processes. Oral readers are engaged in comprehending written language while they produce oral responses. Because an oral response is generated while meaning is being constructed, it not only is a form of linguistic performance but also provides a powerful means of examining readers' process and underlying competence.

Miscue analysis requires several conditions. The written material must be new to the reader and complete with a beginning, middle, and end. The text needs to be long and challenging enough to produce sufficient numbers of miscues for patterns to appear. In addition, readers receive no help and are not interrupted. At most, if readers hesitate for more than thirty seconds, they are urged to guess, and only if hesitation continues are they told to keep reading even if it means skipping a word or phrase. Except that it takes place orally and not silently, the reading during miscue analysis requires as normal a situation as possible.

Depending on the purpose of miscue analysis research, readers often have been provided with more than one reading task. Various fiction and nonfiction reading materials have been used, including stories and articles from basal readers, textbooks, trade books, and magazines. Readers have been drawn from elementary, secondary, and adult populations and from a wide range of proficiency and racial, linguistic, and national backgrounds. Studies have been conducted in many languages other than English and in various writing systems (Goodman, Brown & Marek 1993).

Betsy's oral reading of the folktale "The Man Who Kept House" (from McInnes, Gerrard & Ryckman, 1964, pp. 282–83) will be used throughout this article for examples (Goodman, Watson & Burke 1987). The story has 68 sentences, 711 words. Betsy, a nine-year-old from Toronto, was selected by her teacher as representative of students with reading difficulties. Betsy read the story hesitantly, although in most places she read with appropriate expression. Below are the first 14 sentences (S1–S14) from the story, with the actual printed text on the left and the transcript of Betsy's oral reading on the right.

Text	*Transcript*
S1 Once upon a time there was a woodman who thought that no one worked as hard as he did.	Once upon a time there was a woodman. He threw . . . who thought that no one worked as hard as he did.
S2 One evening when he came home from work, he said to his wife, "What do you do all day while I am away cutting wood?"	One evening when he . . . when he came home from work, he said to his wife, "I want you do all day . . . what do you do all day when I am always cutting wood?"
S3 "I keep house," replied the wife, "and keeping house is hard work."	"I keep . . . I keep house," replied the wife, "and keeping . . . and keeping . . . and keeping house is and work."
S4 "Hard work!" said the husband.	"Hard work!" said the husband.
S5 "You don't know what hard work is!	"You don't know what hard work is!
S6 "You should try cutting wood!"	"You should try cutting wood!"
S7 "I'd be glad to," said the wife.	"I'll be glad to," said the wife.
S8 "Why don't you do my work some day?	"Why don't you . . . Why don't you do my work so . . . some day?
S9 "I'll stay home and keep house," said the woodman.	"I'll start house and keeping house," said the woodman.

S10	"If you stay home to do my work, you'll have to make butter, carry water from the well, wash the clothes, clean the house, and look after the baby," said the wife.	"If you start house . . . If you start home to do my work, well you'll have to make bread, carry . . . carry water from the well, wash the clothes, clean the house, and look after the baby," said the wife.
S11	"I can do all that," replied the husband.	"I can do that . . . I can do all that," replied the husband.
S12	"We'll do it tomorrow!"	"Well you do it tomorrow!"
S13	So the next morning the wife went off to the forest.	So the next day the wife went off to the forest.
S14	The husband stayed home and began to do his wife's work.	The husband stayed home and began to do his wife's job.

Betsy's performance reveals her language knowledge. These examples are not unusual; what Betsy does is done by other readers. She processes graphophonic information: most of her miscues show a graphic and phonic relationship between the expected and the observed response. She processes syntactic information: she substitutes noun for noun, verb for verb, noun phrase for noun phrase, verb phrase for verb phrase. She transforms phrases, clauses, and sentences: she omits an intensifier, changes a dependent clause to an independent clause, shifts a *wh-* question sentence to a declarative sentence. She draws on her conceptual and linguistic background and struggles toward meaning by regressing, correcting, and reprocessing as necessary. She predicts appropriate structures and monitors her own success based on the degree to which she is making sense. She develops and uses psychosociolinguistic strategies as she reads. There is nothing random about her miscues.

Reading Miscues and Comprehension

Since we understand that the brain is the organ of human information processing, that it is not a prisoner of the senses but controls the sensory organs and selectively uses their input, we should not be surprised that what is said in oral reading is not what the eye has seen but what the brain has generated for the mouth to report. The text is what the brain responds to; the oral output reflects the underlying competence and the psychosociolinguistic processes that have generated it. When expected and observed responses match, we get little insight into this process. When they do not match and a miscue results, researchers have a window on the reading process.

We have come to believe that the strategies readers use when miscues occur are the same as when there are no miscues. Except for S3, S8, and S9, all of Betsy's miscues produced fully acceptable sentences or were self-corrected. By analyzing whether miscues are semantically acceptable with regard to the whole text or are acceptable only with regard to the prior portion of text, it is possible to infer the strategies readers actively engage in: S2 provides a powerful example. Betsy reads, *I want you do all day,* hesitates, reads slowly, and eventually—after a twenty-three-second pause—reconsiders, probably rereads silently, and self-corrects the initial clause in this sentence. The verb *said* in the sentence portion prior to her miscue and her knowledge about what husbands might say when they come home from work allowed her to predict *I want you. . . .* After she self-corrects the first part of the dialogue, she reads *when I am always cutting wood* for *while I am away cutting wood* with confidence and continues her reading. These two substitution miscues (*when* for *while* and *always* for *away*) produce a clause that fits with the meaning of the rest of the story. The more proficient the reader, the greater the proportion of semantically acceptable miscues or miscues acceptable with the prior portion of the text that are self-corrected (Goodman & Burke 1973).

In S12 Betsy produces, *Well you do it tomorrow* instead of *We'll do it tomorrow.* Although it seems that Betsy simply substitutes *well* for *we'll* and inserts *you,* the miscues are seen to be more complex when we examine how the phrase and clauses are affected by the miscues. Betsy substitutes an interjection prior to the subject *you* to substitute for the pronoun and the beginning of the verb phrase represented by the contraction *we'll.* In addition, Betsy shifts intonation to indicate that the wife rather than the husband is talking. Apparently Betsy predicted that the wife was going to speak to maintain the pattern of husband-wife conversation that is established by the author in the previous sections (S2 and S11). Although the author's intended meaning is changed, the sentence is semantically acceptable within the story.

A reader's predicting and confirming strategies are evident in miscues that are acceptable with the text portion prior to the miscues. Such miscues often occur at pivotal points in sentences, such as junctures between clauses or phrases. At such points the author may select from a variety of linguistic structures to compose the text; the reader has similar options but may predict a structure that is different than the author's. Consider these examples from Betsy's reading:

Text	Transcript
S38 "I'll light a fire in the fireplace and the porridge will be ready in a few minutes."	"I'll light a fire in the fireplace and I'll . . . and the porridge will be ready in a flash . . . a few minutes."
S48 Then he was afraid that she would fall off.	Then he was afraid that the . . . that she would fall off.

Betsy's predication of *I'll* instead of *the* in the second clause of the first example is logical. Since *and* often connects two parallel items, it is not an unreasonable prediction that the second clause will begin with the subject of the first. However, when *I'll* does not fit with the second clause, Betsy confidently disconfirms her prediction and immediately self-corrects. The miscue substitution of *the* for *she* in the second example is also at a pivotal point in the sentence. Whenever an author uses a pronoun to refer to a previously stated noun phrase, a reader may revert to the original noun phrase. The reverse phenomenon also occurs. When the author chooses a noun for which the referent has been established earlier, the reader may use the appropriate pronoun. Betsy was probably predicting *the cow*, which *she* refers to. These miscues clearly show that Betsy is an active language user as she reads. Ken Goodman has done studies on the control readers have over determiners and pronouns in relation to the cohesion of text (Goodman 1983; Goodman & Gespass 1983).

The idea that miscues often occur at specific pivotal points in any text is important enough to provide an example from another reader. An Appalachian reader, while reading the clause "By the time I got out and over to where they were," inserted *of the water* between *out* and *and*. In the previous paragraph the male character is in the water. The author and the reader have similar options at this point in the grammatical structure. The prepositional phrase *of the water* is understood by the reader though not stated by the author and therefore may be inserted without changing the meaning. In this case, the reader makes explicit what the author left implicit.

Miscues that result in semantically acceptable structures are confirmed as acceptable to readers and, therefore, are less likely to be corrected than those that are not acceptable or acceptable only with the immediately preceding text. Miscues at pivotal points in the text are often acceptable with regard to the preceding text. Of the ten semantically acceptable miscues that Betsy produced in the first excerpt, she corrected only one (*all* in S11). However, of the six miscues that were acceptable only with the prior portion of the text, she corrected four. Such correction strategies tend to occur when the reader believes they are most needed—when a prediction has been disconfirmed by subsequent language cues.

Insights are gained into the reader's construction of meaning and the process of comprehension when we ask questions such as Why did the reader make this miscue? Does it make sense in the context of this story or article? Through such examination, it is possible to see the pattern of comprehending strategies a reader engages in.

We contrast comprehending—what the reader does to understand during the reading of a text—with comprehension—what the reader understands at the end of the reading. Open-ended retellings that always follow the reading during miscue analysis are an index of comprehension. They add to the profile of comprehending, which shows the reader's concern for meaning as expressed through the reading miscues. Retellings also provide an opportunity for the researcher or teacher to gain insight into how concepts and language are actively used and developed throughout a reading event.

Although the concept of retelling is common to present-day research, in the early sixties when we first used this concept, many questioned the term and the appropriateness of its use in reading research. Rather than asking direct questions that would give cues to the reader about what is significant in the story, we asked for unaided retelling. Information on the readers' understanding of the text emerges from the organization they use in retelling the story, from whether they use the author's language or their own, and from the conceptions or misconceptions they reveal. Here is the first segment of Betsy's retelling:

> Um . . . it was about this woodman and um . . . when he . . . he thought that he um . . . he had harder work to do than his wife. So he went home and he told his wife, "What have you been doing all day." And then his wife told him. And then, um . . . and then, he thought that it was easy work. And . . . so . . . so his wife, so his wife, so she um . . . so the wife said, "Well so you have to keep," no . . . the husband says that you have to go to the woods and cut . . . and have to go out in the forest and cut wood and I'll stay home. And the next day they did that.

By comparing our interpretation of the story with Betsy's retelling and her miscues, we are able to analyze how much learning has occurred during Betsy and the author's transaction. For example, although the story frequently uses *woodman* and *to cut wood, forest,* the noun used to refer to setting, is used twice. Not only does Betsy provide evidence in her retelling that she knows that *woods* and *forest* are synonymous, she also indicates that she knows the author's choice is *forest.* The maze she works through suggests her search for the author's language. Her oral language mazes are evidence of her intentions and self-correction patterns. Betsy seems to believe that the teacher is looking for the author's language rather than her own. Additional evidence of Betsy's concern to reproduce the author's language is seen in her use of *woodman* and *husband*. In the story, the woodman is referred to as *woodman* and *husband* eight times each and as *man* four times; the wife is referred to only as *wife*. Otherwise pronouns are used to refer to the husband and wife. In the retelling, Betsy uses *husband* and *woodman* six times and *man* only once; she called the wife only *wife*. Betsy always uses appropriate pronouns in referring to the husband and wife. However, when cow was the referent, she substituted *he* for *she* twice. (What does Betsy know about the sex of cattle?)

The linguistic and conceptual schematic background a reader brings to reading not only shows in miscues but is implicit in the developing conceptions or misconceptions revealed through the reader's retelling. Betsy adds to her conceptual base and builds her control of language as she reads this story, but her ability to do both is limited by what she brings to the task. In the story, the husband has to make butter in a churn. Betsy makes miscues whenever butter making is mentioned. For example, in S10 she substituted *bread* for butter. (Bread making is much more common than butter making as a home activity for North American children.) The next time *butter* appears, in S15, she reads it as expected. However, in S18, *Soon the cream will turn into butter*, Betsy reads *buttermilk* for *butter*. Other references to butter making include the words *churn* or *cream*. Betsy reads *cream* as expected each time it appears in the text but produces miscues for *churn*. She pauses about ten seconds at the first appearance of *churn* and finally says it with exaggerated articulation. However, the next two times *churn* appears, Betsy reads *cream*.

Text		*Transcript*
S25	. . . he saw a big pig inside, with its nose in the churn.	. . . he saw a big pig inside, with its nose in the cream.
S28	It bumped into the churn, knocking it over.	It jumped . . . it bumped into the cream, knocking it over.
S29	The cream splashed all over the room.	The cream shout . . . shadow . . . splashed all over the room.

In the retelling Betsy provides evidence that her miscues are conceptually based and not mere confusions:

And the husband was sitting down and he poured some buttermilk and um . . . in a jar. And, and he was making buttermilk, and then he um . . . heard the baby crying. So he looked all around in the

room and um . . . and then he saw a big, a big, um . . . pig. Um . . .
he saw a big pig inside the house. So, he told him to get out and he,
the pig, started racing around and um. . . . he di . . . he um . . .
bumped into the buttermilk and then the buttermilk fell down and
then the pig, um . . . went out.

Betsy, who is growing up in a metropolis, knows little about how
butter is made in churns. She knows that there is a relationship between cream and butter, although she does not know the details of
that relationship. According to her teacher, she has also taken part in
a traditional primary school activity in which sweet cream is poured
into a jar, closed up, and shaken until butter and buttermilk are produced. Although Betsy's miscues and retelling suggest that she has
only some knowledge about butter making, the concept is peripheral
to comprehending the story. All that she needs to know is that butter making is one of the wife's many chores that can cause the woodman trouble.

For a long time, teachers have been confused about how a reader
can know something in one context but not know it in another. Such
confusion comes from the belief that reading is word recognition; on
the contrary, words in different syntactic and semantic contexts become different entities for readers, and Betsy's response to the structure
keep house is good evidence for this. In S3, where the clauses *I keep house*
and *and keeping house* occur the first time, Betsy reads the expected responses but repeats each several times before getting the words right,
suggesting that she is grappling with their meanings. In S9 she reads
start house and keeping house for *stay home and keep house,* and she reads
the first phrase in S10 as *If you start home to do my work.* The structure
keep house is a complex one. To a nine-year-old, *keep* is a verb that
means being able to hold on to or take care of something small. *Keeping house* is no longer a common idiom in American or Canadian English. *Stay home* adds complexity to *keep house.* Used with different verbs
and different function words, *home* and *house* are sometimes synonyms
and sometimes not. The transitive and intransitive nature of *keep* and
stay adds to the complexity of the verb phrases.

In her search for meaning and her transaction with the published
text, Betsy continues to develop strategies to handle these complex
problems. In S14 she produces *stayed home;* however, in S35 she encounters *keeping house* again and reads *perhaps keeping house . . . home
and . . . is . . . hard work.* She is exploring the concept and grammaticality of *keeping house.* She first reads the expected response and then
abandons it. In the story *home* appears seven times and *house* ten
times. Betsy reads them correctly in every context except in the pat-

terns *staying home* and *keeping house*. Yet as she continues to work on these phrases throughout her reading she finally is able to handle the structures and either self-corrects successfully or produces a semantically acceptable sentence. Thus Betsy's miscues and retelling reveal the dynamic transaction between a reader and written language.

Through careful observation and evaluation, miscue analysis provides evidence of the ways in which the published text teaches the reader (Meek 1988). Through continuous transactions with the text, Betsy develops as a reader. Our analysis also provides evidence for the published text as a mediator. Betsy is in a continuing zone of proximal development as she works at making sense of this text (Vygotsky 1978). Because the text is a complete one it mediates Betsy's development.

The Reader: An Intuitive Grammarian

Reading is not simply knowing sounds, words, sentences, and the abstract parts of language that can be studied by linguists. Reading, like listening, consists of processing language and constructing meaning. The reader brings a great deal of information to this complex and active process. A large body of research has been concerned with meaning construction and the understanding of reading processes and has provided supporting evidence to many of the principles we have revealed through miscue analysis. However, there is still too little attention paid to the ability of readers to make use of their knowledge of the syntax of their language as they read.

Readers sometimes cope with texts that they do not understand well by manipulating the language. Their miscues demonstrate this. The work of Chomsky (1965) and Halliday and Hasan (1976) has helped us understand the syntactic transformations that occur as readers transact with texts. Such manipulations are often seen when readers correctly answer questions about material they do not understand. For example, we ask readers to read an article entitled "Downhole Heave Compensator" (Kirk 1974). Most readers claim little comprehension, but they can answer the question What were the two things destroying the underreamers? by finding the statement in the text that reads, "We were trying to keep drillships and semisubmersibles from wiping out our underreamers" (p. 88). It is because of such ability to manipulate the syntax of questions that we decided to use open-ended retellings for miscue analysis.

In miscue analysis research, we examine the syntactic nature of the miscues, the points in the text where miscues occur, and the syntactic acceptability of sentences that include miscues. Readers often produce sentences that are syntactically, but not semantically, acceptable. In S10 Betsy finally reads, *If you start home to do my work* for the text phrase *If you stay home to do my work.* Her reading of this phrase is syntactically acceptable in the story but unacceptable semantically since it is important to the story line that the woodman stay home.

We became aware that readers were able to maintain the grammaticality of sentences even if the meaning was not maintained when we examined the phenomenon of nonwords. Such nonsense words give us insight into English-speaking readers' grammatical awareness because sentences with nonwords often retain the grammatical features of English although they lose English meaning. Betsy produces only two nonword miscues among the seventy-five miscues she produces. In S58 Betsy reads, A*s for the cow, she hang between the roof and the gorun* instead of the expected response *she hung between the roof and the ground.* She repeats *and the* prior to *ground* three times and pauses for about ten seconds between each repetition. She seems to be aware that the word *ground* is not a familiar one in this context, but she maintains a noun intonation for the nonword. This allows her to maintain the grammatical sense of the sentence so that later in the story when the text reads *the cow fell to the ground,* she reads it as expected without hesitation. Use of intonation also provides evidence for the grammatical similarity between the nonword and the text word.

Nonwords most often retain similarities not only in number of syllables, word length, and spelling but also in bound morphemes (the smallest units that carry meaning or grammatical information within a word but cannot stand alone, such as the *ed* in carried). In one of our research studies (Goodman & Burke 1973), a group of sixth graders read a story that included the following sentences: "Clearly and distinctively Andrew said 'philosophical'" and "A distinct quiver in his voice." The nonword substitutions for each were different depending on the grammatical function of the word. For *distinctly* readers read nonwords that sounded like *distikily, distintly,* and *definely* (all retaining the *ly* suffix) while for *distinct* they read *dristic, distink, distet.*

There is abundant evidence in miscues of readers' strong awareness of bound morphemic rules. Our data on readers' word-for-word substitutions, whether nonwords or real words, show that on average 80 percent of the observed responses retain the morphemic markings of the text. For example, if the text word is a noninflected form of a verb, the reader will tend to substitute that form; if the word has a prefix, the reader's substitution will tend to include a prefix. Derivational suffixes will be replaced by derivational suffixes, contractional suffixes by contractional suffixes.

Maintaining the syntactic acceptability of the text allows readers to continue reading and at the same time to maintain the cohesion and coherence of the text. Only a small portion of Betsy's substitution miscues do not retain the same grammatical function as the text word. Analysis of the word-for-word substitutions of fourth and sixth graders showed that their miscues retained the identical grammatical function over 73 percent of the time for nouns and verbs (Goodman & Burke 1973). Function words were the same 67 percent or more of the time, while noun modifiers were retained approximately 60 percent of the time. In addition, an examination of what kinds of grammatical function were used for substitution when they were not identical indicated that nouns, noun modifiers, and function words are substituted for one another to a much greater degree than they are for verbs. Again this suggests the power of grammaticality on reading. Of 501 substitution miscues produced by fourth graders, only three times was a noun substituted for a verb modifier, and sixth graders made such a substitution only once in 424 miscues.

Evidence from miscues occurring at the beginning of sentences also adds insight into readers' awareness of the grammatical constraints of language. Generally, in prose for children, few sentences begin with prepositions, intensifiers, adjectives, or singular common nouns without a preceding determiner. When, on the beginning words of sentences, readers produce miscues that do not retain the grammatical function of the text, we have never found one that represents any of these unexpected grammatical forms. One day we will do an article called "Miscues Readers Don't Make." Some of the strongest evidence about the reading process comes from all the things readers could do that they do not. These patterns are so strong that we have been able to detect manufactured examples of miscues in some professional texts. The authors have offered examples of errors readers don't make.

Readers' miscues that cross sentence boundaries also provide insight into the readers' grammatical sophistication. It is not uncommon to hear teachers complain that readers read past periods. Closer examination of this phenomenon suggests that when readers do this they are usually making a logical prediction that is based on a linguistic alternative. Although Betsy does this a few times, we will use an example from a story we used with fourth graders: *He still thought it more fun to pretend to be a great scientist, mixing the strange and the unknown* (Goodman & Goodman 1978). Many readers predict that *strange* and *unknown* are adjectives and intone the sentence accordingly. This means that their voices are left up in the air, so to speak, in anticipation of a noun. The more proficient readers in the study regress at this point and self-correct by shifting to an end-of-the-sentence intonation pattern. Less proficient readers either do not correct at all and continue reading, sounding surprised, or try to regress without producing the appropriate intonation pattern.

Interrelations of All the Cueing Systems

Reading involves the interrelationship of all the language systems. All readers use graphic information to various degrees. Our research (Goodman & Burke 1973) demonstrates that the least proficient readers we studied in the sixth, eighth, and tenth grades used graphic information more than the most proficient readers. Readers also produce substitution miscues similar to the phonemic patterns of text words. An examination of Betsy's word substitution miscues reveals that she pays more attention to the look-alike quality of the words than to their sound-alike quality. Although attention to graphic features occurs more frequently than attention to the phonemic patterns, readers use both systems to show that they call on their knowledge of the graphophonic system. Yet the use of these systems cannot explain why Betsy would produce a substitution such as *day* for *morning* or *job* for *work* (S13 and S14). She is clearly showing her use of the syntactic system and her ability to retain the grammatical function and morphemic constraints of the expected response. But the graphophonic and syntactic systems together do not explain why Betsy could seemingly understand words such as *house, home, ground,* and *cream* in certain contexts but not in others. To understand these aspects of reading, one must examine the interrelationship of all the cueing systems.

The integration of all the language systems (grammatical, graphophonic, semantic, and pragmatic) are necessary in order for reading to take place. Miscue analysis provides evidence that readers integrate cueing systems from the earliest initial attempts at reading. Readers sample and make judgments about which cues from each system will provide the most useful information in making predictions that will get them to meaning. All of the miscue examples we have cited point to the notion that readers monitor their reading and ask themselves, Does this sound like language? (syntactically acceptable) and Does this make sense in this story? (semantically acceptable). Finally, if they have to return to the text to check things, they look more closely at the print, using their graphophonic knowledge to confirm and self-correct as they read.

As readers make use of their knowledge of all the language cues, they predict, make inferences, select significant features, confirm, and constantly work toward constructing a meaningful text. Not only are they constructing meaning, they are constructing themselves as readers.

Schema-Forming and Schema-Driven Miscues

Our analysis of oral reading miscues began with the foundational assumption that reading is a language process parallel to listening. Everything we have observed among readers from beginners to those with great proficiency supports the validity of this assumption. The analysis of miscues, in turn, has been the basis for the development of a theory and model of the reading process (see Goodman 1994).

What we have learned about miscues in reading has been applied to aspects of language such as spelling, composition, response to literature, and oral language development. Such research, liberated from the "perfection misconception," has demonstrated the linguistic creativity of humans. Errors children make as they develop oral language have provided insight not only into how the young learn language but into the nature of language—how it develops, grows, and changes (Brown 1973). Children also invent schemata about the nature of written language as they become writers (Ferreiro & Teberosky 1982; Goodman & Wilde 1992). Invented punctuation and spelling are especially good examples of the ways in which children learn to control the relationship between the sound system of their dialects and the conventions of the writing system (Read 1986; Wilde 1992). Adults develop the craft of writing through making miscues (Shaughnessy 1977). Rosenblatt (1978) has long argued for a transactional view of reader response to literature in which all response is seen as a transaction between reader and text that of necessity results in variation among readers as they proceed toward interpretation, evaluation, and criticism. The readers' schemata are vital to the transactions.

What we have learned from the study of oral reading miscues and what we have seen in research on other language processes can help to explain the generation of miscues. The concept of schema is helpful to explore how miscues are necessary to language learning. A schema, as we define the term, is an organized cognitive structure of related knowledge, ideas, emotions, and actions that has been internalized and that guides and controls a person's use of subsequent information and response to experience.

Humans have schemata for everything they know and do. We have linguistic schemata (which we call rules) by which we produce and comprehend language. For example, we know when to expect or produce questions and when a question requires an answer. We have schemata for what language does and how it works. With such schemata, we use language to affect the behavior of others. We have conceptual schemata for our ideas, concepts, and knowledge of the world.

We may reject a Picasso portrait because it does not meet our expectation or schema of the human face.

Our work has led us to believe that humans also develop overarching schemata for creating new schemata and modifying old ones. These we might call schemata for new schema formation. Chomsky's (1965) concept that the generation of language is controlled by a finite set of transformational rules is a case of a schema for schema formation. The rules determine and limit what syntactic patterns may be accepted as grammatical in a language; these same rules also make it possible for speakers to create new sentences that have never been heard before but will be comprehensible to others.

Conceptual schemata work much the same way, and they are also controlled by overarching schemata. That explains why we often use analogy and metaphor in making connections to well-known words and ideas when we talk about new experiences. An example is the use of the term *docking* for space travel. Conceptual and linguistic schemata are at work simultaneously. The schemata must all be in harmony. If more than one complexity occurs, the result is compounding; the possibility of miscues increases disproportionately.

The earlier discussion about Betsy's miscues relating to the concepts of *to stay home* and *to keep house* is a good example. Her complete retelling after reading indicates good understanding of these concepts. In order to build this kind of understanding, Betsy has to work hard during her reading. She relates her own limited knowledge of staying home and keeping house to the meanings she is constructing in transaction with the author. She has to develop control over the syntactic and conceptional complexity of *stay home* and *keep house* and add to her understanding of the relationship of *home* and *house*. She keeps selectively using the available graphophonic cues to produce both expected and unexpected responses. It is important to understand the complexity of thinking that Betsy has to use and that her miscues reflect. Much of children's language learning can be explained in terms of developing control over language schemata. With growing linguistic and conceptual schemata, children use language to predict, process, and monitor expression and comprehension.

Now let's reconsider a concept from miscue analysis: miscues are produced by the same process and in response to the same cues as expected (i.e., "correct") responses. Putting that together with what we have just said about schema formation and use, we can consider miscues from the perspective of two schema processes: *schema-forming* or *schema-driven* miscues. And since schemata can be forming while we use our existing schemata, both processes can go on at the same time.

Piaget's (1977) concepts of assimilation and accommodation are pertinent here. A schema-forming miscue may be seen as a struggle toward accommodation, while a schema-driven miscue shows assimilation at work. Further, the effect of the miscue on subsequent language processing or intent may result in a disequilibrium, which may lead to reprocessing—that is, self-correction. Schemata may need to be abandoned, modified, or reformed as miscues are corrected.

A schema-forming miscue reflects the developmental process of building the rule systems of language and concepts, learning to apply those language rule systems, and delimiting them. For example, Susie responds to the printed name Corn Flakes on a box of cereal by pointing to each line of print successively while drawing out the word *ceeerrreeeeuuuull* until she finishes moving her finger. Although she has not yet developed the concept that English print is alphabetic, she shows through her response that she is developing a schema concerning a relationship between the length of print and the length of oral utterance.

The young child's development of the rules of past tense, number, and gender are reflected in the miscues children make in oral language (Brown 1973). Rebecca, age three, provides a good example when she says to her aunt, who is waiting to read her a story, "I'll come and get you in a few whiles." She shows her control of the schema for pluralization (*few* takes a plural) but she has taken *while*, which functions as a noun in the idiom *wait a little while*, and made it a count noun *(a few whiles)*.

In the view of some scholars, a subject's production of language is dependent on whether the subject is dealing with old or new information. A schema-forming miscue is likely to involve new information, either linguistic or conceptual, which may not be easily assimilated. A schema-driven miscue may involve either old (given) information or new information in a predictable context. Furthermore, the schema, as well as the information, may be old or new.

A schema-driven miscue is one that results from the use of existing schemata to produce or comprehend language. In our research the concept of prediction has become important. Texts are hard or easy in proportion to how predictable they are for readers. They may use their existing schema to predict and comprehend, but sometimes the organization of the knowledge—that is, the schema on which the predictions are made—is so strong that it overrides the text and miscues occur. In the initial paragraph of a story that many adolescents and adults have read for us, the phrase *the headlamps of the car* occurs. The majority of these North Americans read *headlights* rather than *headlamps*. Many of those who did read *headlamps* indicated that they expected *headlights* and had to reread to accept *headlamps*.

Language variations also show evidence of schema-driven miscues. We shift dialects and registers when we move from formal written language to more informal styles or from one regional dialect to another. Tommy was overheard saying to his mother, a Texan, "Mom, Dad wants to know where the bucket is" and then to his father, a midwesterner, "Here's the pail, Dad." Tommy had learned to switch codes depending on the situation, and his schema-driven responses were appropriate to each parent. Understanding that dialect miscues are driven by schemata may help teachers and researchers see them in proper perspective. A rural African American fourth grader in Port Gibson, Mississippi, was reading a story that included the line *the ducks walked in single file*. At this point in the story, mother duck was leading her babies in a proud and haughty manner. The child reading that line produced *the ducks walked signifying*.

The malapropisms that we all exhibit are also evidence of schema-driven miscues at work. We try to use schemata for word formation beyond word-formation limits. These result in miscues in listening as well as speaking. TV's Archie Bunker was upset because of the *alteration* he had had with a boisterous customer. We can't help relating the concept of schema-driven miscues to Tannen's (1990) work on conversations between men and women and among different ethnic groups. "I make sense of seemingly senseless misunderstandings that haunt our relationships and show that a man and a woman can interpret the same conversation differently, even when there is no apparent misunderstanding," she writes (p. 13). By understanding the reasons that underlie our misunderstandings perhaps we can form schemata that will help us "prevent or relieve some of the frustration" (p. 13).

In many cases it is not easy to separate miscues into schema-forming or schema-driven processes since they often occur simultaneously. At any particular point in time, it is fairly easy to explain the schemata that drive the miscues that occur. Schema formation, on the other hand, is less likely to occur at a single point and be easily discernible in a single miscue. The study of children's writing development allows us one way to observe the process of schema formation. It also reveals how both schema-forming and schema-driven miscues can occur in concert. An example from a story that Jennifer wrote in the first grade illustrates invented spelling that is driven by her linguistic schemata. Jennifer produced past-tense verbs about twenty times. Each reflected her invented phonic rules (and her awareness of the phonological rules of her own speech) since each had the letter *d* or *t* at the end, representing the appropriate phoneme. These spelling miscues included *rapt* (wrapped) and *yeld* (yelled). Her phonic schemata at this point led her to invent consistent spellings of single letters for single sounds. But a year later her spelling represented an awareness of the interrelationship of morphophonemic rules (past tense taking one of three forms depending on the preceding consonants) and the orthographic rule that spelling is not determined by sound in a simple one-to-one manner. Of twenty-eight regular past-tense verbs in a story she wrote in the second grade, twenty-five were spelled conventionally. Jennifer was in a classroom where a lot of writing was encouraged but there was no direct teaching of spelling. During this year she continually reformed her schemata and moved toward socially conventional ones.

Readers' miscues often can be driven by conceptual schemata, but at the same time readers can be forming new schemata. This is often revealed through retelling as well as through miscues. In our research, we have had children read a story that has a significant concept represented by an unfamiliar but high-frequency word. One such word was *typical*. Although the children who read this story often reproduced oral substitutions for *typical* in the text (such as *tropical, type-ical,* and *topical*), they usually were able to explain the meaning of the word as it developed in the reading of the text. One Texas youngster said, "Oh, yeah, *tropical* means ordinary, just like all kinds of other babies. But, you know, it could also be a big storm."

Sometimes a new word represents a concept well known to the reader. In this case the reader must assimilate the new term to the old concept. Bilingual students often face this when they begin to read in a second language. We studied Arabic immigrant students who produced miscues on the word *plow* in a story they were reading, substituting *palow, pull, pole, polo, plew,* and *blow,* among other words and nonwords (Goodman & Goodman 1978). However, they all were able to provide evidence that they had a "plowing" schema. One reader's example is representative: "Well, it's a thing with two handles and something pointing down. You got to pull it. But they don't push it with a camel. They push it with a cow. When the cow moves, the one who's pushing it got to go push on it so it goes deeper in the underground." In such a context we see both schema-driven and schema-forming processes taking place in a dynamic way. These fourth-grade Arabic readers are new to English. They use their developing knowledge of English to produce unexpected responses to the word *plow* and their knowledge about plowing to show understanding of the concept (schema-driven). At the same time, they add new knowledge as they encounter the English word for the concept (schema-forming). The example also indicates that the reader rejected the story element that a camel was used to pull a plow as implausible because of his conceptual schema.

We hope that our discussion of the role miscues play in language learning communicates to teachers and researchers that miscues are the positive effects of linguistic and conceptual processes rather than the failure to communicate or comprehend. If a language user loses meaning, she or he is likely to produce a miscue. If the language user chooses a syntactic schema different from the author's, a miscue will likely result. If a reader or listener interprets in a way different from the meaning intended by the speaker or author, a miscue will result. Miscues reflect readers' abilities to liberate themselves from detailed attention to print as they leap toward meaning. Readers make use of their linguistic and conceptual schemata to reverse, substitute, insert, omit, rearrange, paraphrase, and transform. They do this not only with letters and single words, but with two-word sequences, phrases, clauses, and sentences. Their own experiences, values, conceptual structures, expectations, dialects, and lifestyles are integral to the process. The meanings they construct can never be a simple reconstruction of the author's conceptual structures because they are dependent on the reader's schemata.

Risk taking has been recognized as a significant aspect of both language learning and proficient language use. In risk taking there is a necessary balance between tentativeness and self-confidence. Miscues reflect the degree to which existing schemata fit the existing circumstance and the level of confidence of the language user. In speaking a second language, speakers often show great tentativeness, consciously groping for control of developing schemata. As their confidence grows so does their risk taking, and their miscues show the influence either of schemata for the first language (schema-driven) or of their developing schemata for the second language (schema-forming). An example of the former type is this sentence from a native Spanish-speaking adult who is asking his English teacher for advice: "Ms. Buck, please, I hope I do not molest you." This oral miscue is driven by the speaker's schema for the Spanish *molestar* (to bother). In her response to the student, the teacher will provide information that will help the student form a schema to provide semantic limits for the English *molest*.

Oral and Silent Reading

We need to say a word about the relationship between oral and silent reading, since much of miscue analysis research uses oral reading. The basic mode of reading is silent. Oral reading is special since it requires production of an oral representation concurrently with comprehending. The functions of oral reading are limited. It is a performing art used by teachers, entertainers, politicians, and religious leaders. We have already explained why we use oral reading in miscue analysis. But a basic question remains: Are oral and silent reading similar enough to justify generalizing from studies of oral reading miscues to theories and models of silent reading?

In our view, a single process underlies all reading. The language cueing systems and the strategies of oral and silent reading are essentially the same. The miscues we find in oral reading occur in silent reading as well. We have some research evidence of that. Studies of nonidentical fillers of cloze blanks (responses that do not match the words deleted from a passage) show remarkable correspondence to oral reading miscues and indicate that the processes of oral and silent reading are much the same (Anderson 1982; Cambourne & Rousch 1979; Chapman 1981). Still, there are dissimilarities between oral and silent reading. First, oral reading is limited to the speed at which speech can be produced; therefore, it need not be as efficient as rapid silent reading. Next, superficial misarticulations such as *hangaber* for *hamburger* occur in oral reading but are not part of silent reading. Also, oral readers, conscious of their audience, read passages differently from when they read silently. Examples are production of nonword substitutions, persistence with several attempts at problem spots, overt regression to correct miscues already mentally corrected, and deliberate adjustments in ensuing text to cover miscues so that listeners will not notice them. Furthermore, oral readers may take fewer risks than silent readers. This can be seen in the deliberate omission of unfamiliar words, reluctance to attempt correction even though meaning is disrupted, and avoidance of overtly making corrections that have taken place silently to avoid calling attention to miscues. Finally, relatively proficient readers, particularly adults, may become so concerned with superficial fluency that they short-circuit the basic concern for meaning. Professional oral readers (newscasters, for example) seem to suffer from this malady. With these reservations noted, we believe that making sense is the same in oral and silent reading; in construction of meaning, miscues must occur in both.

Parts and Wholes

Too much research on language and language learning is still concerned with isolated sounds, letters, word parts, words, and even sentences. Such fragmentation, although it simplifies research design and the complexity of the phenomena under study, seriously distorts processes, tasks, cue values, interactions, and realities. Many years ago, Kintsch (1974) wrote as follows:

> Psycholinguistics is changing in character. . . . The 1950s were still dominated by the nonsense syllables . . ., the 1960s were characterized by the use of word lists, while the present decade is witnessing a shift to even more complex learning materials. At present, we have reached the point where lists of sentences are being substituted for word lists in studies of recall recognition. Hopefully, this will not be the endpoint of this development, and we shall soon see psychologists handle effectively the problems posed by the analysis of connected text. (p. 2)

Through miscue analysis we have learned that other things being equal, short language sequences are harder to comprehend than are long ones. Sentences are easier than words, paragraphs easier than sentences, pages easier than paragraphs, and stories easier than pages. We see two reasons for this. First, it takes some familiarity with the style and general semantic thrust of a text's language for the reader to make successful predictions. Style is largely a matter of an author's syntactic preferences; the semantic context develops over the entire text. Short texts provide limited cues for readers to build a sense of either style or meaning. Second, the disruptive effect of particular miscues on meaning is much greater in short texts. Longer texts offer redundant opportunities to recover and self-correct. This suggests why findings from studies of words, sentences, and short passages produce different results from those that involve whole texts. It also raises a major question about using standardized tests, which employ words, phrases, sentences, and short texts to assess reading proficiency.

Sooner or later all attempts to understand language—its development and its function as the medium of human communication—must confront linguistic reality. Theories, models, grammars, and research paradigms must predict and explain what people do when they use language and what makes it possible for them to do so. Researchers have contrived ingenious ways to make a small bit of linguistic or psycholinguistic reality available for examination. But then what they see is often out of focus, distorted by the design. Miscue analysis research makes fully available the reality of the miscues language users produce as they participate in real speech and literacy events. Huey (1908/1968) said: "And so to completely analyze what we do when we read would almost be the acme of a psychologist's achievements, for it would be to describe very many of the most intricate workings of the human mind, as well as to unravel the tangled story of the most remarkable specific performance that civilization has learned in all its history" (p. 6). To this we add that miscues are windows on language processes at work.

References

Anderson, J. 1982, July. *The writer, the reader, the test.* Paper presented at the annual meeting of the United Kingdom Reading Association, Newcastle-upon-Tyne.

Brown, Roger. 1973. *A first language: The early stages.* Cambridge, MA: Harvard University Press.

Cambourne, Brian & Rousch, Peter. 1979. *A psycholinguistic model of the reading process as it relates to proficient, average, and low-ability readers* (Technical Report). Wagga Wagga, NSW, Australia: Riverina College of Advanced English, Stuart University.

Chapman, John. 1981. Introduction. In John Chapman (Ed.), *The reader and the text* (pp. 1–15). London: Heinemann.

Chomsky, Noam. 1965. *Aspects of the theory of syntax.* Cambridge, MA: MIT Press.

Ferreiro, Emilia & Teberosky, Ana. 1982. *Literacy before schooling.* Portsmouth, NH: Heinemann.

Goodman, Kenneth S. 1983. *Text features as they relate to miscues: Determiners* (Occasional Paper No. 8). Tucson: Program in Language and Literacy, College of Education, University of Arizona. (ERIC Document Reproduction Service Document ED 297 260)

Goodman, Kenneth S. 1994. Reading, writing, and written texts: A transactional sociopsycholinguistic view. In Robert B. Ruddell, Martha R. Ruddell & Harry Singer (Ed.), *Theoretical models and processes of reading* (pp. 1093–1130). Newark, DE: International Reading Association.

Goodman, Kenneth S., Brown, Joel & Marek, Ann M. 1993. *Annotated miscue analysis bibliography* (2nd ed.). Tucson: Program in Language and Literacy, College of Education, University of Arizona.

Goodman, Kenneth S. & Burke, Carolyn L. 1973. *Theoretically based studies of patterns of miscues in oral reading performance* (Final Report, Project No. 9-0375, U.S. Department of Education). Detroit: Wayne State University. (ERIC Document Reproduction Service Document ED 079 708)

Goodman, Kenneth S. & Gespass, Suzanne. 1983. *Text features as they relate to miscues: Pronouns* (Occasional Paper No. 7). Tucson: Program in Language and Literacy, College of Education, University of Arizona. (ERIC Document Reproduction Service Document ED 297 259)

Goodman, Kenneth S. & Goodman, Yetta. 1978. *Reading of American children whose language is a stable rural dialect of English or a language other than En-*

glish (Research Report No. NIE-C-00-3-0087, U.S. Department of Health, Education, and Welfare). Tucson: Program in Language and Literacy, University of Arizona.

Goodman, Yetta M., Watson, Dorothy J. & Burke, Carolyn L. 1987. *Reading miscue inventory: Alternative procedures*. New York: Richard C. Owen.

Goodman, Yetta M. & Wilde, Sandra (Eds.). 1992. *Literacy events in a community of young writers*. New York: Teachers College Press.

Halliday, M. A. K. & Hasan, Ruqaiya. 1976. *Cohesion in English*. London: Longman.

Huey, Edmund. 1968. *The psychology and pedagogy of reading*. Cambridge, MA: MIT Press. (Originally published 1908)

Kintsch, Walter. 1974. *The representation of meaning in memory*. Hillsdale, NJ: Erlbaum.

Kirk, Stephen. 1974, June. Downhole heave compensator: A tool designed by hindsight. *Drilling-DCW*, p.88.

McInnes, John, Gerrard, M. & Ryckman, J. 1964. *Magic and make believe*. Don Mills, OT: Thomas Nelson.

Meek, Margaret. 1988. *How texts teach what readers learn*. Exeter, UK: Thimble Press.

Piaget, Jean. 1977. *The development of thought: Equilibration of cognitive structures*. New York: Viking.

Read, Charles. 1986. *Children's creative spelling*. Boston: Routledge & Kegan Paul.

Rosenblatt, Louise. 1978. *The reader, the text, the poem: The transactional theory of the literary work*. Carbondale, IL: Southern Illinois University Press.

Shaughnessy, Mina. 1977. *Errors and expectations: A guide for the teacher of basic writing*. New York: Oxford.

Tannen, Deborah. 1990. *You just don't understand: Women and men in conversation*. New York: Morrow.

Vygotsky, Lev. 1978. *Mind in society: The development of higher psychological processes*. Cambridge, MA: Harvard University Press.

Wilde, Sandra. 1992. *You kan red this! Spelling and punctuation for whole language classrooms, K–6*. Portsmouth, NH: Heinemann.

Part Three

Print Awareness and the Roots of Literacy (1980–1992)

While many scholars in reading research and instruction were responding positively to Ken Goodman's model of the reading process, I began to realize that some were skeptical about whether Ken's model could apply to the beginnings of reading development. I began to wonder how I could show that young children were learning to read using the same underlying reading processes as more sophisticated or proficient readers. I decided to study first graders to discover how they were learning to read.

The most important conclusion I came to was that these children were already readers. Regardless of instructional setting, kindergarten experiences, or home background, they knew a lot about literacy before they came to first grade. They knew how to hold books, turn pages, and respond to print in books. They knew word and sentence boundaries and had conceptions of directionality. I realized that there were literacy learning experiences taking place way before the first-grade year, where I, up to this point in my career, had believed children first learned to read and write.

I began to frequent preschools and worked with two-, three-, and four-year-olds, and the beginnings of my print awareness research developed. I quickly rejected the concept of readiness as a time in school where children were being prepared to learn about reading. I began to use the terms *literacy development* and *literacy learning* to distinguish my view from the typical view that children learned to read and write only in school. Children were literate by their membership in a literate family and literate society. Other scholars were beginning to study early literacy, and I was learning about how children construct the knowledge they have about literacy through transactions between their own personal inventions and the written conventions of society.

Researching and asking continual questions about early literacy development has been an exciting part of my professional history. I've worked with kids from a range of backgrounds and realized the varied and rich literate environments that support the literacy learning of a vast number of children. I came to understand that literacy is a major cultural phenomenon that needs to be understood within the context of society and not treated as a simple skill that is taught only in school. My inquiry into and understanding about literacy learning led to the metaphor of the roots of literacy that has continued to be a major focus of my work.

The Roots of Literacy

The environment of three- and four-year-olds in many places in the world is filled with the settings, signs, and implements of a print-oriented society. In Tokyo, the atmosphere is not only filled with the sounds and presences of millions of people moving from one place to another in their busy day, but the senses are bombarded with signs announcing banks, buildings, and stores in three Japanese symbol systems and English. Street signs in Tel Aviv announce themselves on large white rectangles in Roman, Arabic, and Hebrew alphabets. A small boy who could be no more than five in Cuernavaca, Mexico, is lying on his back next to his mother as she sells her beads and wares to tourists. He is reading a small Spanish comic book while his brother, about a year older, is selling newspapers, shouting out headlines to capture the attention of potential buyers. A three-year-old Papago child is sitting on a small chair next to her mother at a teacher aide meeting in Sells, Arizona. She looks around and sees another chair the same size as hers, drags it over, and sets it carefully facing her chair. She then walks over to a table, takes a pencil and paper to her chair, sits down, places her paper on her self-constructed chair-desk and begins to "scribble" with her pencil.

These vignettes are features of a literate society, a society in which literacy plays such a strong role that many young children, years prior to the introduction of formal instruction in written language, are beginning to discover how print is organized and how it is used by the members of their society. They begin to act on the literate forms in their

Originally published in *Claremont Reading Conference, 44th Yearbook,* edited by Malcolm P. Douglass (Claremont, CA: Claremont Colleges, 1980), pp. 1–32. Reprinted with permission.

environment in the same manner in which they act on the rest of their environment. In responding to, interacting with, and organizing the written language in their daily world, they begin to understand

1. The significance of written language;
2. The oral labels used when referring to written language;
3. The purposes written language serves for people of different socioeconomic status; and
4. The variety of forms used to construct the meanings communicated by written language.

It is in these interactions between the learner and his or her world that we must look for the origins of literacy.

In 1965, I began to study first graders to discover the beginnings of reading. Among the six children I studied, three had failed reading readiness tests. Yet even these children were beyond beginning reading. They were doing things and had developed concepts that were part of the reading process of mature, proficient readers. They were aware of the alphabetic nature of print. They knew that written language had a relationship to oral language. They could handle books and follow print in a left-to-right direction. They were predicting, confirming, and comprehending using graphophonic, syntactic and semantic cueing systems with varying degrees of proficiency.

My major questions were:

1. How do children develop early concepts about print?
2. When do children actually begin learning to read?
3. What is the impact of home, community, and environment on learning to read?

At the same time I was considering these questions, developing knowledge from related fields of study helped me organize my thinking about reading development (Brown 1973; Chomsky 1971; Clay 1975; Downing 1970; Read 1975; and others).

Researchers in oral language development provided insight into the large amount of language learning that goes on in young children from birth to school entrance. Children learn to speak and listen and develop the rules for oral language use without the benefit of formal instruction (Brown 1973).

Read (1975) and others were exploring children's development of phonological rules by examining children's spontaneous writing. Again I was able to substantiate a basic principle of language development—that young children prior to instruction are in control of their own learning—since conclusions from Read's research suggested strongly that preschoolers categorize speech sounds and invent their own spelling.

As early as the 1930s, research has provided supportive evidence that to understand literacy development, one must look to very young children involved in reading and writing tasks prior to school entrance. This research provides evidence that young children are actively involved in self-learning in the area of written language, both reading and writing.

It was not enough to look at reading alone. Written language has receptive and productive processes. Both have to be investigated to understand how written language develops. New questions were added to my three original questions. I broadened my concerns about reading not just to writing but to the development of literacy in young children.

The ideas I present are tentative answers to my questions influenced by the work of significant scholars in the field of language development, including literacy development (see references). Most important, these views have been developed and modified by my own naturalistic research with children in response to both reading and writing situations and personal interviews. These children are two to six years of age and represent wide ranges of socioeconomic backgrounds. As I describe my views, I will verify them with examples from the research. I am representing the beginnings of literacy with a metaphor—the roots of what will eventually become the tree of literate life.

In order to understand reading and writing, we have to be concerned with at least five roots of literacy development (Figure 1). Before examining the roots, however, I wish to suggest that just as a tree is influenced by the soil in which its roots grow, the maturing roots of literacy in the young child respond to the variety of nutrients in their soil—the written language environment.

Language development is natural whether written or oral. It develops in a social setting because of the human need to communicate and interact with significant others in the culture. It develops in response to the creative, active participation of the individual trying to understand and make sense out of the world in which he or she is growing. Language is functional because it has immediate and significant bearing on the life of the developing human organism.

It is, therefore, impossible to consider literacy development without understanding the significance of literacy in the culture—both the larger society in which a particular culture grows and develops and the specific culture in which the child is nourished (Halliday 1975; Vygotsky 1978). In a print-oriented society, every child's literacy is fed by the nutrients of the environment in which he or she grows. I won't

Figure 1.
Roots of Literacy. Drawing by Inta Gollasch.

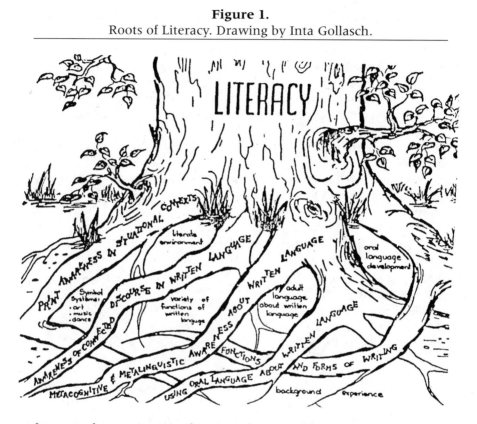

focus on the nutrients in this essay, but in order to explain the development of the roots themselves, we must keep in mind that all the child's personal experiences—(1) the degree of literacy in the environment, (2) the oral language of the child, (3) the attitudes about written language expressed through oral language by adults, (4) the values expressed about language by various significant others toward literacy, (5) the child's degree of awareness of how symbols can be represented in art, music, and dance—all these experiences and no doubt many more nourish the roots of literacy.

The five roots are:

1. Development of print awareness in situational contexts.

2. Development of print awareness in connected discourse.

3. Development of the functions and forms of writing.

4. The use of oral language to talk about written language.

5. Metacognitive and metalinguistic awareness about written language.

As I explore each root, keep in mind that the others are growing and developing simultaneously to varying degrees depending on the nutrients in the soil in which the tree of literacy is planted. At the same time as each of them is developing, all of them are continuously interacting and influencing each other.

Root 1: Development of Print Awareness in Situational Contexts

This is the root of literacy I believe is most common to all learners and the most well developed in the preschool years.

Description of the Social Setting, Function, and Linguistic Components of Root 1

The environment in which the young child is interacting and continuously organizing and analyzing includes the embedding of print in different kinds of settings. The child develops a model, a worldview, rules about the features of written language in situational contexts. In other words, the child is developing a schema about these phenomena.

These young beginning readers are an integral part of the daily transactions that occur between themselves, adults, and print. Many of the daily personal items that children and other significant persons in their surroundings pick up or touch deal with print. Adults or older children will often react to the print in some verbal way as they use or react to an item. Preschoolers either see adults or are themselves involved in reading signs and maps, looking for a particular kind of gasoline station, getting Coke from one type of dispenser or potato chips from another. As children are pushed in their strollers down a street past stores or in a shopping cart through aisles of well-advertised edibles and nonfood items, they observe parents and older siblings making choices based on various criteria involved in communication with the print. Even the decisions about which store to enter may involve knowing if they give or take certain stamps or have particular specials on certain days. In the streets of even a small town in an industrialized society, the young beginner deals with names of stores, restaurants, street signs, highway markers, and other printed matter that advertise or tell the names of places or control the behavior of people.

Preschoolers are not passive bystanders. They are fitting all these experiences into what they are learning about the world. They ask themselves questions about the world of print in which they live.

What does it do? How can I use it? What does it say? Can I use print to tell others?

Children often see others looking in TV listings to make choices about TV viewing. Very young children often play in front of the TV intent on their favorite toys. But as commercials come on or programs change, the change of color, movement, and sound catches their attention, and they watch the print on television and wonder what it is all about. The hucksters of advertising on TV are out to hook children at a young age. Count Chocula sounds like an intriguing item, thinks the toddler, and she pulls it off the shelf the next time she is at the market with her mother and throws it into the basket. At the breakfast table, there is talk about Count Chocula, and the preschooler finds ways to tell it apart from oatmeal and cornflakes.

In talking about the items that labels represent or name, adults can use a variety of names to represent the graphic print. Generic terms are often used regardless of the specific label. Children are more likely to hear, Get the cereal and fix it for breakfast, than Get Kellogg's Special K. Sometimes a specific term has become generic in a home so that Chiffon and Scott tissues may both be called Kleenex by all members of the family when they are talking about them, buying them, or using them. All of these interactions occur in the presence of an active preschooler absorbing knowledge like a sponge. So it is not surprising that to the child Crest and Aim may be called either toothpaste or Colgate depending on whether the child views them as generic or specific, based on the background and experience in the home environment.

The functions of print in the environment are many. The most important function that it serves is communication. The print surrounding the young child can label and name games, buildings, stores, restaurants, TV programs, streets, cities, food items and household items. These same labels in the exact same shape and size can be embedded in different settings and serve the function of advertising. The McDonald's logo can occur on television as an advertisement or it can be seen announcing the eating place as the family drives by on the way to grandma's house. Other kinds of print serve the function of controlling and regulating the behavior of others through signs that warn and advise—STOP, NO PARKING, KEEP OFF THE GRASS, STAY OFF THE VERGES, SQUEEZE RIGHT, 55 MILES AN HOUR.

The form of print takes varying shapes and sizes and is embedded in different ways in the environmental setting. This provides linguistic information for the child to organize. The characteristics of graphic units include distinctive shapes, colors, and sizes. They usually occur in predictable places—on a street corner, high above other structures, on a particular structure, on a carton or bag accompanied by the same pictures every time they occur.

There is no question that there are many cueing systems that support and constrain the embedded print. Color, size, shape, and pictorial cues, each is a system of its own, but to the child developing print awareness—a key discovery is that it is the print that communicates the message. When asked how he knows that a particular boxed toy says LEGO, a little boy points to the print. Just as a child developing oral language uses all the cues in the situational context to communicate, so the child developing written language relies on many cues to comprehend. Lois Bloom (1970) says about context and oral language, "Children talk about events that are immediately, perceptually available in the nonlinguistic context. . . . It appears that child utterances depend directly on the support of nonlinguistic context whereas adult utterances do not." Our research suggests that the same is true of written language.

Directionality is another linguistic principle that begins to develop. Since environmentally embedded print in English is usually presented horizontally, children at a very early age are aware that print takes a horizontal form. However, there are times when environmental print is vertical, and children must make room for this in their developing schema of directionality. Print in environmental settings does not always stand still. There are times when it is movable and the letters, words, and whole logo can be seen from many vantage points as they twirl around and blink on and off. The print may not always begin at the left margin of the object on which it occurs. Aesthetics is an important part of some of the print displayed in the environment, and spacing becomes a significant feature. The shape and size of an item will influence and constrain the directionality of print.

Forms and groupings of letters and words are aspects of print, and the principle that language comes in units becomes significant in development. Children begin to gain some insight into the length of a printed item and the oral response to it. They use voice pointing in various ways to indicate that there is a relationship between length of print and oral language. One child might show evidence of this by saying "Co-Co-Co-Co" pointing to each segment of the scripted form of Coca-Cola. Another child runs her finger under "Kellogg's Raisin Bran," laid out on three different lines of the carton, and holds on to her oral rendition of "Ceeereeeeealll" so that her finger and voice stop at the same time.

Signs that control occur in different places from signs that label or advertise. This may provide an additional cueing system, since children early in their development usually respond to controlling signs with imperative statements and to the other types of signs with naming statements. Shown the traditional school crossing sign or even the word SCHOOL without the picture but with the appropriate yellow background with black capital outline letters, Michael, age three and a half, replied, "Watch out for kids."

Type style varies. Logos like Coca-Cola are most often in a particular script, and many signs use lower case even for the first letter. However, the most common display includes capital letters, boldly presented, flickering from TV sets and neon signs and dominating the world of signs and logos in the environment.

In this highly social, complex, and busy literate environment, the young preschooler becomes print aware.

Development of Root 1

I believe that the beginnings of reading development often go unnoticed in the young child. Neither children nor their parents are aware that reading has begun. This lack of sensitivity occurs because the reading process is misunderstood; because learning to read print and being taught to read it have been conceived as a one-to-one correspondence; and because we have been led to believe that the most commonsense notion about learning to read suggests that it begins in a formalized school environment.

Reading is a receptive process. Like listening, it cannot be observed directly but can only be inferred from other behaviors. Therefore, the very beginnings of reading, like listening, are not readily observable. It is not until the child responds to oral language very deliberately and overtly that people know the child has listened (and understood). Beginning reading, like beginning listening, takes place in a familiar, predictable setting for the child. Since this setting includes color, shape, body movement, and familiar oral language, adults assume that the child is not reading print but decoding from the other contextual cues. I don't deny that the beginning reader uses all the cueing systems available to decode written language. I wish only to argue that the child is also using the print as a cueing system, just as oral language reception or listening takes place in a familiar context in which all cueing systems available are used by the child to decode oral language. It is in an environment with many cueing systems available to support hearing that the child learns oral language and in such an environment, with the inclusion of print, that the child learns to read and write as well.

If we don't recognize these beginnings, we cannot help the child know about the strengths he or she is using in becoming literate.

My research indicates that children develop the ability to read the print embedded in the environment in the following ways:

1. The young child begins to read when printed symbols embedded in situational context are decoded to meaning. A fifteen-month-old child says, "D-D, D-D" jumping up and down in his car seat, every time a Dunkin' Donuts is passed. Or a two-year-old says, "Get Froot Loops," takes the appropriate box off the shelf, and points to the print on the package when asked, Where does it say Froot Loops? For many children in this highly literate society, this behavior develops between the ages of two and four.

2. The child is aware that *print* does the telling. By the time children are four, most will point to print when asked, Where does it say *milk* or *stop*? Children at this age will point to print they are interested in and ask, What does this say? They often can recognize their own name regardless of the context. When Mark was as young as four, he looked at the word TIMEX, pointed to the *M*, and said, "That's my word."

3. As three- and four-year-olds become aware that print does the telling, they react to print ideographically. The whole linguistic unit has a meaning and represents the item directly. A child will point to his own name and spell J-I-M-M-Y. When asked what that is, the child may respond, That's me. All brands of cereal will be called *cereal* at this point—the specific name may not be used. IVORY is soap and STOP is a stop sign. As children move into the four- and five-year-old range, two principles that make them seem less sure about their responses interact: (1) They become aware that "cereal" is not a sufficient response and that a specific name is more appropriate. This will cause a slower response than the three-year-old might make, or even an I-don't-know response; (2) The alphabetic principle begins so that the child might respond as Shana did to a cut-out CREST logo. "That's toothpaste, wait it's Aim, no, Colgate! Colgate!"

When awareness of the alphabetic principle occurs in the situational context of real written language embedded in a real setting, the child will focus first on meaning and then attend to letters. However, if letters, sounds, and words are presented apart from functional language, children will treat these isolated units as unrelated to the act of gaining meaning from context. But more about this later.

4. Children's responses to print even at very young ages tend to be appropriate. When they believe they know an item, they respond confidently. Children also seem to know when they do not know. Their I-don't-know responses are usually appropriate to the situation. When pushed or probed with too many tasks that are unfamiliar, they

begin to change their behavior drastically. A child who can sit and interact with a researcher for up to forty-five minutes responding to familiar items and print will quickly become evasive, restless, playful, and hostile if too much of the task becomes unknown or unfamiliar to the child.

5. Children from three to five are tentative and suggestible. They point to MILK when asked, Where does it say milk? When asked, Does it say milk anywhere else? they may point to all the print on the carton. Or if they say no originally in response to that question and the researcher points to Carnation or some other brand name and asks, Does that say milk? the child may hesitate a bit and then answer yes. Children are still sorting out all the meanings in the environment. They are trying to understand how to answer questions and to respond to strangers who are asking unusual questions, trying to figure out why anyone would ask such questions, and responding to print, all at the same time.

6. Directionality begins very early. As soon as the child points to print as the agent of communication, his or her finger will most likely move horizontally across the page. It is important to remember that the directionality of print in situational context is more varied than in a connected text. Children will move their fingers from left to right as well as from right to left, but in no cases have we had any children move their fingers from top to bottom (although we can predict what children in China and Japan do.)

7. When children respond to print in context, they tend to relate items conceptually even as young as two. Pepsi and Coke may be substituted for each other; stop may be said for a school crossing sign; Rice Krispies may be substituted for Sugar Frosted Flakes. But almost never is Coca-Cola called tuna, Lego, or Johnson's Baby Powder. Children are categorizing and organizing so that their substitutions can almost always be explained in a logical way.

Root 2: Development of Print Awareness in Connected Discourse

Description of the Social Setting, Function, and Linguistic Components of Root 2

Children interact with many kinds of written language that are not situationally embedded in their environment. Another person must bring these materials into the environment and experience of the child. A particular child's experience with connected discourse is therefore probably more idiosyncratic than her experience with situationally embedded print, which is more universally a part of all children's environments. In some homes, books are readily available and adults and siblings can be seen reading silently, reading aloud to each other, and talking about events from books. Winnie the Pooh, Snoopy, or the Borrowers can become part of the creative play in the home. "Speaking of the butter for the royal slice of bread," says a five-year-old to her mother. It's part of their family lore and a neat way to ask for the butter.

In other homes, the daily newspaper may be scanned hurriedly and a popular monthly magazine may be read silently, but there is little oral interaction with others in relation to the reading. In still other homes, a religious work may occupy a special place on the mantel and may be read aloud daily prior to the evening meal with the whole family assembled.

Some homes may receive mail that is shared, while in others mail may be opened and read when children are not around to annoy or disturb. Reading may take place silently, orally, individually, or in groups. A child may sit in a lap and have a very personal experience with the adult and the book being read. Or the child may sit in a care-taking setting among twenty or thirty other preschoolers, listening intently and watching as the teacher holds the book in various ways to share the illustrations with the children.

For each kind of material that includes print in connected discourse there is probably more than one function. Books may be fun and filled with stories, or they may be read occasionally out loud by someone in a stern manner, or the material being read may be incomprehensible to the child. Early on the child learns whether the connected discourse in all books or only in some particular, special books has significant relationships to his or her daily life's experiences. Newspapers may be used to "buy things" or to "turn to channel 4."

At age three, some children may examine each page of a story as an independent entity. They may talk about each page as if it were unrelated to the one that came before or to the next one. At four and five, many children can open books in the appropriate direction and know that the story moves along from page to page even though they are still unaware of the function of print in books. As they have greater experience with written language materials, children begin to know that print is the communication device in connected discourse, just as it is in situationally embedded print; that the written language moves from left to right across the page and back to the left again moving from top to bottom.

Children can begin to read without being fully aware of word boundaries, punctuation, or the concepts represented by the terms *letter, word,* or *number.* Their responses show evidence that they know about the macrostructure or overall organization of what they are reading and can predict how stories will start and how letters begin *Dear Somebody* and end *Love Jennifer.*

Development of Root 2

With connected discourse, young children develop the ability to handle the form of the material in which the discourse is organized, such as books, newspapers, letters, magazines, notes, and so on. Although our research has involved children in response to a number of these items, we have done the most with book-handling knowledge. Therefore, I will focus on this as we turn to the developmental sequence of this root. Each form of connected discourse may develop differently depending on the experiences the child has with the particular form.

Book-handling knowledge develops as the young child learns to open the book in the appropriate direction, knows that the frontmatter and the title page are not significant features, and turns to the first page of the story when asked, Where do you want me to start reading? Early in the development of book handling, the child may indicate that the pictures are providing the language information when asked, "Where am I reading?" By the time children are five or six, most show evidence that they are aware that the print is what does the telling and point to the print when asked, Where am I reading?

There is no automatic or simple relationship between being print aware in terms of print embedded in situational context and being aware of the function of print in books and magazines.

In each specific print experience, the receiver must make decisions about what is significant or not. Even when adults open a book, there is a great deal of print to which they do not attend. It is common for readers to skip five or more pages of print before they come to the page where they start reading. Children must learn this. Some children even as young as three provide evidence that they are aware that some of the early pages of a book are insignificant. For many children this occurs by five.

Developmentally, the child becomes more confident about where the story begins and that it is indeed the print that does the telling. I believe that this generally happens earlier and more often with children who are read to in an intimate one-to-one or small-group setting. Children who are in nursery schools and are read to in large groups without intimate storyreading interactions are more likely to believe that the pictures are the significant features of storytelling.

Even two- and three-year-olds show evidence that they are becoming aware of book handling. When directed, Show me how you read, one very young two-year-old opened a book to the middle and moved her head from side to side, looking at the pages but not moving her lips. This child is growing up in a home with academic adults who do a great deal of silent reading. Another child, when presented with the same request, opened up her picture storybook, held it upright, and turned it so that the researcher could see it. She began to tell a story holding the book facing the researcher and turning the pages every so often. It was obvious she was reading a book just like a teacher might to a group. Both these children are at the beginning stages of developing book-handling knowledge. As they do with so many of the activities of older members of their culture and society, they are role-playing the experiences they eventually hope to participate in. But this "play" provides them with the opportunities to try out or experiment with a variety of forms before they will actually put the process all together and gain mature control. *This, not remote readiness exercises,* is the beginning of reading in young children.

Once children become aware that print does the telling, they begin to develop insights into the conventions of print in books. This seems to go from whole to part. Marie Clay's Sand Test (1979) and an adaptation of the Sand Test procedures that I have developed called Book-Handling Knowledge provide insights into this process. Responses to the tasks on either of these instruments indicate that children seem to develop on their own concepts foundational to reading; not only do children show that print goes from left to right and from the top of the page to the bottom, but eventually children develop the ability to follow along as the adult is reading. First, they follow along until they hear the sentence is almost over, and finally they can point to the word as it is being read.

As the child begins to handle books, oral reading becomes part of the experience as well. At two or three, a child might well say, I can't read, when asked to read a book. However, as children get older, different responses occur.

Some children will respond to the book in a way dependent on what kind of book it is. If cues suggest the book is fiction, he or she will begin to read by saying, Once upon a time. Sometimes the child's response depends on the researcher's request. When prompted, Tell me about this, the child may point to each page and each picture and respond by describing or labeling. When prompted, Read me a story, or Use the book to tell a story, the child more often will use a storytelling discourse. Eventually, between the ages of four and six, children begin to use the print itself to read with. If provided with the opportunity, they will read with adults, predicting words or phrases appropriately. If the story is well known, some children can provide a holistic remembering of the entire story. They develop an awareness of the integrated quality of storyness but are not fully able to use the print continuously. At certain moments in time, the print may take on significance, but children will use the print selectively, perhaps at the beginning of each page or to remember certain names within the story. A lot more work has to be done to gain greater insight into holistic remembering.

I believe that holistic remembering is a significant stage of reading development that goes beyond simple memorization. It provides evidence that children know the essence of storyness. They know stories have a beginning, middle, and end, while their focus is on the reconstruction of meaning. Even when the child has begun to read, making greater use of the graphophonic system, there are moments when the child concerned with story quality will complete predictions that make sense rather than waste the time to go slowly to get the word or to sound out or remember. Like other aspects of language, the more familiar the child is with the book, the story, and the ideas, the more confident and appropriate the child's response to the book will be. Personal background and experience are always significant elements. So it shouldn't surprise us that little Melanie, whose parents read the Bible at home every night, asked her father, "Can I read the Bible tonight?" Dad replied, "When I finish my turn, you can have your turn." When she received the Bible, Melanie wet her two fingers between her lips, squeezed the thin page of the Bible, turned it, and, looking closely at the page, read, "Joseph, three-sixteen . . . He walketh the way."

Root 3: Development of the Functions and Forms of Writing

Description of the Social Setting, Function, and Linguistic Components of Root 3

Since most of my own research has focused on reading, I have treated writing as a single root, knowing that this aspect of the representational scheme of literacy development is oversimplified. I believe that the production of written language is as significant to literacy development as is its reception.

We need a great deal of research to provide the necessary insights concerning the impact reading has on writing or writing has on reading. Although there are some who have suggested that writing may precede reading (Chomsky 1971), the insights I have developed regarding literacy development suggest that reading precedes writing. However, for some children the writing of stories, notes, or letters begins soon after the child is aware that written language communicates receptively.

Writing in homes, communities, and preschools may be even more idiosyncratic than the reading of connected discourse is. Although in most homes reading occurs in some way every day, there are some homes in which a pencil or pen may be hard to find. But even in homes where there is very little letter, story, or expository writing, someone at least occasionally takes a message, makes a shopping list, or fills out some forms. Most children, therefore, see writing occur in many different places and through many interactions. Reports are written at tables or desks, and this often occurs in a particular room of the house. Shopping lists are written in the kitchen in a special listing format and placed in a pocket or a purse. At restaurants, stores, and offices, children see waiters taking orders and clerks writing. The people they are with sometimes read the writing and then write something in response.

Since Hildreth's studies (1936) about how children write their names, it has been obvious that many children as young as three years of age write their own name to represent themselves; to label their possessions, drawings, or dictations; or to sign a letter or card for a family member or friend. Susie, age four, wrote this note to herself as a reminder to put the silver tongue of her shoe buckle in the fourth hole in her sandal so her sandal wouldn't be too loose or too tight:

$$4^{th} \quad \bigcirc \quad in \quad my \quad \ominus$$

Reiss, age four, wrote a note to his mother so she would know that "I'm going to be outside":

$$I\,MG\,OE\,G\,TOO$$
$$BAWTS i D$$

Cards to Grandma on Mother's Day or thank-you notes for presents may also be written, as Rebecca did at age four:

THANK YOU FOR THE NICE BOOK   DEAR KEN AND YETTA,

Children may make lists of things for Santa to get them for Christmas (Baby Alive, Dump truck) or to buy in the store (cookie, syrup):

BABELIV / COCE
DOPTUK / SRP

Or they may write stories or songs. Jerome, age four, wrote a story about LANRD. It was seven pages long. He numbered each page, wrote about Leonard's trip in his TIMMSHYN (time machine) and the last page was appropriately labeled AND (end).

As in other aspects of language development, children are concerned with learning to mean. In addition, they may play with the same form over and over again, because it serves a purpose for them—enjoying the accomplishment of a task. Early writing often looks like scribbling to adults, but as we ask the child about the writing, we often find that it expresses some meaning. Other children, however, after they have written something that seems to be pre-communicative (scribbling), when requested by an adult, to Read that to me, will respond, You know I can't read. As children write their names, they seem to become aware of the distinctiveness of letter forms. When Lynn, two and a half, was asked by her mother to write her name, she produced a series of slashes (/ / / /), saying "L-Y-N-N" as she made the strokes. There are many down strokes in Lynn's name. She had been spelling her name aloud for some time. Using one-to-one correspondence, she showed beginning development of the form of written language.

Many productions of early precommunicative writing seem to look more like cursive writing, while writing that occurs at four or five is often in print form. Perhaps early scribbling is a way for children to role-play the cursive writing style of adults. Children who live in environments where the writing system is not roman seem to have a scribble that looks different from the way the roman-alphabet-writing child scribbles. Once children begin to produce alphabetic writing, the form that written language takes is reflected in the purpose of the child's productions. Lists will be written differently from stories or notes. Envelopes may be scribbled on in the center. As children write connected discourse, they begin to use appropriate syntactic form, experimenting with spacing and punctuation. The child's phonological system is often represented in invented spellings; such spellings provide evidence that children are using articulatory features of language as well as their intuitive knowledge of the phonological system.

Development of Root 3

Each of the following components of writing shows developmental sequencing:

1. *Moving from scribbling to alphabetic writing.* The child moves from precommunicative script (scribbling) to representing meaning alphabetically, first using capital letters for all letters except the *i*. An interesting aspect of this is the response of readers to the child's development. The precommunicative stage can be read only by the child. As children move toward alphabetic orthography, their early attempts may only be decoded by themselves, but soon a devoted parent or knowledgeable and willing teacher is able to read the children's writing, and finally the children's inventions are understood by wider and wider groups of people. This again shows a parallel to the way infants' oral language is understood by others as oral language develops from ages one to three. Initially as children begin to write, a word, syllable, or oral sequence may be represented by a single letter. Letters are strung together without spacing or punctuation. All these aspects move slowly and unevenly toward adult convention, but early attempts indicate children's experimentation with language form. Spacing may occur for some words but not for all. The concept of overgeneralization is also a part of this development. Periods may initially separate children's representations of words before periods are used for sentence markers only. Apostrophes may initially occur prior to the *s* in all words that end in *s* before the child becomes more selective and conventional in using apostrophes. Once children move from writing with capital letters almost exclusively, they seem to use capital letters selectively for nouns, other important words, or the first letter in every line. Use of all capitals in initial writing gives way to more conventional manuscript or cursive writing depending on the environmental setting and the value placed on each by the home or school.

2. *Directionality* is not always from left to right. Children write depending on where their pencil lands, and then fill up the space using logic rather than arbitrary form. Timmy, four and a half, drew his picture first (Figure 2). He then decided to write his name. He happened to put his *T* in the middle of the paper and then moved to the right to write his *i*. He had no place to go, so he then put his *m* in an empty space on the left. He moved again to his right but down to the bottom of the page to write the second *m* and finished to the left because that was the only room remaining. Unless the researcher or teacher is watching at the moment of production, it is possible to believe that Timmy does not know the order of the letters in his name or the direction that he is writing.

Figure 2.
Drawing with Directionality

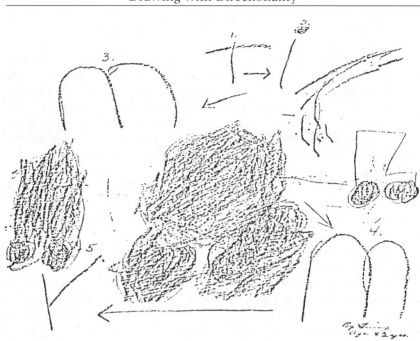

3. In *spelling development* it seems that in most cases, consonants are used appropriately earlier than vowels (except for the preconsonantal nasal: the *m* and *n* in words like *want* and *jump* are often omitted in children's spelling inventions). Sometimes children use only consonants in their first writings except for initial vowels. The long vowel is then introduced in medial vowel positions and finally the short vowels, except for the schwa, which may not develop for some children until they are in third and fourth grade. Children's spelling develops toward conventional spelling over time, but even in the writing of a single story or note, the young author can show spelling development. Jerome, who wrote the story about LANRD, showed his experimentation in that story. On pages 1 and 2 of the story, "time machine" is spelled TIMMSHYN, then the next three times he spelled the word he indicated an awareness that the vowel in *time* was a glide and that there was a schwa at the beginning of machine, using the spelling TIYMMASHYN. He verified his phonological awareness with FLIYING for *flying* and MYTYTING for *meat eating,* consistently using the *iy* for the long i (/ay/) sound and the *y* for the long e (/iy/) sound.

Children's spelling development is receiving deserved attention by researchers (Chomsky 1975; Henderson, Estes & Stonecash 1972; Read 1973). They have shown that children may spell correctly at any early period, but as they develop they look as if they are regressing. Our own evidence suggests that these "misspellings" are overgeneralizations. Early in development children may copy or have adults spell for them, and notes to friends may seem "right." As they develop, they begin to generate or invent their own spelling using developing intuitive rules. Bobby who at age four had written "Dear Grandmother, I love you" wrote her a note when he turned five that said "DER GADMTR. I LUVYU."

Our research also shows that in addition to articulatory and phonological features, graphic shape and length of word also have impact on spelling development. Kristy, age five, was asked by her mother to write *milk*. She carefully said each letter as she wrote: "em" (M), "aye" (I), "el" (l), "kay" (adding the diagonal strokes of the *k* to the vertical line she'd used for *l*). When she was through, her finished production looked like MIK. Kristy stared at her production for some time and then added an M at the end (MIKM). Later after continuous inspection of MIKM, she crossed out the *M*. When asked why she had done this, she replied, "I thought it needed something else but milk has a *K* at the end. Only these letters are milk." She pointed to the MIK.

Because of the way reading and writing are used in our society, writing probably develops more slowly and later than reading. However, in homes where children's writing is encouraged for purposes of communication, writing could develop simultaneously and become more sophisticated at an earlier age than reading.

Before I discuss the last two roots, it is necessary to examine their different nature compared to the first three. The last two roots are developed in relation to the first three. They represent oral language use and thought processes as influenced by the use of written language that children are developing. These will develop in direct response to the social settings, the varied functions, and the linguistic features of the first three roots. Talking and thinking about written language only takes place when children are actively involved in using written language as we explored in the first three roots. Therefore, there are no separate social setting, function, or language features to describe for these last two roots. They are developing at the same time as the first three roots are developing, and they develop *because* the first three roots are developing. If the child did not interact with print in an environmental setting, there would be no need for talking about or thinking about signs or labels or other written language in the environment. If the child has not been read to or has not seen writing in his or her home, there would be no purpose or need to talk about, think about, or develop schemata about written language.

Root 4 is the ability to use language relating to written language, including its vocabulary—*read, write, name, word, page, book, number, Spanish, Arabic, letter,* and so on. It also includes the use of such phrases as What does this say?, Turn the page, Read this to me, What's your name?, I'll read you a book, Don't forget to write, and so on. For both children and adults this usually involves an appropriate context calling for a particular use of language. Root 5 is concerned with overt evidence that there is understanding about how written language is used or processed. At the present time, I believe that Root 4 probably occurs somewhat prior to the development of Root 5 and is always more developed or more sophisticated than Root 5. Even as adults, we are able to talk about reading and writing, about what we do with them, how we use them, and how important they are. On the other hand, even scholars who have studied how children learn to read and write or how the process of reading and writing develops are not able to fully articulate the processes humans use as they read and write.

Root 4: Use of Oral Language to Talk about Written Language

When adults say, I'll write your name on your picture, or Sign your name to Grandma's card, or What does this say? (pointing to the child's precommunicative writing), the picture, the pen, and the child's productions are usually there to refer to and to use as cues to understanding. Even when the specific referent is not immediately available, there are pragmatic constraints in the social context that help the child (and the adult as well) to understand. Mother is on the phone and calls out, Get me a pencil, I need to write down this message for Dad. Or it is bedtime and Daddy says to Tommy, age two and a half, as they are walking toward the bedroom after bath time, Go get me your favorite book to read.

The young child can also respond appropriately in a commonplace situation. A three-year-old says when a page of a book has been read by the adult, Turn the page. Or a two-year-old pulls her favorite aunt into a chair, pushes a book into her hands, and says, Read me, read me.

When these same children are placed in more clinical or research-oriented settings where they are asked for definitions using a question-answer format, they often use language about written language but may use the language less appropriately. Three-year-olds readily say, Turn the page, when the adult reading to them has come to the end of the page. However, they are not very adept at responding when the adult waves a page from a book back and forth and asks, What is this? Typical responses to the latter statement can be *paper, moving,* or *a boy,* referring to the picture on the page being moved. It is not uncommon for a child to be able to spell his own name, R O B E R T, and yet respond inappropriately when an adult points to the letters and asks what they are. The child may reply, Those are numbers, or There are six words in my name. Still, in this type of word substitution, the child in most cases is using terms within an appropriate category, terms for graphic units.

In question-answer settings, children may substitute terms like *word, number,* and *letter* for one another. However, in our research a word or letter or number has never been called a book or a page. It is not uncommon for a two-year-old to overgeneralize the term *daddy* to refer to all men. But this does not mean that the child does not know his or her own daddy from other men. For such children, features of maleness and daddyness are overlapping. The same seems to hold true of our three- to five-year-olds in talking about written language. It is important to keep in mind that the inappropriate use of a label does not necessarily mean that the child is confused about the concepts. In fact, what the child may be providing evidence for is the development of significant features about written language that do not yet match the adult's categories.

The development of oral language about written language is totally tied to the experiences children have with written language. The home and the preschool environments are very important in helping children develop the concepts and the labels related to them. In an environment rich with written language experiences that have very real purpose and function for the children, the concepts of and oral language about written language develop over a period of time, and the appropriate oral language forms begin to be used more and more. Given time, children work out for themselves what items belong in what categories.

In a society such as ours, where people are very concerned with literacy, there are many opportunities even outside school settings for children to encounter oral language about written language that is isolated from its use. Preschools, television shows, and trade materials marketed to parents of preschoolers often deal with letter names, sounds, and the use of terms like *word* and *number*. Such formats are reminiscent of formalized instruction rather than related to the use of language in a functional way in a more natural setting. Although children will eventually learn such terminology, what is important to understand is that the naming of letters, numbers, and words apart from the use of written language may be conceived by some children as a task unrelated to reading. Let me try to explain this through a common analogy. Children learn to use building blocks to build all kinds of structures. Sometimes the blocks they use to build houses or stores or roadways have letters on them. Children can also call out the letters on these blocks or use them to spell out their names or the names of their loved ones. However, to the child, naming the letters or spelling their own name with the blocks certainly has nothing to do with using the blocks to construct castles or airports.

Children can learn to sing the alphabet, read and write numbers, and write letters and call them by name yet never become aware that this activity is related to reading in books, writing letters to friends, or writing their names on paper. For example, Tanya, age four, and a researcher are looking at a red six-sided stop sign pasted on cardboard:

Tanya: That says stop.

Researcher: What else can you tell me about this?

Tanya (*points to* S): X.

Researcher (*points to* T): How about that?

Tanya: A Y.

Researcher (*points to* O): And what about this one?

Tanya: A Z and a P.

Researcher: And altogether it says what?

Tanya: X U Y Z O X P.

Researcher: Now what's that say?

Tanya: A sign that says stop.

Children learn many things ritualistically and enjoy it because they like the rhythm or the sound but may not relate this to anything they are beginning to understand conceptually about reading and writing.

Children begin to read print embedded in environmental settings and even in connected discourse before they are aware of the relationship of the labels *letter* and *word* to reading and writing. I believe it is the use of reading and writing that helps children develop oral language about written language. To isolate one from the other or claim that labeling and overt conceptualizations must precede reading and writing will, I believe, cause confusions that are difficult to sort out as children get older. Very often as teachers see this confusion develop, worry sets in about what a child will be expected to demonstrate on some standardized test. Just at a time when children should be focused on understanding that written language is for the purpose of communication, they are focused on memorizing names, words, and letters, and their attention is turned away from the significance of function, purpose, meaning, and communication in written language.

It is not possible to list the ways in which oral language about written language will develop. The use will be directly tied to the development of the first three roots. Whatever occurs in Roots 1–3 will be talked about, considered, and wondered about.

Through oral language interactions, people express all kinds of attitudes about written language to the child, influencing the development of written language. While doing homework, older siblings will talk about what happens during reading and reading instruction in school. Adults talk about what they read, what they like to read, and what is good to read. People begin to lay the groundwork for the young child's attitudes toward poetry, learning to read, reading instruction, the ability of family members to read, and the difficulty of reading. For some, reading is taken for granted. Everyone does it, and it is assumed that the young child will do it easily and well. For others, reading is a chore. It is something that must be done because it is probably good for people, like castor oil or taking a bath once a day. Attitudes toward and reactions to language by the adults, older siblings, and other children in the environment surrounding the child, as well as that language itself, leave their indelible mark on the language the child develops to use when he or she talks about written language.

Root 5: Metacognitive and Metalinguistic Awareness About Written Language

This last root focuses not just on the use of language and the thinking and conceptualizations necessary for the use of language to occur but specifically on the ability to understand and explain the process of language. It presupposes the ability to analyze language in such a way that the user can define, explain, compare, contrast, or categorize language units. I have narrowed the definition of metalinguistic to the use of language to explain language processing. Metalinguistic awareness has to include some evidence of analysis of the process. This does not mean that the analysis has to be correct by adult standards, but it must show evidence that the child is thinking about how language works. When three-year-old Roberta says, Revco has the same face as my name, her use of terminology is not the same as that which an adult might use, but it indicates an analysis of aspects of language.

Metalinguistic awareness starts early, as Roberta's comment about Revco and her name shows. I believe that metalinguistic awareness develops like other concepts develop (Dybdahl 1980; Smith, Goodman & Meredith 1976). First, as in the Revco-Roberta example, the analysis and the oral response are very personal. Children tend to build their initial concepts upon everyday personal experiences. I have provided a number of appropriate examples already, but two more may be in order. Anders was three years old when he pointed to the *A* in Safeway on a grocery bag and said, "That's one of mine." His mother responded, "One of yours?" Anders said, "Yes, like in Anders." Patrick, age four, responded to the word *milk* on a carton and said, "That says *milk,*" then pointed to the *K* and said, "That's for Kelly . . . she's my lover girl, my lover girl!"

As the child develops, statements providing analysis of language begin to be more similar to adult concepts. These concepts may be called public or commonsense conceptualizations. Again, these concepts may not yet be scientifically accurate, but they are similar to concepts about language that most adults in the community would agree on. Children's public concepts about language begin with some children as early as five. Examples we have collected include this one, from Paula, age five, who is involved in a spelling task:

Researcher: Are you saying the word?

Paula: Yeah, so I won't forget what's at the end or in the middle or at the first.

Researcher: What are you doing now?

Paula: Well, I'm thinking what . . . the letter sounds like . . . so I can spell it right, you know.

Since children can only understand and develop conceptualizations about those activities in which they are actively involved, development of metalinguistic awareness about written language can only occur as children are involved in reading and writing. Children who have never used written language are unable to think about and discuss how its processes work.

The significance of the last root to instructional practices needs to be carefully studied. There is a good deal of correlational research to indicate that those who read and write well can pass tests that focus on language analysis. This has caused some to conclude that metalinguistic awareness is prerequisite to literacy instruction. Yet other conclusions are equally plausible. The ability to use language effectively may be prerequisite to being able to provide evidence about metalinguistic awareness, or both development in metalinguistic awareness and use of language may occur in concert and result from the same nutrients in the soil of growth. On the other hand, development may occur because of a dynamic interaction of all five roots of literacy. In addition, little research has looked at effective readers and writers who are not able to verbalize about written language. We must be careful about our conclusions, because the instructional programs we plan will be very different depending on which conclusion we choose.

Schooling has significant impact on young children's language development, and it isn't always positive. Two examples will suffice. Jonathan had been writing his name in all caps since he was three years old. By the time he was four, he was writing stories that anyone could read using invented spellings that represented his developing graphophonic rule system. One week after school began, he would no longer write anything but his name. His response to the question, Why don't you write a story? was, "I can't write till I'm in first grade." And he didn't.

Mia had a similar experience. She had been writing her name since she was three and a half with a capital *M*, a dotted *i* as large as the *M* and a capital *A*. After three weeks in kindergarten, she came home with a worksheet and on the line that said *Name* was written only *Mi*. Her mother asked, "Mia, what happened to your *a*?" Mia responded, "I don't know how to make *a*'s yet." Two days later Mia's worksheet only had an *M* on the name line. The mother again asked why, and Mia's response was, "I don't know how to make *i*'s yet." Three days later, Mia didn't sign any parts of her name on her school work. It took a number of months before Mia would write her name in school, although she continued to write at home. She was not as completely intimidated by school policies as Jonathan was.

I hope these incidents are rare. Whether they are or not, the significant implications of these examples is that instructional practices are singularly important in helping extend literacy development or stopping its growth in serious and dramatic ways.

Conclusions

Those of us responsible for literacy development in school can only be successful if we understand and appreciate the multiplicity of forces that influence how children learn to read and write. We must be aware of the social, cultural, and economic forces that influence the development of literacy. We must understand the impact of the complex attitudes and views various members of society have toward literacy. We must understand the child's own involvement in and control of learning to become literate. We must understand the teacher's impact on the child's learning through both instructional techniques that enhance learning to read and those that interfere.

Development of curriculum for literacy must take into account what all children already know. We must stop preparing children to read but rather expand on their immersion in all kinds of reading and writing activities. Curriculum needs to be organized in ways that provide the greatest opportunities for children to build on their developing literacy roots in order to grow a vital and strong tree of literacy.

My research has shown that literacy develops naturally in *all* children in our highly literate society. I'm certainly not the first person to recognize natural literacy development, but maybe we are more ready now to understand its significance. Edmund Huey concluded his 1908 study of reading with the following pedagogical statement:

> The home is the natural place for learning to read, in connection with the child's introduction to literature through story-telling, picture-reading, etc. The child will make much use of reading and writing in his play, using both pictures and words.

I can only hope that seventy-two years from now it isn't necessary for someone to quote me to prove their point about natural literacy development.

References

Bloom, Lois. 1970. *Language development: Form and function in emerging grammars*. Cambridge, MA: MIT Press.

Brown, Roger. 1973. *A first language: The early stages*. Cambridge, MA: Harvard University Press.

Chomsky, Carol. 1971. Write first, read later. *Childhood Education, 47,* 296–99.

Chomsky, Carol. 1975. How sister got into the grog. *Early Years, 6,* 36–39.

Clay, Marie. 1972. *Sand: The Concepts About Print Test.* Portsmouth, NH: Heinemann.

Clay, Marie. 1975. *What did I write?* Portsmouth, NH: Heinemann.

Clay, Marie. 1979. *Reading: The patterning of complex behavior* (2nd ed.). Portsmouth, NH: Heinemann.

Downing, John. 1970. The development of linguistic concepts in children's thinking. *Research in the Teaching of English, 4,* 5–19.

Dybdahl, Claudia. 1980. Learning about language. In Yetta M. Goodman, Myna Haussler & Dorothy Strickland (Eds.), *Oral and written language development research: Impact on the schools* (Proceedings from the 1979 and 1980 IMPACT Conferences) (pp. 21–30). Newark, DE & Urbana, IL: International Reading Association & National Council of Teachers of English. (ERIC Document Reproduction Service Document ED 214 184)

Halliday, M. A. K. 1975. Learning how to mean. In Eric H. Lenneberg & Elizabeth Lenneberg (Eds.), *Foundations of language development: A multidisciplinary approach* (Vol. 1) (pp. 239–66). New York: Academic Press.

Henderson, Edmund, Estes, Thomas & Stonecash, Susan. 1972, Summer. An exploratory study of word acquisition among first graders at mid-term in a language experience approach. *Journal of Reading Behavior, 4*, 21–31.

Hildreth, Gertrude. 1936. Developmental sequences in name writing. *Child Development, 7*, 291–303.

Huey, Edmund. 1968. *The psychology and pedagogy of reading*. Cambridge: MIT Press. (Originally published 1908)

Read, Charles. 1973. Children's judgments of phonetic similarities in relation to English spelling. *Language Learning, 23*, 17–38.

Read, Charles. 1975. *Children's categorization of speech sounds in English* (Research Report No.17). Urbana, IL: National Council of Teachers of English.

Smith, E. Brooks, Goodman, Kenneth S. & Meredith, Robert. 1976. *Language and thinking in school* (2nd ed.). New York: Holt, Rinehart & Winston.

Vygotsky, Lev. 1978. *Mind in society: The development of higher psychological processes*. Cambridge, MA: Harvard University Press.

Beginning Reading Development: Strategies and Principles

Many of my colleagues in the field of reading support a model of reading as a psycholinguistic guessing game. However, they say, it's a model that seems to describe the developing reader well but certainly that's not how kids learn to read. A carefully controlled reading program is necessary at the beginning stages.

This statement was a challenge to me and since 1971 I have been on a search to find out more about the onset of learning to read. All of the work done in relation to Kenneth Goodman's model of reading (Goodman & Goodman 1978) suggests that processing written language is similar to processing oral language, so I looked to the research on oral language development to understand more about the development of written language.

In order to understand the beginnings of oral language development, linguists and psycholinguists studied two-, three-, and four-year-olds. They were amazed at what young children know about language at such an age. Though children cannot talk about this knowledge, their daily language use provides insight into it. Now psychologists are looking at children only a few months old to gain additional insights into the process of oral language development.

I began to wonder what we could discover about the emergence of reading and writing by studying very young children before the age

Originally published in *Developing Literacy: Young Children's Use of Language,* edited by Robert P. Parker & Frances A. Davis (Newark, DE: International Reading Association, 1983), pp. 68–83. Copyright 1983 by the International Reading Association. Reprinted with permission.

at which it is commonly assumed that beginning reading occurs. As my own work developed I became aware of an international group of scholars who were also beginning to think about young children and their interactions with print (Clay 1975; Downing 1970; Ferreiro 1980; Read 1975; Reid 1966; Smith 1976; Söderburgh 1977). A number of questions emerged. In a print-oriented society, do children develop an intuitive awareness of the nature of print at two, three, and four years of age? Do most children learn to read in some sense prior to schooling? As researchers, have we overlooked this early learning of written language because our models have caused us to ignore what is happening in the child's head? Have we so confused literacy development with schooling that we have ignored what children learn about written language prior to formal instruction?

I began to study children from the ages of two through six. I used print that I expected to be familiar to them from TV, streets, freeways, and supermarkets. I asked them to handle books and newspapers in various ways.

I am interested in written language development not because I believe reading should be taught in kindergarten or preschools. Rather, if we can discover (1) how children learn to interact with print in the real world, (2) what developmental patterns are involved in written language acquisition, (3) what significant features of written language children attend to, and (4) the nature of written language development, then we can set up curricula that build on the knowledge about written language that children bring to school.

Based on the research and theories of these scholars, and my own research with preschoolers, I have some tentative conclusions. Many two-, three-, and four-year-old children are learning to read by themselves through their interactions with print. This self-teaching happens only in literate societies and cultures where print bombards the senses of children. Think of the streets and supermarkets where preschoolers walk, the highways young children are driven along, and the written displays they encounter on TV. Children learn to organize and make sense of print just as they learn to organize the rest of their world. As they understand how four-legged animals differ from two-legged animals, they learn that print says things in one way while pictures say things in another. Early in my own research, I realized that preschoolers would often point to print and ask, What does that say? They were aware that print communicates—that it involves an act of meaning. Reading begins at this point of awareness.

Beginning reading at this stage is not alphabetic. Children are aware that print does the telling but view the written display as symbols of meaning. Therefore, the cut-out front panel of Rice Krispies is *cereal*, the Crest panel is *toothpaste*, and Pepsi-Cola can be called Pepsi, Coke, pop, or soda. It is interesting that children most often respond appropriately within the category of items. Even though they may know the names of some letters, understanding the alphabetic nature of written language comes later. The important questions for children seem to be, What is written language for? and, What does it mean? Through this exploration, children begin to make all kinds of intuitive decisions about *how* written language means. This supports Halliday's notion (1975) that form follows function. Just like proficient readers do, young children use print and its meaning, interacting with it through their own knowledge about the world—their own developing system of language and concepts. In addition they use pictorial cues, including color and situational context. Given a cut-out from a McDonald's french fries envelope, one child yelled, "That's McDonald's french fries!" She only had a two-dimensional form but could construct what the whole was from her previous experience. "Where does it say McDonald's french fries?" we asked, and the child pointed to the small black boldface letters, moving her fingers from left to right saying "McDonald's french fries" quickly and moving her finger slowly so it all came out even. She could have pointed to a whole line of golden arches, but rejected that graphic display as the written language communicator. This child is using the whole situation to construct meaning but knows it's the print that does the telling or saying of the meaning. One more example can support this point. We use a magazine picture of a large automobile in our studies. As the picture comes in view, our subjects most often say car. "Where does it say car?" we ask. Our subjects will respond by quickly finding a very small printed *Chevrolet* in the upper lefthand corner and moving their fingers back and forth under the printed word.

When print is totally decontextualized, preschoolers no longer treat it as meaningful language. For example, given a wrapper (pasted on cardboard) that says *Ivory* in large blue letters on a design of blue and white wavy lines, there is enough context so that almost all of our three- and four-year-olds respond with either soap or Ivory. When the word *Ivory* is printed in manuscript on plain white paper, the little ones react in three different ways. Some respond immediately with, "You know I can't read." Others start naming the letters, often but not always appropriately. One four-year-old who read Ivory and pointed to the appropriate print in the earlier contextualized task, pointed to each letter saying, "One-five-zero-r-e." The third group acted bored, fidgety, or silly. Being able to read in a situationally embedded context but not out of it is similar to the way young children develop oral language.

Bloom (1970) says children talk about events that are immediately perceptually available in the nonlinguistic context—adults do not talk about what they see and what they are doing when a listener is there to see for himself. It appears that child utterances depend directly on the support of nonlinguistic context, whereas adult utterances do not. This seems to be as true of written language development as it is of oral.

Use of Reading Strategies

Children make use of all the reading strategies described by the Goodman model of the reading process (Goodman 1980). Early on, readers recognize print and select the cues they believe to be significant. One four-year-old subject, upon seeing a label from Chicken of the Sea tuna, said, "That's chicken, no, tuna!" She then concluded, "No, dog food." Her first prediction was based on some cue from the graphic print *chicken*; she then realized it was not really chicken by picking up additional cues. We're not sure which ones, but she disconfirmed her original prediction as she changed her response to tuna. We couldn't understand the dog food response until one of the research assistants noticed a red-and-white checkered symbol on the can, the symbol used by the Ralston Purina Company, the manufacturer of dog food that also manufactures Chicken of the Sea tuna. With a lot of experience with a variety of print in many different situations, readers learn which are the significant language cues and which are not. It is very important to be selective in language learning and language use. Our early readers show they are beginning to be selective. They'll need lots of experience with real print in natural language environments to set it all straight.

Another predicting example comes from a four-year-old who responded to the picture of a Chevrolet by saying Bruick. "Where does it say Bruick?" I asked. He pointed to the small print in the upper part of the picture (Chevrolet) and said, "No, it's a Cadillac; no that's a Chevette. I thought it was a Bruick 'cause my auntie drives one."

Confirmation strategies are shown in both of the previous examples. In each case, the subjects use their knowledge to select minimal cues and predict. They disconfirm their initial guesses and responses and select additional cues to come up with responses more satisfactory to themselves. Through these examples, it is obvious that young readers are using print embedded in a known context to construct meaning.

Young readers are also tentative. They begin to form generalizations about the alphabetic nature of print and often begin to know when they do not know. Three-year-olds are quick to respond to Rice Krispies as cereal, while five-year-olds may respond more slowly. They may respond initially with, "I don't know," but when encouraged to guess, some say, "It's not Raisin Bran" or "I know it's some kind of cereal." I believe these children are at a more mature stage than the quick-to-respond three-year-olds. By five, children begin to relate sounds to letters and to know that names should be specific, not generic. With their greater knowledge, they become more tentative, acting as if they know less than some of the three-year-olds.

As children develop concepts about print, the labels they use may be inappropriate, although in responding to print in context, three-year-olds often respond with a two-word response for a two-word text item. Children often use the terms *word, letter,* and *number* interchangeably. (It is important to realize that these terms are all conceptually related.) In addition, children can use language appropriately in context but when asked to define the same item, they often cannot. For example, part of the task we have given our readers is book handling. I hold up a page in a book, wave it back and forth, and say, What is this? None of the twelve three- and four-year-olds I last did this with could answer the question. However, as I read them a story and came to the end of the print on the page, I'd say, What should I do now? Every one of the children I asked replied, Turn the *page.* Using language appropriately in a common, real-experience setting is much easier than defining a term or explaining what something is in the abstract.

Principles of Beginning Reading Development

So far I have provided a general picture of what children do in response to print and some tentative conclusions about written language development. As children interact with print, they not only begin to read and write—that is, actually use reading and writing for various purposes—they begin to develop principles about the nature and meaning of written language. They begin to decide which aspects of written language are significant for communication to take place and which aspects are insignificant and merit little attention. Designers of commercial logos make use of color. Color seems to be a feature of familiar print that provides some cue to aid in prediction early in development, but children soon seem to respond almost as well to the same print environment when color is missing. For example, children respond to a black-and-white reproduction of a stop sign, the McDonald's logo, or an Ivory wrapper almost the same as to the item retaining the original color.

Children construct a variety of principles about language relevant to their developing literacy, though they may essentially need to discard some and construct others if they are to move on. For a period of time, some of these principles may actually interfere with the development of other principles that may be more important. For example, if a child decides that in order for an aspect of language to be readable it must have no less than three characters or letters (Ferreiro 1980), then at some point a conflict or disequilibrium develops between concepts of wordness related to a minimal number principle and the reality of words such as *in,* and *on,* or phrases such as *he is to go to a Dr.* To complicate matters even further, many of these developing principles overlap and interact and children have to sort out which principles are most significant to meaning in written language and which are not very useful, are used infrequently, or have no relationship to reading or writing. Most important for everyone involved in curriculum development, however, is that these principles really cannot be taught through traditional, structured reading programs. Rather, they develop as children personally interact with a great deal of written language in appropriate environmental contexts that highlight the need for written language and the significant functions it serves.

These principles, I believe, emerge idiosyncratically for each child. Some principles may be considered together from the beginning and others may not. Children may reject one principle for another, depending on the text, the item, the significance of the reading or writing experience to the child, or the function of any particular literacy event. Also, children may decide that some principles have certain qualities in reading but are different for writing and still different for spelling or for talking about writing. For example, when Denise wrote her name, she wrote each letter with a capital letter except for the *i,* which was the same size as the others except dotted: DENiSE. As she formed each letter, she said, "D. . . E . . . M . . . L . . . C . . . E." After she was finished, she was asked, "Now tell me, what does that say?" She responded, "Denise Roberts." When asked, "Can you read that?" she looked at each letter as she responded appropriately, "D. . .E. . .N . . .I. . .S. . .E." Reading, saying, and spelling as one writes do not all result in the same kinds of productions. Different principles seem to be operating in each one of these situations.

In my research on the roots of literacy (Goodman 1980) and through an awareness of the research of others, I have begun to delineate these principles as I understand them at the present time. Additional research will cause adaptations, changes, or deletions in the principles and their various aspects; other principles will be expanded and developed. The more researchers gain insight into which principles children develop, how they are used, and how they develop, the more we'll understand about written language development.

What's most significant, in my view, is that children are involved in developing a writing system for themselves. In many ways, as individuals, they are going through the same problems and raising the same questions for themselves that the world's communities went through when they became literate. The needs, the environment, the attitudes, the knowledge, the significant others, are all merging to aid each child in becoming a literate human being. If the significance of each "literacy event" (any experience with reading or writing in which the child is involved) in the life of the child is not well understood, educators will continue for hundreds of years to teach children, prior to the development of literacy, aspects of linguistic study that they do not need, and will ignore the intuitive knowledge children have when they come to school. This intuitive knowledge about the principles of written language is their greatest asset in becoming literate.

The major principles are best viewed as developmental, since children grow into and through all of them. They develop idiosyncratically, depending on each child's environment, and they overlap and become integrated. Over time, children must sort out which principles are the most significant in any particular written language event or situation. The three major kinds of principles include (1) functional principles that emerge as children discover when and how written language is used and for what purposes; (2) linguistic principles that emerge as children discover how written language is organized in relation to the graphophonic, syntactic, semantic, and pragmatic systems of language; and (3) relational principles that emerge as children discover how the systems, units, or aspects of written and oral languages relate to the systems, units, or aspects of meaning and how they relate to each other.

Functional Principles

Functional principles develop through children's responses to specific uses of literacy. The degree to which literacy events are meaningful and the value that any particular literacy event has for any particular child in any particular cultural setting will have impact on the development of the functional principles. Most written language that the child experiences can be divided into two categories: (1) print in environmental settings (on TV; names for people, toys, games; print used to direct and control our lives on streets and highways and in buildings and stores) and (2) print embedded in connected discourse, which includes more traditional forms of written language (books, magazines, comics, newspapers, letters).

Experiences with print will be different for different children. Children whose parents are college students, computer programmers, or authors, where a great deal of writing and reading goes on in the home, will discover the significance of literacy events differently from children whose parents read the Bible daily before dinner or children whose parents use writing selectively for shopping lists, filling out forms, and taking phone messages. The statements adults and siblings make about literacy events also have their effect on children's developing notions about the function of literacy. Negative statements about schooling, reading, and writing will have as much impact on children's developing literacy as will the influence of enjoying books and reading. Literate parents who show anxiety about literacy development in young children and denigrate the schooling experience may leave marks on the child's view of the value of reading and writing and its learning in the school setting. Educators can do little about these situations in any immediate sense. It is important, though, to build awareness of the impact of home experiences on literacy development through parent and community education.

We know children are influenced by the great diversity of literacy events they experience in developing ideas and concepts about the function of written language in society by the time they come to school (Wells 1981). Children encountering literacy events will construct important knowledge about the nature and function of print in their daily lives many years prior to schooling. Children will show through their responses that some functions of written language in the environment control the lives of others. Jon, as he passes a school sign, says to his mother, "That says, Watch out for kids." Darryl's mom is driving him to school and stops by a park-parallel sign to let him out near the school playground. He points at the sign and says to his mom, "Ya better not park here." Roberta may be indicating that the names of people and the names of places serve similar functions when she says to her mother as they are driving past the drug chain, "Revco has the same face as my name." By age four, some children know that newspapers serve many functions. A number of four-year-olds, shown the advertising page in the newspaper, respond with: "Take that to the market," "Buy ketchup," and "It says coffee costed less." When shown the TV page, they say: "Channel Four,"."Sesame Street," and other favorite programs. These children are categorizing and organizing the function of one form of written language in their world. They even discover their own personal use for written language. Reis was scolded one day for leaving the house and not letting his mother know where he went. The next day, when his mother was looking for him, she found this note on the table. It said, IMGOEGTOOBAWTSID.

(I'm going to be outside.) When you don't have an immediate face-to-face situation, written language, this child discovered, can be used for long-distance communication.

A seven-year-old was very concerned about a problem she had. Instead of confronting her mother directly, she decided that if she wrote a note it might soften matters somewhat. Her mother found the following on her pillow when she woke up in the morning:

> Dear Mom   plese don't get mad
> I dremed that i was sitting on
> the toylit
> you no what I mean do you and by axidint
> i pede my bed

When children write shopping lists or lists for Santa Claus, they most often place one item appropriately after the previous one. Not only have they learned the function of lists, but they seem to know something about the form as well. Children discover a variety of functions of written language through everyday literacy events, but through story reading they learn the function of connected discourse. They are able to point to the print in books when someone asks, Can you show me where I am reading? Children who are not as personally involved in book reading may point to the picture as the place adults are reading. Also, a child will show the function of language even by reading a wordless book, starting on an appropriate beginning page and saying in an appropriate tone, Once upon a time. Children discover the function of written language through every literacy event in their experience. If those events are positive, warm, and significant to their lives, children will grow into literacy easily and naturally. Literacy events may be unpleasant or meaningless for some children; for them, growth into literacy will seem to be an overwhelming chore.

Linguistic Principles

A second group of principles is linguistic in nature. The child comes to know (1) how the written language system is organized, (2) what its units are, (3) which features are most significant, and (4) the stability of its organization.

For example, children learning English develop notions about the alphabetic nature of that written language, while Chinese children develop notions about the logographic nature of writing. English-language children must come to know that the alphabet includes letters such as B K A, and not such letters as ‫ע‬, as in Hebrew. Many children play at making letters or characters before they know that letters have names or that letters are related to reading and writing. English-language children's letters look remarkably like the alphabetic system known as roman letters, while Arabic-language children's letters have the sweep and character of the Arabic alphabet. Over time, children discover that English words have a specific pattern or organization, and this is revealed through their invented spellings. They become aware, especially as they read and write stories, that punctuation is used for a variety of purposes. They sometimes begin using punctuation before they have total control over its function and purposes. Other times they experiment with punctuation in nonconventional ways. Rudy, age six, used periods instead of spaces to show word boundaries for a time in his development of the writing system.

As children learn that written language takes up space, the directionality of the written language system and the various forms it takes also develop. Although in schools we are sometimes concerned that children write from right to left, we take it for granted that almost all of these children do write horizontally and not vertically. In most cases, when children are asked to show where it says something, they move their fingers from left to right and sometimes from right to left across the print. Early in their schooling, they seem to know that the story in a book goes from the top line to the bottom and across to the next page.

Observation of children as they write often shows their developing control over directionality. They may start their explorations into directionality by writing in the same way they draw. It goes in many directions and it doesn't make any difference where it starts or ends. Soon more deliberate directionality is observable.

When Bryan was three and a half, he drew a large dinosaur on the right side of a large sheet of paper. When he finished his drawing, he was at the bottom of the paper but he wanted to write the name of the dinosaur so he asked for the spelling and as he was given the letters, he wrote TY on the bottommost part of the paper and, because of the amount of space left, put RAN USOR US REX each on separate lines snaking up to the top of the page. He was writing from left to right and returning to the beginning of the line each time, but the direction he went seemed to relate to the spacing of his drawing and aesthetic qualities rather than all the appropriate writing conventions. Since we have not observed children carefully in their writing development during these periods of time, we have been ignorant of the development toward horizontal directionality by English-speaking children. We become nervous when we look at a finished piece of writing, see it in reverse order, and assume that something is organically wrong with the writer. Most children, except the hearing impaired and those with some other disabilities involving speech, generally control the linguistic principles of oral language prior to the development of written language. Many of the syntactic and semantic aspects of oral language are similar to written language. However, directionality, space, and form in written language have no counterpart in oral language and children need to organize this system from the beginning as they use it. They also must develop ideas about spelling, punctuation, and variations in spacing, typography, and handwriting, as well as aesthetic uses of written language. None of these features is obvious in oral language, so children need to explore written language and its components widely in order to understand the complexities of writing as a system. This is developed through use. Children most easily control those aspects of the syntactic and semantic systems that are similar in both oral and written language. However, some features of written language occur only in that system. Direct quotes, for instance, are used frequently in children's literature but are not represented formally in oral language. Children represent direct quotes in their own writing very early but don't use conventional spacing and punctuation until later in their development.

Relational Principles

Children learn to relate written language to meaning and where necessary to oral language. They develop the knowledge that some unit of written language is linked in some way with some unit of meaning or some unit of speech or both. This linkage may be words or letters, but it is not restricted to them. It also includes propositions, ideas, concepts, images, signs, symbols, and icons.

Early in their development, children may develop the belief that somehow written language should express in writing some of the characteristics of the object being described. Therefore, it is not surprising that Ferreiro (1980), after assigning children Piagetian-type tasks in written language, concludes that they often use the size of the object, the characteristics or the number of items being referred to, or their age. ("Father's name must have more letters than mine because he is so much bigger and older than I am." If *kitten* is written with three characters, then *three kittens* is written by reduplicating the same set of characters three times.) Again, the active development of children's involvement in their own written language development is evident. As children develop the notion that written language is alphabetic, the phonological system and the graphic system of language become interrelated. The child may write AED at the end of a story. Usually at this stage, the child is generalizing the sound that *e* represents in words such as *bent* and *set* to the letter *A*. (Read, 1975, explains this phenomenon in his study of children's phonological development.) When asked why there is both an *A* and *E* in that word (AED), one child said, "It has to have three and that letter has to be *D* 'cause it's at the end. It's got an *E* in it, but I know it has to have an *A* here." The child cannot fully articulate the graphophonic relationships, but a careful analysis of this and other aspects of children's spelling suggests a complicated interrelationship developing between the graphic and sound systems of language.

It is not uncommon to find children using *e* and *y* interchangeably at the end of words to represent the silent *e* or *y*. *Play* and *make* have been spelled as PLAE and MAKY. Think of the complex relationships and rules children must work through: *y* often represents the sound of *e* in final position in many dialects of American English as in *kitty, Betty, marry*. In addition, both *y* and *e* are final markers and each can be in final positions without having its own sound representation, patterning instead with other letters in order to represent sounds. Both *make* and *play* are good examples of this latter phenomenon. As in so many other areas of language, children's errors or miscues provide considerable insight into their developing knowledge of the principles of written language.

During their development children also relate story structure and voice pointing to written language. They indicate as they start to "read" a book that they know it has a story structure. They use phrases such as *Mother said* or *The witch cried* as they retell a book they've heard read to them often. They will start such a book with a story opener such as *Once upon a time* or *A long, long time ago*. These are all aspects of language that tend to occur in written texts for children. As they use written language forms, they show they know that certain kinds of language occur in certain texts and not in others. Given a joke or riddle book, children change the kinds of language they use. They relate certain kinds of language to certain kinds of written texts. They have insights into the context of the situation.

Another kind of relational principle develops as children seem to discover that the written line and the oral utterance have some relationship in common in certain contexts and may match an oral rendition syllable by syllable with the words of a written text. Eventually, as children are read to or asked to follow along as an adult reads, there is evidence that they are developing ways of relating the oral and written language. Clay (1979) has called this phenomenon "voice pointing."

Children need active experiences with literacy in order to grow and to develop the roots of literacy (Goodman 1980). Through such active experiences with literacy events, children develop principles about written language. We can't teach these principles. Children construct them through interactions with their literate environment and through asking questions about it. What we can do as teachers is to organize a literate environment that will invite children to interact and to ask questions.

References

Bloom, Lois. 1970. *Language development: Form and function in emerging grammars.* Cambridge, MA: MIT Press.

Clay, Marie. 1975. *What did I write?* Portsmouth, NH: Heinemann.

Clay, Marie. 1979. *Reading: The patterning of complex behavior* (2nd ed.). Portsmouth, NH: Heinemann.

Downing, John. 1970. Children's concepts of language in learning to read. *Educational Research, 12,* 106–12.

Ferreiro, Emilia. 1980. *The relationship between oral and written language: The children's viewpoints.* In Yetta M. Goodman, Myna Haussler & Dorothy Strickland (Eds.), *Oral and written language development research: Impact on the schools* (Proceedings from the 1979 and 1980 IMPACT Conferences) (pp. 47–56). Newark, DE & Urbana, IL: International Reading Association & National Council of Teachers of English. (ERIC Document Reproduction Service Document ED 214 184)

Ferreiro, Emilia & Teberosky, Ana. 1982. *Literacy before schooling.* Portsmouth, NH: Heinemann. (Original work published 1979)

Goodman, Kenneth S. & Goodman, Yetta. 1978. *Reading of American children whose language is a stable rural dialect of English or a language other than English* (Research Report No. NIE-C-00-3-0087, U.S. Department of Health, Education and Welfare). Tucson: Program in Language and Literacy, University of Arizona.

Goodman, Yetta M. 1980. The roots of literacy. In Malcolm P. Douglass (Ed.), *Claremont Reading Conference, 44th Yearbook* (pp. 1–32). Claremont, CA: Claremont Colleges.

Halliday, M. A. K. 1975. *Learning how to mean: Explorations in the development of language.* New York: Elsevier.

Read, Charles. 1975. *Children's categorization of speech sounds in English* (Research Report No. 17). Urbana, IL: National Council of Teachers of English.

Reid, J. F. 1966. Learning to think about reading. *Educational Research, 9,* 56–62.

Smith, Frank. 1976. Learning to read by reading. *Language Arts, 53,* 297–99, 322.

Söderburgh, Ragnhild. 1977. *Reading in early childhood: A linguistic study of a preschool child's gradual acquisition of reading ability.* Washington, DC: Georgetown University Press.

Wells, Gordon. 1981. *Learning through interaction: The study of language development.* New York: Cambridge University Press.

Early Literacy Development: A Sociotransactional View

I became interested in studying how children learn to read about twenty-five years ago. I was naive about when learning to read started, so I examined the reading experiences of first graders, believing at the time what many still believe today, that literacy learning started in school and that if I wanted to study beginning reading I had to study first graders. But I learned through my study of first graders that even children who had taken tests that predicted that they should not be able to read provided evidence that they knew a great deal about reading. All the children I worked with knew about the alphabetic nature of English print. They knew that print in books and on other objects in the environment communicated messages. They knew how to open books and which way was up, how and when to turn pages, and which parts of print in books were meant for reading aloud and which could be ignored. (Has a child ever read to you the bibliographic information on the back of the title page?) The children I was carefully observing knew that print was read from left to right. They were predicting as they read and confirming their predictions. They made use of all language cueing systems: *the graphophonic system*—they sounded out as they read, and read quite a bit of text without any miscues; *the syntactic system*—as they read orally, their intonation

Originally published in *Perspectives on Whole Language: Past, Present, Potential* (Selected proceedings from the First Whole Language Umbrella Conference), edited by Mary Bixby, Dorothy King, Susan Ohanian, Shirley Crenshaw & Patricia Jenkins (Columbia, MO: University of Missouri Press, 1992), pp. 16–22. Copyright 1992 by Yetta M. Goodman.

showed that most of the time they knew when sentences started and when they ended; and *the semantic system*—their miscues usually indicated that they knew that reading had to make sense. Not only could they do many things with reading, but they knew about how writing worked as well. They could use pencils, pens, and magic markers appropriately. Their writing resembled the English writing system. They knew that what people wrote could be read.

It became obvious to me that in a literate society such as ours, children learn initially about written language not as a result of instruction in reading and writing in school but because they are members of a literate society—a society whose members, regardless of socioeconomic status, use reading and writing daily and in many different ways. Most members of our society can use written language to accomplish the basic tasks they need to live in their communities. It is in this environment that children learn very important things about literacy. They come to understand and to explore the purposes for which people use literacy. They come to know how reading and writing are organized so that people can make sense from the forms they take. They learn that reading and writing represent ideas, meanings, and concepts. They become sensitive to which people are considered more literate than others and begin to develop values about different kinds of literacy. They learn how others value literacy events. They begin to realize that they belong to a society and culture in which literacy plays significant and important roles, sometimes even controlling ones. They learn that people even talk about literacy events.

As I've continued to study how children learn to read and write in this literate society of ours, I have become convinced that children must invent literacy for themselves as they become aware that in order to be a fully functioning member of society, they must be literate. Of course they take their lead from the ways in which literacy is used in society, but people must invent aspects of literacy for themselves. Children invent forms of writing, so they experiment with cursive and print forms before producing them in readable forms; they experiment with how spelling and punctuation work. They invent stories as they interact with print in books.

The Roots of Literacy

In 1980 I wrote an article (Goodman 1980) exploring what I called the roots of literacy, helping to explain the written forms that children invent as they are immersed in literate settings and exploring their moves toward conventionality in their reading and writing. I suggested that children develop complicated roots of literacy, each with a number of offshoots. They develop the roots of writing, the roots of reading, and ways to talk and think about reading and writing. These roots are developed not in isolated settings but in collaboration with the members of children's particular cultural groups and through their intimate contact with routine and significant literacy events that occur daily in their lives. The roots of literacy develop as children transact with all the symbol systems in their world, such as art, music, and dance. Written language is an additional symbol system, and children come to understand that written language is used and formed differently from the other symbol systems. Every experience that they have with TV, in shopping centers, and in watching family members cook and clean, write lists, pay bills, and read newspapers and Bibles is an important influence on children's learning to read and write. These add to their history of experiences.

Children want to participate socially in the same events their loved ones do, so they experiment with reading and writing. They play at reading books. They write notes to family members and ask that they be read. They snuggle up to adults in order to participate in the warmth of being read to. They participate in literacy events. As they write and read they invent forms and functions for their personal literacy uses. So children put up signs on their doors that say KEPE AWT because they have experienced that written signs control the behavior of others, or they write on paper to simulate tickets for their shows or circuses, money for when they play store or house, or labels for their Teenage Mutant Ninja Turtles. As they transact with their environment—through their talk and their play and the thousands of acts and tools of literacy they encounter every day—they develop important concepts about how literacy communicates. In other words they use language to learn "how to mean" (Halliday 1975).

Principles of Literacy Development

I have identified three important principles that children develop as they become literate. I call these the functional, linguistic, and relational principles.

Children develop the functional principle of literacy as they come to understand the reasons, the purposes, and the functions for reading and writing in their world. They come to know that the different significant people in their lives use literacy in different ways and for different purposes. Some are always involved with a book of some sort. Some people read newspapers daily and react to them emotionally. Some people receive mail and cry or laugh over letters from family members. Others react to receiving junk mail or bills by wincing or swearing. Some people do homework for school and make statements about its importance and the purposes it serves. Children become aware that their written language labels and personalizes objects and places. They come to know that when people want to remember things, they write down phone messages or notes and put things away in special places. Written language can be used to contact other people, and sometimes it is used when people want to build things, cook, clean, or take medicine. Each of these kinds of daily acts influences the ways in which children learn the functions of written language.

A second principle is the linguistic principle. Through this principle, children come to understand how literacy is organized so that it can be read or written. They learn that written language is usually organized in different ways when it serves different purposes. Written language in books looks different from written language in magazines or on a letter from Grandma. Children come to understand the formation of letters, paragraphs, books, and advertisements. They realize that written language has a syntactic organization and needs to be written or read in certain ways in order for communication to occur. As they develop this principle, they learn the systems of spelling, punctuation, and the other forms of writing necessary to organize coherent texts.

The third principle develops simultaneously with the others. Children come to know that written language represents, symbolizes, or stands for meanings or concepts of various kinds. They learn that written language sometimes represents oral language but that oftentimes written language represents meanings directly. I call this principle the relational principle, suggesting that kids come to understand the complicated ways in which written language relates to meanings. They come to know that written language is a complex symbolic system.

What is difficult for teachers and parents and people developing curriculum for schools to grasp is that all the roots and all the principles develop simultaneously and that they are in progress and well underway years before children come to school. Children who are read to for five thousand hours prior to kindergarten have a different history with written language than children who have a lot of books in their room that they peruse whenever they wish without an adult around and a small desk filled with all kinds of writing and drawing implements at which they write or draw whenever they wish. And the history of those children who see writing used primarily for very practical purposes such as getting a job, paying bills, and reading advertisements that come in the mail is different still. In most cases

Figure 1.
Birthday Card

schools are organized to be more receptive to some kinds of these histories than to others. Sometimes we even believe that children who haven't had the kind of experiences that we believe are most conducive to literacy learning in school are not living in literate environments. And our beliefs color the ways in which we react to such children when it comes to their literacy learning.

A set of texts written by Aaron over a three-year period are examples to provide evidence of the principles that a beginning writer comes to understand and the roots of literacy that influence development. Aaron knows that writing serves different purposes and is organized in different ways. The three texts each have a different overall format. His birthday card for Grapa Ghne (Grandpa Kenny) (Figure 1) has the greeting in the most prominent place with the signature ("by Aaron") written up the left-hand side. The note to his mom (Figure 2) has the prose written straight across each line in letterlike fashion.(The cursive *mom* was written on the top section of the note, which was folded over with the message written inside.) The receipt (Figure 3) is organized differently still, with short appropriate phrases and a line drawn for the signature.

Figure 2.
Note to Mom

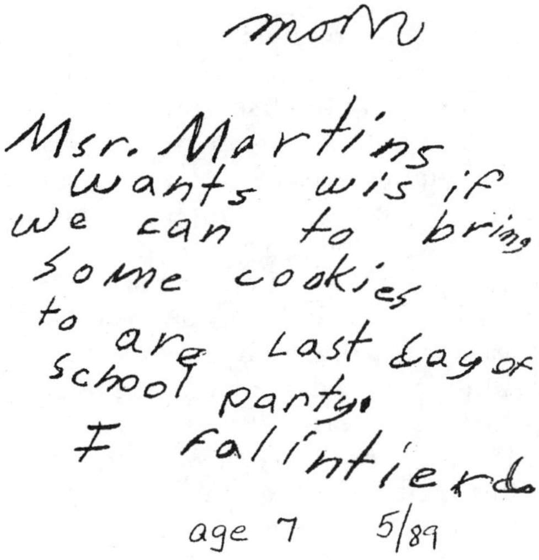

mom

Msr. Martins
  wants wis if
we can to bring
some cookies
to are last day or
school panty.
I falíntierd.

age 7   5/89

Figure 3.
Receipt

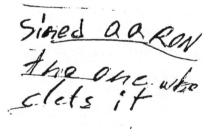

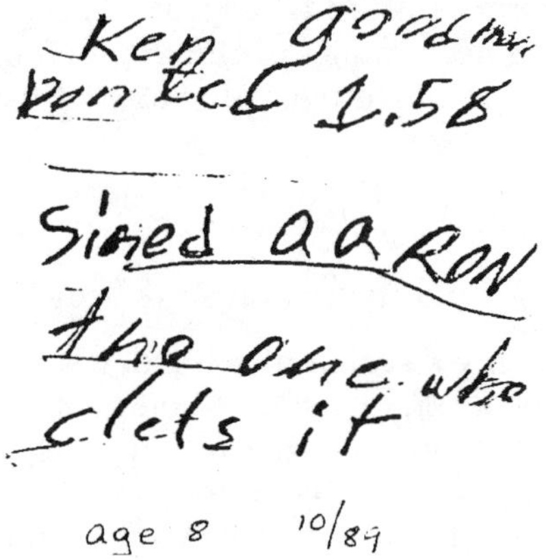

Ken goodman
ponted 1.58

Simed aaRon
the one who
clets it

age 8   10/89

None of these forms was taught to Aaron in any formal sense, but the community in which he lives has immersed him in literacy experiences so that he could write such texts spontaneously at appropriate times. He shows his knowledge of that relational principle by representing what he needs to say in writing in an appropriate format. The language he uses in each text shows that he can change the syntax and semantics of his messages to fit the appropriate contexts.

"Happy Birthday Grandpa Kenny" is enough language for a card. In his note to his mom, he seems to want her to know that the teacher is only making a request, not a demand. To accomplish this he embeds a subordinate clause into his first sentence: "Mrs. Martins wants us *if we can* to bring some cookies to our last day of school party." He uses a period at the end of the sentence and then continues to explain: "I volunteered." By using short phrases in the UNICEF receipt, Aaron is able to show who donated the money, how much was collected, who collected it, and even that he, Aaron, was the one who collected it. His note has complex syntax and vocabulary.

The birthday card was written when Aaron was five. The note to his mother was written two and one half years later, and the receipt six months after that. Each was written without adult direction, although he was asked to supply a receipt when he was given a pocketful of change for his UNICEF carton. The three texts provide insight not only into the roots and principles of language but into Aaron's development as well. He develops concepts of word boundaries, spelling, handwriting, and complex syntax and meanings moving toward adult convention.

Every piece of children's writing that has a real purpose in the real world provides evidence of children's developing knowledge. The best way to capture this knowledge is to keep examples of children's writing over time. Samples of children's reading can be audiotaped and kept and examined over time as well (Goodman, Watson & Burke 1987).

A Sociotransactional View

As I have continued my research into the development of literacy in children, I have come to a rather simple notion of how these roots and principles develop. I should say that my notions are simple but the process of development is very complex indeed. I call this developmental model "a sociotransactional view of literacy development." Literacy develops and is influenced by the transactions people have with literacy use in their communities. The home and the school are indeed the child's first literacy teachers. For me human development is synonymous with the social and personal history of each individual. Thus children become literate as a result of their personal and social histories with literacy events. Literacy events include all the various transactions such as the ones I've been discussing that children have with reading and writing. Literacy events include not only the reading and writing that children participate in directly but the reading and writing and talk about reading and writing in which they are immersed. These aspects of literacy constitute the social history of literacy for each child. But each child responds to literacy in different ways based on his or her unique self. Children make individual decisions about literacy, the purposes it serves, the forms it takes, and the ways in which literacy makes sense. They often invent forms and functions of reading and writing themselves as they explore and experiment with the uses of literacy. These individual responses reflect the child's personal literacy history.

As teachers and researchers, in order to understand how each individual becomes literate, we must know and understand the uniqueness of the individual's personal and social experiences as she or he is immersed in literacy events, and we must understand the influence of context on each event. Through Aaron's examples, I showed how his experiences with written language helped me understand why he did what he did and why he chose the specific forms of written language that he did to express his meanings.

The *contexts* in which these experiences occur also impact learners. Children are only influenced regarding how written language communicates when they are in environments where written language does communicate. Children only learn that reading is pleasurable if they are in contexts where reading is pleasurable. People learn what bus signs mean or what is meant by "cholesterol free" on a package only if they have had real reasons to be in contexts to understand the functions and forms of such writing and reading and how these relate to the meanings being conveyed. Not only is the quality of the experiences as they occur in particular contexts important, but the *amount of time* spent in literacy events in those particular contexts is also significant for each learner.

This discussion, which has explored the roots of literacy, the principles of literacy learning, and the fact that the social and personal histories of individual children influence their literacy learning, demonstrates the complexity of written language development. For many children the complexity of literacy learning is not difficult. Schools are important places that influence children's personal and social literacy development. In schools the learning of literacy can be exciting and stimulating. It can build on the learnings children have already begun and extend and expand on literacy development. This is happening in many whole language classrooms.

However, children can also learn that reading and writing are too difficult for them to achieve, that written language in school is boring and has no relevance to their lives. Marilyn French, in her novel *Her Mother's Daughter* (1987), describes the first day in school for Bella, an immigrant non-English-speaking five-year-old. Bella is bewildered by this new experience:

> The teacher poked open the lid of the inkwell and showed Bella how to dip a pen in it and how to hold the pen to write. But when Bella tried it, she made a big blot. . . . Bella copied meaningless words from the blackboard: BOY GIRL DOG CAT. In time she came to understand what these words meant, but she could not put them in a sentence. . . . She could hear the word "stupid, stupid" running through her brain and knew that was what they all thought. . . . And she was stupid.

Needless to say, Bella does not do well in school.

Many of us can describe experiences of children who have had a good start in literacy development but who have become discouraged by what they come to believe reading and writing are in the school setting. I believe that whole language teaching builds on the literacy that children bring to school. It values and respects children's social and personal histories and extends and expands on them. Teaching children literacy with holistic understanding about language has been advocated for well over a century (Huey 1908/1968; Iredell 1898; Shannon 1990).

I'd like to conclude by thinking about curriculum and schooling when we take into account the roots of literacy, the principles of literacy learning, and the issues of experience, context, and time. Many of these ideas have come from discussions with whole language teachers.

Experiences

Children need to be immersed in a wide range of learning experiences. They can explore environmental issues in their communities. They can discover how people use reading and writing by taking walks through the school and the community. They can learn about democracy by participating in the important roles necessary to organize and manage a classroom so it is a pleasant learning environment. Bringing community experiences into the classroom and taking trips to places where important things are happening provide opportunities to examine issues such as space exploration, death, roles of family members, or high prices for gasoline. And as children play with a wide variety of resources, they develop many concepts about literacy. Accompanying such play experiences taking place daily in the classroom are hundreds of literacy activities that are necessary for the experiences to be successful. Letters must be written to local government employees to ask questions or raise issues. Wheeled-toy areas contain automobile and bicycle catalogues and blank receipts for gasoline stations or auto shop repairs.

These experiences demand that the classroom environment must include a wide variety of uses of literacy, a wide variety of forms of literacy, and opportunities for choice in what to write and read. In early grades especially, such experiences may become part of everyday play, and opportunities to read and write during play activities must be planned for. There will need to be all kinds of reading and writing resources to help children and teachers get through the day. Classrooms need paper on which to write notes and lists of what will be served at the cafeteria or what to use for cleaning sinks and floors in the classrooms, for example. At the same time it is necessary to provide opportunities to read and write to each other in the classroom, to other members of the school community, or to the community at large; these opportunities grow out of the planned or spontaneous experiences that are taking place daily in the classroom. Because so much is being learned, and reading and writing are usually involved in the learning, there will always be the need to talk about literacy events.

Contexts

The experiences that children have and the resources that they use will involve students in using literacy in many different places in the classroom and as part of most of the activities during the school day. Teachers may build lofts or have some quiet reading corners. Tables or grouped desks are more conducive to writing than separate desks because they provide social settings in which children can discuss their reading and writing with each other. Some individual space is also necessary for those children who like to find a single desk in a quiet corner to write for a period of time. Children are helped to become aware of how they use literacy both inside and outside the school setting. Teachers respect the literacy events that take place in the homes of children and discuss who reads and writes and why they need to do so in all kinds of home and work settings. All kinds of literacy use are considered legitimate. Children are helped to see how literacy is used by all members of the school community for all manner of functions. Teachers know that children provide evidence that they do not know the same things about reading and writing in every setting. Writing signs to display art work may show that kids know more about written language than is seen only in their writing a letter to the editor of the daily newspaper. Expectations for such differences are built into the instructional program.

Time

For too long in schools there has been an expectation that children must be at a particular point in their literacy development at a particular time. Curriculum planning must take into consideration the time necessary for children to become confident readers and writers. Learning to read and write by having separate reading and writing instructional periods does not provide the in-depth time children need to become literate. Children need lots of time with reading and writing. We have for too long spent more time in school on learning how to read and write than in the actual use of reading and writing to get things done, to learn new things, and to enjoy reading and writing.

Teachers must consider carefully the amount of time that they plan for different experiences. Children who read and write only fictional narratives or focus mostly on journal writing will develop these genres, but this will not help in the development of the reading and writing of directions or nonfiction materials. On the other hand, changing types of reading and writing experiences too quickly without time for young readers and writers to build an in-depth knowledge of a particular genre is also problematic. Whole language teachers who take such notions into consideration will balance these varieties of reading and writing with the time available. In whole language schools, committees are able to schedule appropriate time for different literacy genres and assure that children get a wide range of experiences across the years as well as explore and develop the knowledge necessary to be successful.

In addition to curriculum planning that takes into account the issues of context, experiences, and time, there is one additional key to literacy learning. Teachers and curriculum planners must continue to build their knowledge about what kinds of literacy experiences children have at home and what children's reading and writing reveal about their knowledge of literacy. With such information teachers will find ways to help children connect their new literacy learning in school with their social and personal histories. Through such connections, school literacy learning is compatible with children's prior social history within the family and the community and with their unique personal histories. In this way literacy learning can be made easy for all children. That is the challenge we must face and work toward.

References

French, Marilyn. 1987. *Her mother's daughter*. New York: Summit.

Goodman, Yetta M. 1980. The roots of literacy. In Malcolm P. Douglass (Ed.), *Claremont Reading Conference, 44th Yearbook* (pp. 1–32). Claremont, CA: Claremont Colleges.

Goodman, Yetta M., Watson, Dorothy J. & Burke, Carolyn L. 1987. *Reading miscue inventory: Alternative procedures*. New York: Richard C. Owen.

Halliday, M. A. K. 1975. *Learning how to mean: Explorations in the development of language*. New York: Elsevier.

Huey, Edmund. 1968. *The psychology and pedagogy of reading*. Cambridge, MA: MIT Press. (Originally published 1908)

Iredell, H. 1898. Eleanor learns to read. *Education, 19*, 233–38.

Shannon, Patrick. 1990. *The struggle to continue: Progressive reading instruction in the United States*. Portsmouth, NH: Heinemann.

Part Four

The Writing Process (1963–1992)

Writing informs the development of reading and reading informs the development of writing. Most researchers who were initially interested in one of these expressive forms, either reading or writing, have come to realize that they had to consider the role of reading in the composing process and the role of writing in the development of reading. I came to this realization after my initial forays into reading miscue research.

In a study of the writing process that a team of researchers and I participated in with Tohono O'odham third and fourth graders (Goodman & Wilde 1992), it became quickly evident that reading served many purposes for these young writers. They used stories and nonfiction texts as resources for ideas and information. As we observed, children would remember a word or phrase from a particular book, search for it in the classroom library, and return to share their finds with their classmates. In this setting, we became aware of the importance talk and illustration and other print media—in the community and on the walls of the classroom—had on the writing development of the students. We realized how interested the students were in one another's writing and we began to write about and discuss the importance of the social community on writing development.

We were able to document how the young authors responded to using writing for different functions. Letters to friends were written in ways different from letters to professional authors or governmental officials. Articles about sports events were written in forms different from social studies or science reports. Children reached for different linguistic formats to serve the different functions of writing that they needed. This principle that form follows function supported the examples of writing I had been collecting from younger children in my early literacy studies. Children invent forms for birthday or Mother's Day cards that are different from those they invent to leave reminder notes for themselves or to tell their mothers they did something wrong.

As I consider the first article in this group, I realize that although the article focuses on spelling and is part of a section on the writing process, the research was done as part of a case study of my daughter Karen as a self-taught reader. This particular article was the culminating project for a linguistics class that I took in my doctoral program. My husband Ken audited that class because he was applying linguistic principles to miscue analysis and wanted to know more about the nature of language.

What is interesting to me at this point is that the term *invented spelling* was not yet in common use at that time, but we were examining Karen's spellings and her strategies for spelling from a linguistic perspective in order to understand her reading proficiency. I realize now the importance of one of the conclusions from that work. We realized that Karen knew when she did not know. When learners know that they do not know, they remain tentative about their conclusions and they continue to search for additional solutions to problems such as how to spell or what to predict during reading or what to do when reading does not make sense. Eleanor Duckworth (1987) shares my belief about the virtues of not knowing:

> It would make a significant difference to the cause of intelligent thought in general, and to the number of right answers that are ultimately known, if teachers were encouraged to focus on the virtues involved in not knowing, so that those virtues would get as much attention in classrooms from day to day as the virtue of knowing the right answer. (p. 69)

Miscue and writing research makes the concept of invention obvious. Because they know that they don't know, children are tentative about their learning, are willing to take risks and invent all aspects of their oral and written language to express meaning. These inventions are executed in the environment of conventional language used by families and communities. The tension between invention and convention is continual throughout one's life but is especially open to examination during the early years and the primary grades in school.

References

Duckworth, Eleanor. 1987. *The having of wonderful ideas and other essays on teaching and learning.* New York: Teachers College Press.

Goodman, Yetta M. & Wilde, Sandra (Eds.). 1992. *Literacy events in a community of young writers.* New York: Teachers College Press.

Spelling Ability
of a Self-Taught Reader
(with Kenneth S. Goodman)

Some children learn to read before they go to school (Durkin 1961). This is a fact that teachers and educators have been aware of for some time, for considerable attention has been given to early reading. Less attention has been given to other literacy skills—spelling, for example—that children may develop before they begin formal instruction. We have undertaken a study of the language and literacy skills of one self-taught reader. We are reporting here our findings on the spelling techniques she used and the generalizations she developed.

At the time of the study, our daughter Karen was six years and five months of age. She was an intent child who loved to learn. Her keen attention and her love of learning may have accounted in part for her ability to read and comprehend materials at a fifth-grade level, as measured by Gray's Standardized Oral Reading Paragraphs.

Karen's environment was rich in language experiences. She had always been read to, listened to, and talked to. Singing, poetry, nursery rhymes, and oral family language games were daily fare in her home. She had puzzles and picture lotto games, but her favorite recreation at home was to pretend that she was a teacher or a librarian; she set up three or more dolls in front of her and read to them.

With no instruction, Karen was reading independently by the age of five years and six months. At the time she was studied, she had had

Originally published in *Elementary School Journal* 64 (1963), pp. 149–54. Copyright 1963 by the University of Chicago Press. Reprinted with permission.

four months of formal reading instruction in school. Her teacher used a sight-word approach and paid some attention to beginning consonant sounds. Karen had received no formal instruction in spelling. For those who feel that such knowledge is pertinent, at the age of six years Karen had an intelligence quotient of 117, as measured by the Kuhlmann-Anderson Intelligence Tests.

Karen was given sixty-five words to spell. The words were taken from "Billy Whitemoon," by Ruth M. Tabrah, a story in a third-grade book-two reader (Betts & Welch 1963). To prepare the test, we divided all the words in the story into five groups: nouns, verbs, adjectives, adverbs, and function words. (Function words have little lexical meaning but play vital roles in signaling the structural meaning of utterances. Some linguists call these structure words [Goodman 1963].) To assure an adequate sampling of the five types of words in the story, the first thirteen words of each type in the story were selected for the spelling list.

Karen was given the first spelling test before she saw or read the story. To minimize the effect of fatigue she was given about ten words at a sitting over a period of several days. Each word was pronounced and used in a sentence. After the spelling test, Karen was asked to read the story aloud. She was then retested on the words she had originally misspelled (see Table 1). As a third and final test, she was given a list of all the words. In this test each word was presented three times across the page. One spelling was correct; two spellings were incorrect. Whenever possible Karen's misspellings were used. Karen was told: "Look across the row at all three words. I will say the word and then use it in a sentence. You decide which one word is correct and put a circle around it. Only one word in each row is correct."

On the first test Karen spelled these words correctly: *alike, any, back, boxes, closer, dance, fish, happy, hear, his, home, hunt, ices, leap, long, most, off, out, over, pick, poor, push, same, sit, soon, summer, things, this, too, very, who, win,* and *with.* On the second test she spelled six additional words correctly: *carry, just, or, spring, there,* and *when.*

On the first test, Karen spelled thirty-three of the sixty-five words correctly. During the postreading test, she correctly spelled an additional six of the thirty-four words she was given. (In her oral reading, Karen mispronounced two words: *swamps* and *Winnebago*. The two words were added to the spelling list on the second test.) When she was presented with the list of sixty-seven words in the third test, she was able to recognize the correct spelling of sixty-one of the sixty-seven words presented. *Winnebago* and *swamps* remained on this list. Therefore, although Karen could write correctly 58 percent of the words, she could recognize 91 percent of the correct spellings and was able to handle adequately in her reading close to 100 percent.

Table 1. Words Spelled Incorrectly on Each of Three Tests

		Incorrect Spelling	
Test Words	First Test	Second Test*	Third Test*
beauty	butey	butey	
bright	bragt	brigt	
broke	brook	brrok	
carefully	carfulle	carfully	
carry	cary		
color	coler	coler	
cotton	coten	coten	coten
dead	did	daid	
every	eavry	avery	
heavy	havey	havey	havey
highway	hiheway	higeway	
hunters	hanters	hanters	hanters
Indian	Indien	Indin	
just	jist		
leaves	leves	leves	
little	littial	littil	
much	mah	mush	
or	ouer		
own	oen	oen	
prove	proove	proove	
quickly	cucklie	cuckly	
rustle	rasal	rasel	
shoot	shot	shoet	
should	shood	shod	
shoulder	sholder	sholder	
spring	spreng		
straight	srat	strat	strat
there	thar		
travelers	travlars	travalers	travalers
weather	wather	wather	
when	whne		
young	yong	yong	
swamps†		swap	
Winnebago†		Winnie ba-go	Winnie bago
Total	32	28	6

*A blank space indicates that words were spelled or circled correctly at that testing.
†Given in second and third tests only.

Table 2. Words Spelled by Karen, Grouped by First
Occurrence in Five Basal Readers

Composite Word List* Textbooks by Grade Level	Number of Words Spelled Correctly On:		Number of Words Spelled Incorrectly On:	
	First Test	Second Test	Second Test	Third Test
1-0 (pre-primer)	4	0	0	0
1-1 (primer)	5	2	1	0
1-2	6	2	2	0
2-1	10	1	3	0
2-2	4	1	5	2
3-1	1	0	2	0
3-2	3	0	15	4
Total	33	6	28	6

*Whenever a word did not appear, it was considered a 3-2 word.

To see whether the words Karen spelled correctly had any relationship to their appearance in basal texts, these words were compared with a composite list from five widely used reading series (Stone & Bartschi 1963). Table 2 shows that the words that Karen consistently misspelled did not appear in first-grade textbooks and thus were perhaps less readily available for frequent observation in her reading to date.

Karen used at least three patterns in her spelling. The first is remembered configuration. When she used this technique, she spelled the words correctly or almost correctly by remembering how they looked. During the test, she often closed her eyes tight, as if she were trying to see the word. Silent letters were a problem for Karen. *Straight* she spelled *srat* in the first test and *strat* in the second; in the third test, she circled *strat*. (However, *bright* was spelled *bragt* in the first test and *brigt* in the second test, and she circled the correct spelling in the final test.)

Karen also used sound-symbol generalizations that she had developed. For example, she spelled *prove* as *proove* in both the first and the second tests. In the final test she was able to choose the correct spelling. Between the first and the second tests she apparently acquired a generalization of the *ly* morpheme. In the first test she spelled *carefully* as *carfulle* and *quickly* as *cucklie*, using different spellings of the suffix. In the second test, however, she used the correct digraph in both: *cuckly* and *carfully*. In the final test she chose the correct spelling for each word.

It is important to note that Karen never let her sound-symbol generalizations interfere with spellings she was sure of. She spelled *some* and *summer* correctly even though they do not follow a consistent generalization. This finding seems to imply that she also learned some of the limits of the applicability of her generalizations. In the few instances where Karen said she could not spell a word and required urging, she used sound-symbol generalizations.

The third technique Karen used in spelling was to look for recurrent spelling patterns. When she was asked to spell *own*, Karen said, "How come *only* is spelled o-n-e-l-y, but we say the word *one*." She was not correct, but she was looking for recurrent patterns in the spelling of words.

In the first spelling test, Karen showed that she had no problems with so-called sounded consonants. She had difficulty with silent consonants, although she remembered some configurations, so that *highway* was spelled *hiheway* in the first test and changed to *higeway* in the second.

Karen's greatest problem in spelling was vowel phonemes. Her sound-symbol generalizations were least useful there. In this difficulty she confirms what Fries wrote: "The heart of the practical spelling problem for English lies primarily in the representations of the vowel phonemes" (1963, p. 195). She used the wrong graphic representations of vowel phonemes in thirty-one of thirty-two errors on the first test and twenty-six of twenty-eight errors on the second test.

One problem was the type of word in which a single vowel phoneme is represented by a digraph or trigraph (for example, *beauty, heavy, leaves, own, straight, there,* and *weather*). Sixteen errors on the first test were of this nature.

Karen's spelling performance was analyzed by word types to see whether certain types were especially easy or especially difficult for her (see Table 3). She found verbs and function words somewhat easier than other types. She had little difficulty with adverbs. It is probable that the controlled-vocabulary story she read has more variety in nouns and adjectives than in other categories.

Karen's ability to handle function words is interesting. These words have little or no meaning out of context and are thus difficult to learn in spelling lists, even though they may be short and very common in language. Karen may have had less difficulty with these function words than other children do because she learned them in context.

Karen could read and understand a large number of words that she was unable to spell. She could also recognize the correct spelling of many words that she was unable to write correctly. She used several approaches to spelling that she developed as she learned to read

Table 3. Relative Difficulty of Types of Words for Karen

Word Type*	Correct Test 1	Additional Correct Test 2*	Additional Correct Test 3†	Incorrect	Total
Nouns	5	0	7	3	15
Verbs	7	1	5	0	13
Adjectives	4	1	5	3	13
Adverbs	10	1	2	0	13
Function Words	7	3	3	0	13
Total	33	6	22	6	67

*Words spelled correctly on Test 1 were not given on Test 2.
†No words that were spelled correctly on Test 1 were misspelled on Test 3.

without formal training. She seemed to rely chiefly on remembering the whole word, though when she was attempting to spell a word that she did not remember, she used sound-symbol generalizations and common spelling patterns. She appeared to be aware of the limitations of applicability of spelling generalizations. Vowel phonemes, particularly those represented by two or more letters, appeared to cause her the greatest difficulty. This study has shown that spelling can be learned naturally without instruction. At least one child has learned to spell without studying lists of words in isolation and without learning rules or generalizations.

The child who has achieved some language competence before coming to school highlights the importance of individual differences. The question is not what to do with this child but what to do about differential rates of learning and readiness development of all children.

Can teachers justify teaching spelling generalizations to all children at the same time, even if they are grouped, when it is obvious that some are not ready for the generalizations and some have long since developed the generalizations for themselves? Even more difficult to justify is the teaching of lists of spelling words to children who already know the words or are in no position to learn them. The teaching of subsidiary skills in language arts in reading, spelling, composition, grammar, handwriting, or literature must be approached diagnostically, and appropriate remedial measures should be taken at the proper time with the proper child. We hear the advice: "What's good for one is good for all." The slogan is not appropriate in helping children become literate.

References

Betts, Emmett A. & Welch, Carolyn M. 1963. *Along friendly roads.* New York: American Book Company.

Durkin, Dolores. 1964. Children who read before grade one. *The Reading Teacher, 14,* 163–66.

Fries, Charles C. 1963. *Linguistics and reading.* New York: Holt, Rinehart & Winston.

Goodman, Kenneth S. 1963. A communicative theory of the reading curriculum. *Elementary English, 40,* 290–98.

Stone, David R. & Bartschi, Vilda. 1963. A basic word list from basal readers. *Elementary English, 40,* 420–27.

Do We Really Need Those Oversized Pencils to Write With?

(with Richard E. Coles)

For the past few years Virginia had tried to make sense out of the print in her environment and the world in general. She had enjoyed creating words and messages on unlined paper or on frost-covered windows. She had composed messages on original birthday cards with paints or felt markers. Often she imitated the writing behavior of her parents while scribbling an important message on a piece of lined paper with a pen or pencil. In all this she was not unusual. She was doing what children who grow up in a literate society do.

Now she was going to school, and looked forward to learning to print and compose "like the big kids." What she found during the first few weeks at school was that the variety of writing instruments and materials that she used at home were not considered appropriate for her at school. Instead, Virginia and her fellow classmates were each given a large "primary pencil" without an eraser, and wide-ruled paper. They were being treated as novices with no prior experience with writing.

This common practice raises several questions for researchers and teachers who are interested in the composing process of young children. Does the use of special materials in primary grades enhance or interfere with a child's composing? What is the research base for the use of such materials? Why are they widely used in schools today?

Originally published in *Theory into Practice* 19 (Theme issue on Learning to Write) (1980), pp. 194–96. Copyright 1980 by The Ohio State University. Reprinted with permission.

A historical investigation of these questions revealed that (1) there is very little research compared with research on other aspects of handwriting; (2) there are disagreements between authors; and (3) there is a lack of empirical evidence to support many recommendations about the use of special writing implements and specifically ruled paper in primary classrooms.

Children of all ages used the same-sized handwriting tools until the 1920s, when the "primary pencil" and paper with wide ruling became available from school supply houses. At that time it was believed that these tools would help compensate for a young child's lack of muscular coordination and would be consistent with the development of large arm muscles.

Freeman (1936) made several references to handwriting materials in his many articles and books concerning this subject. He thought all children should learn to write at the blackboard and use a "fairly large pencil" with a smooth lead when writing at a desk. Taylor (1926), West (1927), and McKee (1934) agreed with Freeman that children should learn to write at the blackboard. When writing at a desk, McKee recommended a "beginner's pencil," while West believed students needed experience using different instruments in anticipation of out-of-school writing demands.

Publishers and authors of systems of handwriting also gave conflicting advice. The A. N. Palmer Company suggested the use of pencils with a small or medium diameter. The Zaner-Bloser Company, which has paid a great deal of attention to handwriting tools, strongly recommended a large, soft-leaded pencil (Freeman 1936). Foster and Houston (1927) emphasized the use of "an ordinary pencil of a medium grade of softness," while Cavanah and Myers (1937) and Hill and Savage (1934), Billington (1938), and Severance (1924) were in agreement in recommending larger-than-ordinary pencils. Billington, however, did warn that many beginner's pencils were too large or heavy for many young children to handle comfortably. Since a fountain pen was always sharp and used by most adults, Cole (1938) preferred this instrument to a pencil, which she considered informal and unsatisfactory.

Most authors agreed that the writing surface should be lined with initial spacing from one inch to an inch and a half. Gradually this distance would be reduced in the later grades. Most of these recommendations were not based on research. Several authors stressed the need for future study in this area, which seems never to have been done. The most complete piece of research was conducted by Wiles (1950). In her study, Wiles used pencils with different diameters and paper ruled at different widths. Over eight hundred first-grade pupils who had not received writing instruction were assigned to nine different groups using different lined paper and handwriting instruments over a period of a number of months. The handwriting was checked for fluency, alignment, form, spacing of letters, size in relation to space, and slant. Wiles concluded:

> In light of these findings plus knowledge of principles of habit formation, there seems little justification for use by beginners of tools other than those already standardized and recommended for use throughout life. (p. 98)

In recent reports, Tawney (1967) found that children learned to write as well with ballpoint pens as with primary pencils. Krzesni (1971), after his study, recommended that a variety of instruments, such as pens, pencils, felt pens, and lined or unlined paper, be available for children in the primary grades.

This review of the literature provided little empirical evidence for the exclusive use of primary pencils and wide-ruled paper for all primary children in school or for any gradual change from one type of instrument to another or from one kind of lined paper to another. A child who has trouble controlling the writing instrument and becomes concerned with placing words between the lines focuses on the mechanics of composing and not on the expression of thought and ideas. In such a situation the use of these materials could interfere with the child's composing. Graves (1978) described the teaching of handwriting with an emphasis on mechanical correctness and out of the context of composition as the "main event" in many classroom writing programs. Children immersed in a literate environment that provides a variety of purposeful composing experiences learn the different aspects of the composing process, including handwriting, as they grow.

There are many children like Virginia who have used a variety of writing instruments when composing for different purposes in out-of-school settings. Informal interviews with parents, teachers, and children reveal that in homes and preschools, there are all kinds of writing implements and paper available and used by children. Yet when they enter kindergarten, children who have already been exposed to No. 2 pencils with erasers, ballpoint pens, stubby small pencils and grubby large ones, who have used narrow-lined writing paper and unlined note paper, are relegated to using a specified kind of writing implement and paper. Teachers are often prohibited from using paper and pencils that are not designated for the grade level that they teach.

We believe the kinds of materials used in writing are an insignificant aspect of any composition curriculum in schools if flexibility and opportunity for choice are available to teachers and children. If, however, there are stringent rules about the kind of paper and writing implements teachers and children must use, it is possible that such practices may interfere with the composing processes of young children. Sometimes comedians have a way of putting things professionals take too seriously into proper perspective. In his comedy album "Why Is There Air?" Bill Cosby talks about the use of paper and pencils in first grade once learning to write is started:

> They give you this paper, grade Triple Z with wood still floating in it. . . . You got to write around the hunks of wood. The lines are about eight feet apart. They don't want you to miss getting in between them lines, man. . . . They give you these pencils as big as a horse's leg. And you rest them on your shoulder as you write.

We believe that a writing center with different writing instruments and kinds of paper can make composing in the classroom a natural extension of previous writing experiences. To become proficient writers, children need an opportunity to write for different functions and audiences. In an informal setting, teachers provide children with the opportunity and materials for rehearsal, composing, and self-correction. While using a comfortable tool and not worrying about spacing or lines, the child focuses on composing and not the mechanics of writing.

The current research on composing in young children suggests that the purpose of the writing and the need to communicate to others provide the impetus for the development of composition. Research in this area does not support current restrictions on implements and paper.

A number of questions still deserve investigation: Does handwriting change with different functions and materials? Does a lack of focus on formal handwriting instruction lead to poor writing? Has the use of typewriters in the classroom had an effect on handwriting? Until such questions have been addressed, let's provide Virginia and her age-mates with materials of wide variety, encourage composing, and expect development of handwriting to follow the functional use of written language.

References

Billington, L. E. 1938. *The Laurel handwriting series* (Teacher's Manual). Chicago: Laurel Book Co.

Bloser, Elmer W. 1920. The value of large writing for beginners in the elementary schools. Columbus, OH: Zaner-Bloser.

Cavanah, L. & Myers, A. 1937. *Handwriting for expression* (Teacher's Manual). New York: American Book Co.

Cole, Luella. 1938. Heresy in handwriting. *Elementary School Journal, 38,* 606–18.

Cosby, Bill. 1967. *Why is there air?* [Vinyl Recording]. Burbank, CA: Warner Bros.

Foster, M. E. & Houston, H. 1927. *Correlated handwriting practice.* New Haven: Harry Houston.

Freeman, Frank & Zaner-Bloser Co. 1936. *The Zaner-Bloser Correlated Handwriting.* Columbus, OH: Zaner-Bloser.

Graves, Donald H. 1978. Handwriting is for writing: Research update. *Language Arts, 55,* 393–99.

Hill, H. M. & Savage, J. A. 1934. *Handwriting made easy* (Teacher's Manual). Dallas: University Publishing Co.

Krzesni, J. S. 1971. Effect of different writing tools and paper on performance of the third grade. *Elementary English, 48,* 821–24.

McKee, Paul G. 1934. *Language in the elementary school.* Boston: Houghton Mifflin.

Severance, Leta. 1924. *Penmanship teaching and supervision.* Los Angeles: J. R. Miller.

Tawney, Shirley. 1967. An analysis of the ball point pen versus the pencil as a beginning handwriting instrument. *Elementary English, 44,* 59–61.

Taylor, J. S. 1926. *Supervision and teaching of handwriting.* Richmond, VA: Johnson Publishing Co.

West, Paul V. 1927. *Changing practice in handwriting instruction.* Bloomington, IL: Public School Publishing.

Wiles, Marianna E. 1950. The effects of different sizes of tools upon the handwriting of beginners (Doctoral dissertation, Harvard University, 1950). *Dissertation Abstracts International,* p. 155.

The Writing Process

In the beginning there was a question: In what ways would children in a public school in a Native American reservation community develop as writers in a classroom where daily writing was an ongoing part of the curriculum? Along with Ann Francisco, a dedicated educational practitioner who was the principal of such a school, we began to formulate a proposal to try to answer that question and others, and the story of these children began to unfold.

> Dear Pen Pal,
> My name is Dana. I go to school at Topawa. I got one sister. My favorite sports are basketball and baseball. I live in Crowhang. I have lots of friends. My best friends are Harrington and Cody. Everytime it is fun here and hot. How is it over at your place?
> Sincerely yours, Dana

Just as Dana sketched a profile of himself for his pen pal, I will provide a backdrop for the (re)search we did to answer our questions. Dana was one of a group of Tohono O'odham students from southwestern Arizona that a group of researchers observed on a fairly regular basis. (The names of all students and teachers, except for Ann Francisco, have been changed to protect their privacy.) We became fascinated with the collaborative nature of writing, reading, and learn-

Originally published as a portion of Chapter 1 in *Literacy Events in a Community of Young Writers,* edited by Yetta M. Goodman & Sandra Wilde (New York: Teachers College Press, 1992), pp. 1–16. *Literacy Events in a Community of Young Writers* describes the findings of a two-year study of Native American children's writing. A few changes have been made in the text to make it appropriate for this context. Also, in most cases, we have edited the students' spelling and punctuation, except where we have used uppercase letters to represent students' invented spellings.

ing in the classroom. We interviewed students about what they knew about their writing, what they liked about it, and what they believed were their teachers' perceptions of their writing. We observed the teachers as they were giving assignments and leading discussions about writing. We observed the settings in which the children wrote. We became aware of the influence of what was placed on chalkboards, walls, and bulletin boards, and of what books and other print materials were available and accessible to the students. It became obvious that our own interactions with students and teachers were influencing the students' writing, so we noted our involvement with the literacy community.

This research employed naturalistic techniques, imposing minimal control on the setting in which the data were collected. Such techniques seem especially appropriate when the object of study is to focus on the process as well as the products of writing:

> As a general premise, it is probably safe to assert that the best way to study process is to observe it directly, rather than to infer its nature from the known input and the observed output. When process is the issue, naturalistic inquiry seems to offer a more useful means for its study than does the experimental model. (Guba 1978, p. 25)

As a team of researchers, we interacted with two grade levels, three classrooms, three teachers, several classroom aides, two principals, approximately seventy students, and some of their parents, although we worked most closely with ten children the first year of the study and six of those children the second year.

The story of our research begins with a profile of the complex transactions that we now believe make up every literacy event in the classroom setting. One of the most striking conclusions that emerged from our study has to do with the social nature of writing. Writing is strongly influenced by societal views about literacy, by the nature of the social community within and outside classrooms, and by the ways in which schools and classrooms are organized. These social influences strongly impact the personal writing history of every student in the classroom.

Our profile of the social nature of composing emerged over the two-year period and generalizes what we learned about the writing process as we carefully observed the complex influences on the writing development of young third- and fourth-grade authors engaged in the making of meaning through written language. It is by understanding this complexity and by valuing all students as makers of meaning that teachers and curriculum developers can organize schools and classrooms for students to make the most beneficial use of the literacy community as they write. Our purpose is not merely to understand the influences on the writing of these particular children but also to suggest how all children learn to write, learn through writing, and learn about writing (Halliday 1980).

This research narrative starts with a question about Tohono O'odham children as young authors in school. It includes characters such as researchers, teachers, paraprofessionals, principals, elementary school students, and parents participating in plots and themes influenced by their languages and cultures, which changed and developed over a two-year period. Old questions were answered and new ones raised. We began to see patterns in all this activity, to discover myriad transactions that made up the literacy events that are at the heart of this narrative. Every piece of writing produced by the children resulted from a complex literacy event represented by the diagram seen in Figure 1. The diagram reveals the complexities of the processes involved during composing, which is a dynamic transaction across a variety of constraints and influences that can be organized into three broad categories to highlight their significance: the literacy community, the writer, and the written text.

Figure 1.
The Literacy Event

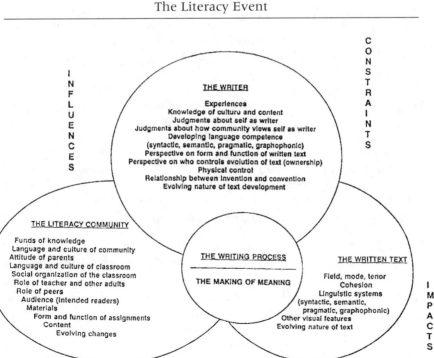

The Literacy Community

The writing of these third and fourth graders took place in the social context of the classroom: the classroom literacy community. At the same time, each member of that classroom community was also a member of family and cultural groups, a broader literacy community. The classrooms that we studied were part of the Indian Oasis school district, located on the Tohono O'odham Reservation about seventy miles west of Tucson, Arizona. At the time of our study and today, 85 percent of students are bused to school, some as far as fifty miles. Approximately 50 percent of the students live in or within ten miles of the largest town on the reservation, site of the elementary school where we first conducted the research. Other students live in villages scattered throughout the reservation. Villages may be as far as twenty miles apart, with homes within a village often separated by one to five miles. Two languages are used in the community. At the time of our study, the Tohono O'odham language was generally spoken fluently by the schoolchildren's grandparents, who in some cases spoke little English. The children's parents were typically bilingual in Tohono O'odham and English, and many of the children were primarily English speakers, although they did have varying amounts of receptive understanding of the O'odham language. The majority of the community are practicing Catholics as well as active participants in Tohono O'odham religious and cultural events. This community has many informal networks through which knowledge of the community and culture is shared and passed on to the children.

Every time the children wrote, their language and culture, formed by multiple influences, were reflected in their writing. These children called on their language repertoire as members of varied linguistic and social groups. Their writing reflected aspects of the English spoken by the Tohono O'odham, the English spoken by the dominant, mainstream population of the region, and also an awareness of the kinds of language appropriate to different kinds of writing. Although the children heard the Tohono O'odham language spoken with varying degrees of frequency by parents and grandparents, it never appeared in the compositions we saw, probably due to its out-of-school association and oral language form.

Culture was also reflected in the children's writing. Their writing revealed that they were part of the Tohono O'odham and at the same time members of the culture of all eight- to ten-year-old North Americans who are influenced by television, movies, and the school curriculum. For instance, Darren created an episode in which the movie character E.T., popular among all third and fourth graders at the time, received his powers from E'etoi, the deity and protector of the Tohono O'odham.

Children represented their personal histories—their language and the worlds of their homes and communities—in their writing. Teachers' writing assignments and the extent of choice within those assignments also had an impact on the children's writing. During the first year of the study, the research was conducted in a single third-grade classroom. In the second year of research, the same children were in two classrooms in two different schools. Each of the three teachers had her own individual style and philosophy about teaching writing; the main common ground was that all provided for writing on a regular basis. Because of both choice and circumstance, we focused on examining the writing process as it was organized by the teachers in their classrooms rather than on trying to change those environments. Therefore, although we responded to the teachers' questions and talked with them frequently about the students, their writing, and the classroom curriculum, we did not systematically attempt to influence their instructional practices. By observing different classroom practices, we were able to conclude that constraints and freedom in areas such as assignments, scheduling, and organization certainly affect writing.

Although we agree with Donald Graves (1983) that assignments often narrow what and how children write, some good writing was done in response to assignments. Both narrative and expository topics were assigned, although the latter tended to be more highly constrained. In most cases, the narratives the children wrote were more engaging and interesting than their attempts at report writing, although the students did not always keep these two genres in neat categories, especially when writing reports. Marian, for instance, showed a blending of genres in her assigned social studies report on the state bird:

> One day the state bird is going to get a worm. He's going to eat the worm and he wants to get some more of the same worm. He's going to eat lots of it, lots of the worm. He likes worms. The End.

Our examination of genre in the children's writing raised the question of whether young children's writing can be categorized as neatly as the traditional genre classifications that are used to discuss literature.

We found that classroom scheduling also strongly influenced the developing text of a writer; children's writing reflected the amount of time they were given to write. When they had only a specified short writing time daily, with the expectation of a finished product at the end of the period, story endings were often quickly conceived, as in Gordon's piece:

> One day when I was at the circus a man was whipping the lions so they would jump through the circle that's on fire. After the circus

was over the lion's trainer asked me if I wanted to be a trainer like him. I said, "O.K."

When the students were asked to write about what circus act they would like to be, Gordon was able to create an exciting image in his story. Needing to finish in twenty minutes, however, he didn't have time to elaborate on his response to the lion trainer. Although the teacher didn't impose a time limit, the children assumed that a piece of writing had to be completed within one twenty-minute writing center period; it didn't occur to them that they could continue the next day. So if a classroom is organized to provide time to finish writing later in the day, if students are encouraged to continue writing as other activities take place, or if writing is seen as an ongoing process that continues from day to day, students will have time to think about the ending of a piece and to shape it appropriately.

Classrooms can be organized to include opportunities to interact with peers and teachers during writing episodes. Even when interactions seem to be boisterous, students gain a lot from questioning teachers and peers, listening to one another read aloud, answering each other's questions, thinking aloud, and discussing pieces of writing. One writing episode provided a glimpse into the impact of classroom organization on the writing community. Walter, Dana, Carl, and Vincent were all writing at the same table. The researcher was observing Dana's writing and taking notes meticulously. Walter asked Dana the spelling of a word; Dana responded appropriately. Dana then wrote the last sentence of his story and said, "I'm finished." The researcher asked Dana to read his story onto an audiotape. Vincent, who was sitting next to Dana, interrupted his own writing, crawled onto the desk, and listened intently to Dana read his story. Then he also listened to Carl read his story. By this time, the rest of the class had lined up for lunch and gone out the door, but the group at this table did not break up; they were too immersed in sharing their writing and talking about their stories. This event was made possible by both the seating arrangement and the students' freedom to get out of their seats and move about the classroom.

The classroom literacy community provides an audience for the writer's evolving text as well as for the completed version. The impact and expectations of various audiences and the ways in which those audiences interact with the writer all have their influences and can support the construction of text, as it did in the following example. Gordon was deciding how to spell *butterfly.* He looked at the dictionary Anna was using; he then went over to the bookshelf and examined another dictionary but still didn't find the word. He looked in yet a third dictionary for a while and then brought that dictionary back to his table and said *butterflies* out loud as he wrote the word. During this time Gordon also gave Ann an eraser, told her how to spell *dragon,* helped David find a word on the wall chart, helped Mark with a spelling, talked with David about playing drums, and chatted with the researcher about her trip out to the school. The other children knew that Gordon was a good person to ask for help with spelling and dictionary use, and most of his assistance came about because he was tuned in to the needs of the others and eager to help them. Not all his activity was directly related to writing, but his attention always returned to his text.

This vignette featuring Gordon helps explicate a concept being explored by Luis Moll and his associates (1990). The concept of *funds of knowledge* suggests that within any community there are members who are recognized as experts with special knowledge in specific contexts. As we studied these classrooms, we observed Gordon as a spelling and grammar expert, Vincent as an expert about the traditional life style of the Tohono O'odham, Anna as an expert on modern life on the reservation, and so on. As teachers understand more about the funds of knowledge that exist in a classroom, they can help support the insights that students build about their personal abilities and those of their classmates. This is how a community of writers (or readers, or learners) in a classroom becomes a force to enhance everybody's learning.

There are dramatic differences between classrooms. Some classrooms are exciting literacy communities in which reading and writing represent important parts of children's daily world. Children are involved in what they are writing about; they know why they're writing and what purposes it serves. Children see their writing as authentic experience, important to their personal lives, and they take their work seriously. In other classrooms children see reading and writing as instructional: assignments that must be completed at a particular time and in a particular way in order to get an appropriate grade.

The decisions made about the kind of writing environment to establish will depend on how teachers and administrators view the impact of classroom organization and accessibility of resources on children's writing. It will depend on the values school personnel place on student interaction or on silence. Such decisions, which are based on beliefs about the empowerment of teachers and learners, significantly affect children's writing development.

The opportunity to move around the classroom and the availability and accessibility of appropriate writing materials and resources invite writers to "live off the land," a metaphor Donald Graves uses to describe how writers make use of a rich classroom environment. Such an environment provides opportunities and resources for children to think about, read about, talk about, and extend their composing. The freedom to use reference books and dictionaries and to stare out the window or at the ceiling, as well as to interact with teachers, peers, paraprofessionals, and others who participate in the community life of the classroom, dynamically influences children's writing.

The Writer

Every time we watched a child write, we saw evidence of the strengths of a writer who was developing as an author. The young writers brought their personal histories, including their background and experience, to their writing. They reflected in their writing their unique experiences as individuals, as well as experiences shared by their peers in school or by other children of the same age throughout the United States.

All the students we examined in depth were native speakers of English, competent oral users able to communicate appropriately with both their peers and adults. Both oral interviews and writing samples revealed the children's control over the major linguistic features of English, even though the students had a range of abilities. They produced the syntactic structures of English in many appropriate variations. They wrote dialogue, questions, and imperative and declarative sentences. They showed an intuitive knowledge of linguistic units such as words, phrases, and clauses and of genres such as stories, letters, narratives, and reports. They used the first person to reveal themselves as speakers in a story or letter, and in their third-person narratives they used pronouns to refer to appropriate characters and objects. They provided evidence of the dynamic ability of humans to invent written language forms for a variety of purposes and functions.

Every writing episode involving our subjects showed that the writers knew that they could produce a written message that others could read. They wrote about personal concerns, real events, and imagined experiences embedded in descriptions of the cultures in which they lived. They wrote about Native American legends that they had heard at home, about becoming medicine men and going to rodeos, about playing PacMan at the video game arcade and going to the Arizona State University Sun Devils football game. They were aware of audience expectations. In their letters, narratives, and expositions, they used different types of language appropriately, showing insights into the pragmatics of different genres and audiences. They exploited different written forms for letters or stories or lists. Dana showed in his letter at the beginning of this chapter that he knew how to introduce himself appropriately. He told about himself, asked his pen pal a question, and used *sincerely* in this formal first letter to someone he had never met before—a form of language he would never use in any oral setting, and that he changed in subsequent letters to *your friend.*

These young writers were very sensitive to one another and to the daily social interactions of a classroom. They were able to discuss what they were writing with their classmates and to suggest ideas about writing to others. They had reasons for why they liked their own writing, why they believed they were good or bad writers, and which of their writings their teachers would appreciate the most. Their reasons reflected their knowledge of the expectations of the school and community.

Gordon illustrated some of these attitudes. To Gordon, writing was fairly straightforward and uncomplicated: "I just sit there and then I think and then I write it." When asked why he chose some of his stories as being better than others, he usually referred only to the interesting parts of the content, such as "the parrot got to talk." But he was also able to give a global assessment of why he liked a story: "It's the words, and the letters, and how it sounds." He knew how to tell if someone was a good writer, because "their stories are sometimes funny and sometimes sad." According to Gordon a good writer "writes straight . . . and never makes no mistakes. A good writer doesn't write sloppy or crooked," in contrast to bad writers who have messy papers when they erase, which "makes black marks and tears the paper." He also believed that his teacher would prefer his longer stories, because he had learned through his varied school experiences that length is an important measure of a story's worth. He saw these surface aspects of writing as important for success in the adult world. Spelling was important because "if you're like a police then you're going to learn better . . . if they don't write straight and it doesn't look good . . . they just throw it away and start on another copy." Many adults had to deal with forms, where "they have to fill out all the blanks," and "if words are misspelled, he'll give it back to you." In contrast, Gordon believed that in writing a personal letter, spelling wasn't important because "it's your writing."

The writers in this study wanted others to read what they wrote, and appreciated the questions and responses they received from their peers, the researchers, and their teachers. They used their interactions to edit and revise when they had the opportunity to do so. However, like Gordon, they were especially concerned about how their products looked, so that the majority of the editing they did was really proofreading, making their papers look neat or correcting their spellings.

They sometimes asked others about topics and looked for topics on lists and in books. They selectively asked others to verify their spellings and appropriate language use, depending on the degree to which they wanted to control conventions for a particular piece of writing. They used information in dictionaries and books and on charts, chalkboards, and wall charts to help them with vocabulary and conventional spellings. They showed that they knew that some dictionaries had easy words and that others included words with a wider range of difficulty.

   All these strengths were evident in the very first writings the subjects produced. Although they didn't control this knowledge according to adult conventions, they showed in various ways that they were moving toward control and understanding of the social conventions of writing. An analysis of the data collected over two years revealed development across many features that can be measured quantitatively. It is easy to show quantitative growth in areas such as conventional spelling, punctuation, embedded clauses, longer and more cohesive texts, and exploration of a greater variety of topics. But this development does not follow a straight ascending line from one writing episode to the next. As Wilkinson says, "Development obviously takes place, but does not take place obviously" (Wilkinson et al. 1980, p. 2). However, development does not mean simply doing something better according to an adult standard. Rather, development must be seen from the writer's perspective. Development reflects the growing experience of writers and their personal histories within a specific cultural context as they begin to control written language to express their meanings (Vygotsky 1986). Even for professional writers, their latest work is not always their best.

   In discussing development, it is important to include the writer's willingness to wade into uncharted waters and to take appropriate risks. Development in writing means using more complex language and expressing more complex ideas, resulting in written texts that sometimes look on the surface as if control over some aspects has been lost (for instance, spelling may be less conventional). However, these controls usually return later in the student's writing, often with greater sophistication.

   In January of the second year of the study, Elaine wrote a story called "The Day the Sioux Came to Town" that helps to illustrate the complex nature of development in writing:

> One day the Sioux came to TONW [town]. BECUES [because] they were dancing . . . and she was a good dancer. They live way out in the DESTX [desert]. . . . The men WAR [wear] MOUCSNS [moccasins].

This was just the beginning of a four-page composition, Elaine's longest ever. She participated in the class unit on Native American peoples by selecting a picture of a man and woman in the traditional dress of the Plains Indians. She was excited about writing a story based on the picture. She had never written such a description before and referred constantly to the picture. She had few interactions with those sitting near her. She showed little concern for conventional spelling (contrary to her usual pattern). Because she made many exophoric references—references to material outside of the actual written text (in this case, to the picture)—the writing was not always internally cohesive. In other words, in order to fully understand Elaine's pronoun references it was necessary to refer directly to the picture she was writing about. Elaine selected the story as one of her favorite stories of the year, and her mother reported that she had a photocopy of the picture hanging in her room four months later. This story had the most complex syntactic structure of any story she wrote in two years and also had the lowest proportion of conventional spellings.

Periods of intense growth for a writer are often not reflected in the product or are reflected in only one aspect of writing. New processes need to be explored and experienced many times before they become integrated and can be used often and easily. As a writer attends to a new concern in composition, energy and attention are often directed to that new problem, and writing conventions that the writer usually controls seem to fall apart. The result is a written text that may look much less sophisticated than an earlier piece. This view of development is in keeping with the notion that development is discontinuous, with highs and lows, leaps and descents, rather than being a simplistic process of gradual ascending transitions in neat and orderly increments (Werner & Caplan 1950).

This developmental view of the writers in our study is grounded in a focus on strengths, building on the social and historical experiences of the child in the context of a literate community. Another view of development might have focused on "problems." Spellings were not 100 percent conventionalized, grammatical structures were not always complete, antecedents were not always clear, narrative and expository forms often appeared in the same composition. However, such "problems" reveal the abilities of young writers. They must have knowledge about literature in order to mix genres, they must understand aspects of the English alphabetic system in order to invent spellings, they must control aspects of cohesion in order to produce ambiguous references. If we understand this view of development in writing, schools and curriculum can be organized to help students become better writers, and teachers can organize their classrooms to be developmentally supportive writing environments.

In considering the role of the learner in written language development, Kenneth Goodman and I (Goodman & Goodman 1990) have explored a learning concept regarding the role of personal invention of language by the individual, in tension with social language conventions of the society, as part of a social view of language development. We see language development as influenced by both invention and convention. Language is developed by people (including children) individually to express new experiences, feelings, and ideas. At the same time, socially shared language forms and functions constrain language inventions. Language is social, and in written language as well as oral language there is an audience to be considered.

> There is almost an explosive force from within children that propels them to express themselves, and at the same time there is a strong need to communicate that pushes the direction of growth and development toward the language of the family and the community. (p. 232)

This research, as well as research on miscue analysis and other aspects of language learning, has helped explicate the notion of personal invention and social conventions. It helps us be confident that children are always learning language, inventing forms and functions; but at the same time, because they want to be understood by their social communities (their peers, their families), they keep balancing their need for new language uses and forms with what they know about how language is used and formed in the world at large. These social forces strongly influence and/or constrain the personal literacy development of learners. The home, the school, and the community are crucial social sites where written language learning occurs.

The Text

The third influence and constraint in the making of meaning is the most visible and permanently available for continuous scrutiny: the author's text. The text includes both the evolution of what is being composed and the author's final text. Both are important in understanding how the composing process develops in writers.

Halliday and Hasan (1976) define text as "the basic semantic unit of linguistic interaction" (p. 295). It is through the written text that writers express their meanings to their perceived audiences. Although the written text is an act of creation, authors learn that in order for their expression to be meaningful to others, they must conform to certain conventions based on the expectations of their audiences. These conventions in turn constrain the production of the text. Our young authors showed that they understood these constraints.

Every written text is part of a larger context of situation, and the students in this study reflected their awareness of this through their use of the various linguistic systems they controlled, as well as the form their writing took, as represented by a variety of visual text features. The students' writing reflected their understanding of field, tenor, and mode within the context of a particular situation—the social community of the classroom (Halliday and Hasan 1976, p. 22).

The children's texts showed their awareness of the *field* in which the writing took place. The concept of field refers to the subject matter, the events, and the experiences that the author brings together to create meanings. The students' writing reflected the assignments given by their teachers and discussions among both the whole class and smaller communities of young authors who often sat together and talked about their writing—discussions that also included the important news of the day within the classroom community. Rodeos, trips within or outside the reservation, television programs, movie and rock stars, suicides, accidents, and the lives of their teachers and friends appeared in their writing either explicitly or implicitly.

Tenor refers to the relationships between the writer and her or his perceived audience. Tenor was represented by the relationships between characters within the narratives themselves, reflecting the cultural relationships in the lives of the children, but it was also shown in the relationship between the author of a piece and its various audiences: peers, teachers, researchers, paraprofessionals, pen pals, and others. For example, when letters were written, the recipients influenced the creation of the text. A letter to a known pen pal or a relative would be signed appropriately with *your friend* or *your son*. A letter to an unfamiliar or important person would have a more formal closing. When Vincent was writing to Jamake Highwater, an author he admired greatly, he spent a long time thinking through an appropriate ending, then finally turned to the researcher and asked, "How do you spell *sincerely?*" The language in the body of the letter also reflected the relationship between the writer and the person to whom the letter was being sent.

The field and tenor constrained the *mode* and resulted in the choice of the language and form of the composition. The concern for appropriate content and form was represented in both the writing conventions used by the students and their oral interviews with the researchers. They were quite confident about what they believed to be the views of the school and business communities toward writers and writing conventions. They believed that teachers liked neat, perfectly spelled, and long compositions. They understood that various people such as nurses and police officers needed to spell accurately and write carefully in order to function properly in society.

Whenever these young writers wrote, they provided evidence that they were aware of the cohesion of a text. Although they were not always successful in providing all the necessary cohesive ties for the reader to make the most appropriate inferences, as shown earlier with Elaine's Sioux piece, their distinctive types of cohesive tie did not spill over from one kind of text to another. In other words, sports stories maintained the language appropriate to those kinds of texts, and folktales had many of the appropriate features that enabled readers to recognize that genre. The language of the story a child was working on stayed within the boundaries of a particular text. When a new composition was begun, new cohesive ties were introduced and maintained in the new text.

Of course these young writers did not control all the necessary features of a text, but they controlled many of those features even from the very beginning of the time we observed them and developed greater control over various textual features as they wrote more, as well as more varied, texts over the two-year period. Most of the texts we analyzed in this study were first drafts that were not revised after their initial production, although the students did revise various aspects of their compositions as they were writing them for the first time.

Change, Development, and the Evolving Nature of Text

The dynamic nature of change must always be considered whenever researchers are involved in responding to and analyzing any literacy event. Each of the intersecting categories I have been discussing is in flux even during the act of one literacy event, let alone across the many literacy events that occur daily and weekly in the classroom. The literacy community is always recreated as teachers, peers, and nonhuman resources change, move, and develop over time. The writer is also developing, growing, and changing. The text itself also evolves as it is written. These changes may not always result in better written productions or better writers. These complexities can have either positive or negative influences on writers.

It is necessary for teachers to understand the influences and constraints that the schooling community has on their students' writing development. Curriculum is often organized without consideration of the dynamic nature of the classroom. There is a tendency to point to good instructional practices when students produce well-written compositions and subtly to blame students when writing is less than successful. I believe that certain kinds of instructional practices in sterile and rigid settings develop writers who produce compositions that are less than adequate. In other words, instruction can result in teaching people to write ineffectively.

This profile and discussion of the many factors involved in any literacy event reveal the complexity of the writing process. Every literacy event is influenced by many factors that teachers and researchers must consciously take into account whenever writing research, instruction, or evaluation is undertaken. In order for writing research to be meaningful, it must consider the dynamic nature of these transactions. Curriculum developers and teachers must acknowledge these complexities to facilitate the writing process for students. There is enough evidence from this study and many others to know that in order for children to write well and develop confidence in their writing, they need to be free from classrooms where they must stay in their seats quietly writing in response to a single narrowly conceived assignment with little purpose or meaning for the author. Teachers who know how to exploit the richness of the literacy community and to value the evolution of written text and the development of the writer take into consideration the complexity of every writing event, including the strengths and knowledge inherent in every writer.

References

Goodman, Yetta M. & Goodman, Kenneth S. 1990. Vygotsky in a whole language perspective. In Luis C. Moll (Ed.), *Vygotsky and education: Instructional implications and applications of sociohistorical psychology* (pp. 223–50). Cambridge: Cambridge University Press.

Goodman, Yetta M. & Wilde, Sandra (Eds.). 1992. *Literacy events in a community of young writers.* New York: Teachers College Press.

Graves, Donald H. 1983. *Writing: Teachers and children at work.* Portsmouth, NH: Heinemann.

Guba, Egon. 1978. *Toward a methodology of naturalistic inquiry in educational evaluation* (CSE Monograph Series in Evaluation No. 8). Los Angeles: UCLA, Graduate School of Education, Center for the Study of Evaluation.

Halliday, M. A. K. 1980. Three aspects of children's language development: Learning language, learning through language, learning about language. In Yetta M. Goodman, Myna Haussler & Dorothy Strickland (Eds.), *Oral and written language development research: Impact on the schools* (Proceedings from the 1979 and 1980 IMPACT Conferences) (pp. 7–19). Newark, DE & Urbana, IL: International Reading Association & National Council of Teachers of English. (ERIC Document Reproduction Service Document ED 214 184)

Halliday, M. A. K. & Hasan, Ruqaiya. 1976. *Cohesion in English*. London: Longman.

Moll, Luis C., Vélez-Ibáñez, C., Greenberg, J., Whitmore, Kathy, Saavedra, Elizabeth, Dworin, J. & Andrade, R. 1990. *Community knowledge and classroom practice: Combining resources for literacy instruction* (OBEMLA Contract No. 300-87-0131). Tucson: University of Arizona, College of Education and Bureau of Applied Research in Anthropology.

Vygotsky, Lev. 1986 *Thought and language*. Cambridge, MA: MIT Press.

Werner, Heinz & Caplan, Edith. 1950. The acquisition of word meaning. *Monographs of the Society for Research in Child Development, 15* (Serial No. 51, No. 1).

Wilkinson, Andrew, Bornsley, Gillian, Hanna, Peter & Swan, Margaret. 1980. *Assessing language development*. Oxford: Oxford University Press.

Part Five

Kidwatching (1978–1989)

My interests in early literacy and reading and writing processes and my knowledge of miscue analysis led me to popularize the term *kid-watching*. I came to understand the significance of careful and knowledgeable observation of students as they are immersed in their own learning and language use. Kidwatching is a conscious process on the part of teachers as they take field notes standing near a group of kids experimenting with a science project, sitting next to a reader marking miscues, or making notes about the resources used by a group at the writing center. Many researchers and administrators and much of the public are enamored with "objectivity" to such a degree that we have minimized the power of knowledgeable subjectivity.

Teachers know more about students in their classrooms than anyone else except their parents. Teachers have insider views of students and their classrooms because they are knowledgeable members of the classroom community. In ethnographic research, the insider's view is considered extremely important to understanding a cultural community. Ethnographers value careful observation of phenomena by knowledgeable participant observers who spend days and nights carefully watching, taking notes, and making professionally informed interpretations. Yet in schools, there is a tendency not to trust the people most knowledgeable about the students to evaluate and make informed decisions. Teachers' observations are often denigrated as subjective or idiosyncratic.

We must learn to trust the judgments of teachers, their professional subjectivity, if we expect them to know their students well and to use what they know to develop supportive curricula and instruction. My concept of kidwatching developed as I perceived the need to help teachers (and those who critique teaching) legitimize teachers' expertise as observers. The language stories that teachers tell about what their students do highlight their insights into how kids learn and how they adapt to new learnings. Knowledgeable kidwatching provides insight into what kids are interested in, what motivates them, and what allows them to immerse themselves in important learning experiences. As I continue to explore the kidwatching concept, I realize that these ideas are extensions of the child-study movement of the 1930s. The importance of a classroom curriculum's emerging from knowing students well through careful observation and interpretation was supported by the exemplary work of early childhood educators.

As I began to discuss ways to observe children—to gather information, to interact with students in conference time and during other learning experiences, and to analyze the collected information—the similarities between research and evaluation became clear to me. Teachers who want to know their students and understand what and how they learn are inquiring into the nature of teaching and learning. Many of the projects students in my graduate and undergraduate classes do are for the purpose of discovering more about their own students and using this important knowledge to plan ongoing learning opportunities and experiences. Thoroughness in kidwatching is evaluative, but the decisions about evaluation come from teacher research: inquiring into the nature of teaching and learning.

Kidwatching:
An Alternative to Testing

Since 1960, our knowledge of how children learn language and how people use language has exploded. While many questions remain unanswered, we do know that children are actively involved in their own language learning. Indeed, the evidence shows that children initiate and create language years before they come to school (Brown 1973). Through interaction with the society into which they have been born, children discover rules about language, and they use their language to make sense out of the world and to share their meanings with others (Halliday 1975).

In the last few years, it has been discovered that even preschool children are learning to read the print in their environment, responding to signs in the streets and commercials on television (Forester 1977; Goodman & Goodman 1977; Ylisto 1977). In addition, children invent their own spellings to match their generalizations about the sound system of English (Read 1975).

At the same time that scholars are discovering significant information about how children develop language, we have heard a growing cry to test children's language in schools. But the credence that has been given to language tests in the last few years is misleading, to say the least. It suggests that we know enough about language and testing to rely on test results to make claims about literacy and language development in all populations in our society. The fact is, the items in tests and the way tests are carried out are often at odds with the knowledge

Originally published in *National Elementary Principal* 57 (1978), pp. 41–45. This journal is now defunct and copyright has reverted to Yetta M. Goodman.

we get from the psychologists, psycholinguists, and sociolinguists studying language development. These two directions in education—testing language in standardized tests and learning how language develops in human beings—provide contradictory evidence for educators about children. Clearly, if educators are to make decisions that will support children's language development, they will need a firm knowledge of both testing and language development theory.

The misuses and abuses of tests have been well documented in the pages of journals, through resolutions by national groups, and in speeches all over the country. I do not intend to repeat that data. Instead, I hope to support the growing national concern about the negative effects of our reliance on tests and to provide some suggestions for alternative ways to observe the development of language in the classroom.

Children are language learners by virtue of being born into human society. The role of the school can never be to *teach* language since children *learn* language naturally through their interaction with others. The role of the school must be to provide an environment in which children will expand their use of language in a variety of settings and situations and for a variety of purposes.

In a supportive, rich environment where language is encouraged and there are plenty of opportunities to read, write, speak, and listen, children will make many discoveries about language. They will not always be right in their discoveries, but they will be in good company. Scientists have always made mistakes and learned a great deal from them; in fact, in the scientific world, making mistakes is expected. Scientists generally hypothesize something and expect that when they test their own hypotheses, they may often go astray. If scientists were sure that their hypotheses were always right, they would not even bother experimenting in the first place. Why work on problems when you already know the answers?

Learning language is similar to scientific method. Children hypothesize about certain features of language and test out a variety of options. Depending on the responses of the community to their hypothesis testing, children add to their knowledge about language. In the preschool years, most children are rewarded for trying out their options. Parents, grandparents, neighbors, peers, and siblings are often excited by young children's attempts to communicate and seldom correct their language in the home setting, since communication is the purpose of the language.

In some settings, however, certain aspects of language learning are frowned on and actually discouraged. Children can learn very early that it is better to use language as little as possible in certain settings—notably, and regrettably, in the classroom. Their language will continue to grow with their peers and in the community, but they do not find it comfortable to share what they know in the classroom— especially if their exploration of language is viewed as a deficiency.

The stifling of language development is supported and enhanced by the way standardized tests are used. If tests were used simply as one tool among many in the evaluation of children, the results would not be so damaging. But that is not the case. It is assumed that tests of reading measure the reading process; that tests of writing measure writing achievement; that tests of language measure language ability; that tests of intelligence measure thinking—even though such assumptions have been challenged by knowledge that is emerging from the study of language development.

The way tests are used today leads teachers to believe that they need to focus on the most meaningless parts of language. The names of letters and sounds, the rules for spelling, syllabication, and punctuation, and the definition of words are aspects of language that children eventually may learn through a lot of experience with reading, writing, speaking, and listening. But teaching these specifics out of the context of real language experiences does not help children become effective and flexible users of language, and it surely does not make them aware of its power.

If language specifics are central to the tests, however, many teachers believe it is their duty to focus on them in the classroom. The curriculum narrows and becomes a matter of teaching to the test. People begin to call for mastery learning, and publishers begin to push programs designed to help students pass tests. Isolated skills in reading, writing, and math are stressed in response to these concerns, leaving no time for reading, writing, or the humanities; no time for taking field trips, for discussing controversial issues, for exploring the world. The learning environment becomes sterile as teachers put away the woodworking materials, store the easels and paints, and move away from block play and the care of animals and plants. Even excellent teachers often have to divert their energies from the exciting activities through which children can expand their language effectiveness and spend time instead on narrow prescriptions to help kids get ready to pass the test. New teachers or teachers who are somewhat insecure about trying new ideas with students find the risks too great. They retreat into using textbooks exclusively or teaching in ways that diminish the use of oral language in the classroom and focus on single correct answers and fill-in-the-blank worksheets.

Students' responses to testing have a great impact on their view of themselves as learners. All children are learners. Yet when children are told repeatedly that they are not working as well as they should and when they see that half of the children who take standardized tests are, by definition, below the mean, they begin to lose belief in themselves. Children do not try as hard or work as hard when they believe that they can't do it anyway.

Those children who do well on tests sometimes *do* get opportunities for expanding language activities. They may be encouraged to write stories and read to younger children. They may work in the library and go to plays. These richer experiences help them expand their language learning.

In many cases, however, the kids who don't do as well are drilled even more on the specifics. Sometimes they are not permitted recess until they've filled in all the blanks. They may be kept from Rodeo Day or International Activities Week because they haven't yet been checked off for a particular blend or vowel digraph. Their learning experiences are narrowed, and their opportunities for expanding their language in the school setting are poor. Bluntly put, the rich get richer and the poor get poorer. There is little time for talking and even less time for actually writing a story or reading a good book.

Moreover, the one right answer required by standardized tests encourages students to believe that there are single answers to complex personal and social problems. Experimenting and exploring issues becomes a frill, as even good students begin to believe that finding the one right answer is what learning is all about. Children begin to do what they must in order to please teachers, and the notion that the essence of learning is for the self is lost.

If we truly want to find out about the development of children and, through that knowledge, to develop educational experiences for them, then standardized testing is not the most effective means to that end. Many evaluative activities that teachers can use in the classroom are less expensive than standardized tests and provide a lot more information about the child.

The best alternatives to testing come from direct and, in most cases, informal observation of the child in various situations by the classroom teacher. Since the process itself is somewhat informal, perhaps the term *kidwatching* is preferable to the more formal *observation*. Either way, the process is the same.

The basic assumption in kidwatching is that development of language is a natural process in all human beings. Two important questions explored through kidwatching are (1) what evidence is there that language development is taking place? and (2) when a child produces something unexpected, what does it tell the teacher about the child's knowledge of language?

When Susie says to Mr. Farrell, her first-grade teacher, "That's the goodest story I've ever heard," she is providing evidence that she is developing rules about how comparatives are generated. Mr. Farrell can now observe Susie in many different situations. Susie seems to use *best* and *very good* as well as *goodest*. If Mr. Farrell keeps a record, he may discover four months later that Susie never says *goodest* any more, although her friend Mary may not eliminate the use of *goodest* from her language until some time later.

When Fred reads *headlights* for *headlamps* in a story, he is providing evidence that he understands what he is reading well enough to interpret the written language into the oral system he uses and understands best.

When Tony has written his teacher's name correctly for six months as *Miss Willis* and then in January begins to spell it *Mes Welles*, he is providing evidence of growth because he is moving away from simply copying from the board to generating his own phoneme-grapheme rules. This evidence is supported by a sentence in a letter he writes to his grandmother: "It is wentr and stel cold."

The first step in observation is having up-to-date knowledge about language. Many myths and misunderstandings are reflected in test items. For example, simple dialect differences or speech immaturities are often marked as errors on tests, rather than viewed as normal parts of language development and use. To help correct such misunderstandings, administrators would do well to provide inservice programs on language development for teachers. In addition, schools of education should provide courses in this area for both preservice and inservice teachers.

The kidwatcher must also understand the role of error in language learning. Research in all areas of language—speaking, listening, reading, and writing—suggests that errors are not random and in most cases can be explained by understanding how people learn language.

Mistakes can reveal a great deal about children's language development. Errors often indicate that children are involved in organizing all of their knowledge and searching for additional information. What did these two fifth graders understand when they wrote down the pledge of allegiance? One student wrote, "to the republic of Richard's stand," while a second wrote, "to the republic of richest stand." The teacher has some information now about what the children are learning about their own nation. They are bringing knowledge together and trying to organize it into something meaningful. When teachers have insight into such responses, they can plan curriculum experiences to help youngsters rethink their understanding and expand their views of the United States.

Mistakes, errors, and miscues provide a great deal of knowledge about a child's language responses, but children are not permitted errors on tests. An error is defined as something that is wrong and must be corrected or righted immediately. Only the test author has the correct answer. Such significance is attached to a test author's correct answers that even teachers of very young children feel inadequate to correct tests, workbooks, or questions at the end of chapters without using answer books. Yet when children are asked for explanations of their answers to test questions, they often give reasoned responses to wrong answers, while right answers are sometimes reasoned through in an inappropriate fashion.

Of course, what a teacher thinks of as a mistake may simply be a different view of the world based on the child's personal experiences or cultural background. In a what-goes-with-what question, for example, an Orthodox Jewish child may have trouble grouping eggs with meat and other proteins or with milk items found in the dairy case. Eggs are often classed with either meats or dairy products in many health or science units, but to an Orthodox child, eggs are in a separate category according to dietary laws.

The kidwatcher observes the child in a variety of social and cultural settings reacting to print on the playground, in the hallway, or on the school bus. Ms. Roberts becomes aware that Bobby may respond to *McDonald's* and *stop* signs although he is still opening books upside down. She knows that he is aware of print and using written language to create meaning but that he needs a lot of experience with books. Maria is observed as she speaks with her mother, grandmother, siblings, and teacher. She talks to her grandmother in Spanish, speaks a mixture of English and Spanish to her mother and siblings, but speaks only English to her Spanish-speaking teacher. She is showing that she believes only English should be spoken in school and that she knows for whom each language form is most appropriate.

The environment in which learning takes place must provide opportunities for the teacher to observe children using language in a variety of settings, on a variety of topics, and through interaction with a variety of people. Reading must include much more than workbooks, worksheets, or texts. Signs, instructional magazines, personal letters, tickets, newspapers, clocks, and maps must be available for children's interactions. Writing must go beyond filling in blanks or completing sentences. It must take place continually in responding to science experiments, writing stories or notes to classmates, typing up invitations, and printing class newspapers.

Records should be kept of kidwatching. The teacher should keep notes on the degree to which children talk, write, listen, and read. Observations need to be made in one-to-one interactions, small-group discussions, question-and-answer sessions, and large-class settings. A chart can be kept on each child, indicating the various settings and responding to such questions as: Does the child use language to a greater extent in one situation than another? Does the child appear to be more comfortable in one setting than another? Is the child attentive during discussions even if someone else is speaking? With which classmate does a less talkative child communicate the most?

When watching children read, it is important to note if they read on their own or only at the teacher's request. Does the child come up to the teacher and share something read at home? How much reading does the child do? What different kinds of things does the child read? Does the child go eagerly to the library? When reading aloud, do the miscues the child produces suggest that the child is understanding the content of the reading selection? Such miscues tend to change the meaning of the text only minimally, even though the miscues may not look much like the text.

In addition, tapes can be kept of a child's oral reading and retelling of a story or article at different times during the year. At the end of the year, the tapes can be compared to see if the child is reading material of increasing conceptual difficulty and if the miscues show that the child is really interpreting what is being read. Together, the child and the teacher (and the parents if possible) can examine the development that has taken place during the year and select areas that need more work. Some growth will almost always be obvious, and the child will be excited and encouraged by it.

To observe writing development, samples of writing should be kept in a folder for each child. At the end of a week of work, the child might select the piece of writing he or she thinks is best to place in the folder. The others can be taken home. At the end of the month, the child and the teacher can discuss the growth that has taken place and choose the best selection of the month to leave in the folder until the end of the year. Together, the teacher and the child (and, again, the parents if possible) can examine development in handwriting, spacing, punctuation, spelling, and, most important, the content of the material.

As kidwatching goes on, the teacher will find that the various questions used as the basis for observation will change as children mature and change. The questions should be rethought regularly, according to the teacher's knowledge of the class and his or her developing knowledge about language. A group of teachers in a school can often work out a list of questions and keep reevaluating them and changing them as the need arises. In fact, it is through kidwatching that the best questions can be formulated.

These kinds of observation techniques have often been criticized because of the time they take. A considerable amount of the teacher's time is already being spent nonproductively, however, in giving children pretests and posttests. Then even more time is spent checking off the items children need to know in order to pass the tests. Kidwatching takes place as the teacher interacts with the child in the many language experiences available for children in every part of the school day. The times the child is actually reading, writing, speaking, and listening are the best times for observation. Kidwatching is not something apart from ongoing learning experiences.

These ideas have come from my own teaching, as well as from the many talented teachers I have had the privilege of working with over the last twenty-five years. Good teachers have always been kidwatchers. They have always observed the language learning of the children in their classes. That kind of teaching should be encouraged and applauded. Teachers and administrators who feel they need a test score that compares their children with others in the nation in order to gauge their effectiveness as educators are not tuned in to the language development of their children.

School people who are concerned with how young children learn language cannot allow inadequate measures like standardized tests to get in the way of the best kinds of learning experience for every child. Whether children expand their language effectiveness in the classroom or narrow their vistas to minimum competencies depends on the teacher. The school environment must support teachers to advance their own professionalism by developing the ability to observe children and understand their language strengths.

References

Brown, Roger. 1973. *A first language: The early stages.* Cambridge, MA: Harvard University Press.

Forester, Anne D. 1977. What teachers can learn from "natural readers." *The Reading Teacher, 31,* 160–66.

Goodman, Yetta M. & Goodman, Kenneth S. 1977. Learning to read is natural. In Lauren Resnick & Phyllis A. Weaver (Eds.), *Theory and practice of early reading* (Vol. 1) (pp. 137–54). Hillsdale, NJ: Erlbaum.

Halliday, M. A. K. 1975. Learning how to mean. In E. H. Lenneberg & E. Lenneberg (Eds.), *Foundations of language development* (Vol. 1) (pp. 239–66). New York: Academic Press.

Read, Charles. 1975. *Children's categorization of speech sounds in English* (Research Report No. 17). Urbana, IL: National Council of Teachers of English.

Ylisto, Ingrid P. 1977. Early reading responses of young Finnish children. *The Reading Teacher, 31,* 167–72.

Kidwatching:
Observing Children
in the Classroom

Three first graders were grouped around the flotation bowl. They were trying to discover what things could float and why. Elana put a wadded piece of foil in the bowl. Just as it sank to the bottom, Mr. Borton walked up and observed the scene. He noticed a wet, fair-sized aluminum boat next to the bowl. He addressed the group. "What did you just learn?"

Elana responded quickly, "Big things float and small things sink."

Robin reacted, "Uh, uh. I don't think that's always true."

"What might you do to prove the hypothesis Elana just made?" said Mr. Borton.

"Well," said Lynn, "maybe we could make a small boat and a big ball and try those things to see what will happen." As the children got involved in the new tasks they set for themselves, Mr. Borton walked on to another group.

Good teachers, like Mr. Borton, have always been kidwatchers. The concept of kidwatching is not new. It grows out of the child-study movement that reached a peak in the 1930s, providing a great deal of knowledge about human growth and development. Teachers can translate child study into its most universal form: learning about children

Originally published in *Observing the Language Learner,* edited by Angela Jaggar & M. Trika Smith-Burke (Urbana, IL & Newark, DE: National Council of Teachers of English & International Reading Association, 1985), pp. 9–18. Reprinted with permission.

by watching how they learn. The term kidwatching has caught on among those who believe that children learn language best in an environment rich with opportunities to explore interesting objects and ideas. Through observing the reading, writing, speaking, and listening of friendly, interactive peers, interested kidwatching teachers can understand and support child language development.

Evaluation of the progress of conceptual and language development for individual children cannot be provided in any useful sense by formalized pencil-and-paper tests. Evaluation provides the most significant information if it occurs continuously and simultaneously with the experiences in which the learning is taking place. Mr. Borton knows a lot about how children conceptualize and develop new insights into the physical nature of the world and what kinds of language they use and have developed during the activity in which they were involved.

Similarly, in the home, parents are aware of how much taller their children have grown, whether they have become better ball players, or how much more considerate they have become toward other family members. Parents know this by their constant attention to and involvement with the size of clothes, the faster and harder return of a pitched ball, or some deed a child does for a parent or sibling. Scales and yardsticks may provide some statistical data for parents to use to verify their observational knowledge, but it is never the only measure on which they rely.

Unfortunately, especially in recent years, scores on tests have been viewed as more objective than the judgment of a professional observer, since test results are often presented under an aura of statistical significance, which for many people has an unquestionable mystique.

Formal tests, standardized or criterion-referenced, provide statistical measures of the product of learning, but only as supplementary evidence for professional judgments about the growth of children. If teachers rely on formalized tests, they come to conclusions about children's growth based on data from a single source. Tests do provide evidence of how children grow in their ability to handle test situations, but not in their ability to handle settings where important language learnings occur. Studies of the role that context plays in how children learn have made it clear that children respond differently in different situations. Teachers who observe the development of language and knowledge in children in different settings become aware of important milestones in children's development that tests cannot reveal.

The term *kidwatching* is used to reinstate and legitimatize the significance of professional observation in the classroom. Those who support such child study understand that the evaluation of pupils' growth and curriculum development are integrally related. The energies of teachers and other curriculum planners must go into building a powerful learning environment. The key question in evaluation is not, Can the child perform the specific tasks that have been taught? Rather, the question is, Can the child adjust language used in other situations to meet the demands of new settings? The teacher must be aware that children learn all the time. The best way to gain insight into language learning is to observe children using language to explore all kinds of concepts in art, social studies, math, science, or physical education.

Teachers screen their observations through their philosophy, their knowledge base, and their assumptions whenever they are involved in kidwatching. Following are some of the basic premises that underlie kidwatching notions:

1. Current knowledge about child language and conceptual development must be a part of continuous education for teachers. Such knowledge guides observations. Not only does it help teachers know what to look for as signs of growth and development, but it also helps teachers become consciously aware of their knowledge, their biases, and their philosophical orientation.

2. Language and concepts grow and develop depending on the settings in which they occur, the experiences that children have in those settings, and the interaction of the people in those settings. The richer and more varied these settings and interactions, the richer the child's language and concepts will be.

3. Knowledgeable teachers ready to assume responsibility for observation and evaluation of children play a very significant role in enriching the child's development of language and concepts.

Current Knowledge About Language

During the second half of this century a knowledge explosion has occurred in the study of language or linguistics. Much of this knowledge is contrary to the ideas about language that have been taught in the past under the labels of phonics, spelling, vocabulary, and grammar. In addition, there have been enormous gains in understanding how children learn language. When old beliefs are being questioned and new knowledge is not fully understood, a great deal of controversy is often generated. This is especially true of those who have to apply the knowledge, as teachers do in classroom situations. Knowledge about language variation and the role of error in language learning can be especially useful to teachers.

There are many issues concerning language differences in the areas of both dialect and second language learning that teachers must consider. Too many children have been hurt in the past because of lack of knowledge about language differences. Not only teachers but test makers and curriculum builders often produce materials that reflect myths and misunderstandings. The more knowledge teachers have about language variation, the better position they are in to evaluate materials and tests in order to use them wisely and appropriately. Attitudes such as *these children have no language* or *bilingualism confuses children* are still too prevalent. Kidwatching can help teachers be aware of how such statements are damaging to language growth, if they are armed with up-to-date knowledge. By observing the language of children in a wide variety of settings such as role-playing, retelling of picture books, or playing games during recess or physical education, teachers gain many kinds of information that help to dispel myths about language and language learning.

For example, Sorita, age six, would use the following types of construction often in oral conversations with other children or during sharing sessions:

"Lots of my friends was at my house."
"We was going to the store."

However, during her narration of "The Three Billy Goats Gruff" that accompanied the acting out of the story by some of her classmates, her teacher heard, "There were three billy goats." Sorita used this more formal construction throughout the narration.

Retelling a story about a farmer and his son, a recent nine-year-old immigrant from Lebanon said, "They were working at to plant something."

Both examples provide insight into each child's language development. Sorita shows the ability to use the more formal *were* form in storytelling, although she uses the colloquial form in informal settings. She is aware of formal and informal language settings and that each permits different language.

The second child shows growing control over two kinds of complex English structures—the verb plus particle *working at* and the infinitive form *to plant*—even though as this child combines the structures, they may sound a little unusual to a native English speaker's ear.

Errors in language and in conceptual development reflect much more than a mistake that can be eradicated with a red pencil or a verbal admonition. What an adult perceives as wrong may in fact reflect development in the child. Errors, miscues, or misconceptions usually indicate ways in which a child is organizing the world at that moment.

As children develop conceptually and linguistically, their errors shift from those that represent unsophisticated conclusions to ones that show greater sophistication. The previous examples are evidence of this kind of growth. Sometimes teachers expect certain responses or "correct answers" because of a school-based cultural view of the world. The child's unexpected responses, if observed with understanding, may broaden a teacher's conceptualization about the child's world. "Errors" also indicate interpretations that may in no way be wrong but simply show that the child has used inferences about reading or listening that were unexpected.

For example, a kindergarten teacher prior to morning snack time gave her class a short talk about what was wrong with wasting milk. Tomasa was observed taking a small sip of milk. She then carefully closed the milk carton, wiped her place with her paper towel, and slowly placed the carton of milk in the waste basket, holding it tight until it reached the bottom. "Didn't we just talk about not wasting milk?" Miss Dasson asked. "I ain't waste my milk," Tomasa responded. "I keeped everything real clean!" Miss Dasson now knows that *waste* has an alternate meaning in the language of Tomasa's community—*to spill*. She and Tomasa can now share each other's meanings.

The kidwatcher who understands the role of unexpected responses will use children's errors and miscues to chart their growth and development and to understand the personal and cultural history of the child. There are no tests available that can provide this kind of data to the professional educator. These insights can emerge only from kidwatching based on a sound knowledge of language and language learning.

Individual teachers may not be in a position to keep current about the dynamic information so vital to understanding language learning. However, courses of study or programs can be organized through setting up teacher support groups, working cooperatively with teacher educators at local universities and colleges or with inservice personnel at the district level, and holding discussion groups. Although courses in linguistics, the science of language, may in themselves be helpful, it may be more useful if teachers encourage and participate in the development of programs that have an applied orientation for the classroom.

Variations of Setting, Function, and Material

Thoughtful observation of children takes place in a rich, innovative curriculum in the hands of a knowledgeable teacher who demands and accepts responsibility for curriculum decision making. With such teachers, children are involved in exciting educational experiences and make the greatest growth in language learning and conceptual development.

Curriculum becomes sterilized when it is based on pupils' results on standardized tests or progress on "criterion-referenced" behavioral checksheets. In order to achieve appropriate gains, curriculum experiences must narrow to those safely entombed in the test itself. Curriculum becomes repetitive practice with the same kind of "skills" on workbooks and worksheets as in the test. The only individualization is how much practice each pupil must endure.

Where kidwatching is an integral part of the curriculum, the teacher's focus is on providing rich learning experiences for children. There is an awareness of the dynamic relationship among the teacher, the children, and the experiences. Evaluation is ongoing. Although teachers should certainly be expected to document and discuss the growth of their children, the most important role of the teacher is involving children in learning through the richness of the curriculum. Only when children have a variety of materials available to read and many good personal reasons to want to learn about new ideas and concepts will they read varied genres, write for different purposes, and grow in their ability to use written language effectively.

As functions and purposes for learning new concepts change, so will the settings, the language, and the materials needed for the learnings change. These broadened experiences enrich language learning for children and provide many opportunities for kidwatching to occur. Children must go to the library to solve certain problems, to the principal's office to solve others. They interview some people orally, read about others, or write letters as it serves the purposes of their explorations. Language learning reaches out to meet new challenges, and teachers can evaluate the flexibility with which children can expand language use.

For example, keeping copies of children's letters written to different people over the course of a few months provides evidence about (1) the appropriateness of the language of the letters, depending on their purposes; (2) the degree to which children change the language and style of the letters, depending on their audience; (3) the increase of conventionally spelled words over time; (4) changes in the complexity of grammatical structures; and (5) concern for legibility.

The Teacher's Role Is Significant

Concepts from three scholars in different fields of child study provide a jumping-off place from which to explore the significance of the teacher's role. Jerome Bruner (1978) talks about *scaffolding*; M. A. K. Halliday (1980), about *tracking*; and L. S. Vygotsky (1962), about the zone of proximal development. Each of these concepts is used to express the significance of communicative interactions between adults and children that are basic to the expansion of language and the extension of learning in children. If parents play as significant a role in a child's language development as these scholars suggest, it seems logical that a teacher who understands how children learn language might capitalize on these ideas and be at least as effective as parents in supporting child language growth and extending it once the child comes to school.

Focusing on mother/child interaction, Bruner (1978) defines scaffolding by quoting Roger Brown: "A study of detailed mother/child interaction . . . shows that successful communication on one level is always the launching platform for attempts at communication on a more adult level" (p. 251). Bruner continues: "The mother systematically changes her BT (Baby Talk) in order to 'raise the ante' or alter the conditions she imposes on the child's speech in different settings" (p. 251).

According to Bruner, the adult always takes the child's ideas seriously, thinking through what the child is trying to communicate, allowing the child to move ahead when capable of doing so, and supporting the child only when the child seems to need help: "Once the child has made a step forward, [the mother] will not let him slide back. She assures that he go on with the next construction to develop a next platform for his next launch" (p. 254).

Halliday (1980) uses a similar notion about language learning in children that he calls tracking. From his extensive study of language development, Halliday concludes that the adults and older siblings who live with the child "share in the language-creating process along with the child" (p. 10). He suggests that teachers take on a similar role when the child comes to school, helping children find new ways to say or write things as children find new reasons to express themselves or to understand.

Vygotsky (1962), who adds additional perspectives on the significance of child/adult interaction, believes that educators can make use of cooperation between adult and student and "lead the child to what he could not yet do" by himself (p. 104).

Vygotsky defines the "discrepancy between a child's actual mental age and the level he reaches in solving problems with assistance" (p. 103) as the child's zone of proximal development.

> With assistance every child can do more than he can by himself. . . . What the child can do in cooperation today, he can do alone tomorrow. Therefore, the only good kind of instruction is that which marches ahead of development and leads it, it must be aimed not so much at the ripe as at the ripening functions. (p. 103–4)

Although there may be some theoretical differences between these scholars, there is little disagreement about the significance of the role of the teacher or other adults involved in children's growth. Teachers who continually observe children using knowledge about language and cognition can ask the appropriate question or pose a specific problem or place an object in front of children so that learning is extended. As they observe, they also gain information for planning new experiences or instructional activities, leading the child toward new explorations. Observation, evaluation, and curriculum planning go hand in hand.

Teachers can develop a variety of ways to keep records of these developments for reporting to parents, to remind themselves of children's growth over the year, to involve students in self-evaluation, and to leave records for continued school use. However, the records of kidwatchers are not simply statistics used to compare children or to have them compete with one another. Whether they are anecdotal records of children's interactions; selected writing samples of students' letters, logs, and stories; or tapes of children's reading or oral reporting, their purpose is to provide profiles of children's language growth in different settings, with different materials, and through different experiences.

Where to Start? What to Do?

My own observations of outstanding kidwatching teachers are reflected in the following suggestions:

1. *When a child achieves success in some communicative setting (including reading and writing), the teacher may find a number of ways to extend this to a new and different setting.* For example, a child who is responding orally to a patterned language book such as "I Know an Old Woman Who Swallowed a Fly" can be encouraged to write a book either alone, with the teacher, or a peer, perhaps entitled "Johnny Swallowed a Bumblebee." This would extend the holistically remembered oral reading of a book to writing a book to share with others, using similar language structures but personalizing characters and experiences in writing. But don't expect the new use of communication to look as successful as the one previously achieved. When a child tries something new, it is bound to seem less sophisticated at first than something the child does that is familiar.

2. *When children are involved in exploratory activities, the teacher might raise questions such as, I wonder why this is so? or What do you think is*

happening here? The questions may help children reflect on their own thinking and see contradictions in their hypotheses.

3. *When children are observed to be troubled with an experience, the teacher can move in and talk about the situation with them and lead them to what they cannot yet do by themselves* (Vygotsky 1962). It is at a moment of frustration that a kidwatching teacher can help children resolve conflictive situations à la Piaget (1977) and move on to expand their language and conceptualization.

4. *Teachers need to trust in children's learning and in their own ability to learn along with their children.* Language learning involves risk taking. When teachers believe in their own professional judgment and respect children's abilities, success occurs as part of the curricular experiences. With such a sense of security, teachers can become kidwatchers and with children build a community that contains many launching pads from which children and the teacher can reach the next level of language learning together.

References

Bruner, Jerome S. 1978. The role of dialogue in language acquisition. In A. Sinclair, R. J. Jarvella & W. J. M. Levelt (Eds.), *The child's conception of language* (pp. 241–56). Berlin: Springer-Verlag.

Halliday, M. A. K. 1980. Three aspects of children's language development: Learning language, learning through language, learning about language. In Yetta M. Goodman, Myna Haussler & Dorothy Strickland (Eds.), *Oral and written language development research: Impact on the schools* (Proceedings from the 1979 and 1980 IMPACT Conferences) (pp. 7–19). Newark, DE & Urbana, IL: International Reading Association & National Council of Teachers of English. (ERIC Document Reproduction Service Document ED 214 184)

Piaget, Jean. 1977. *The development of thought: Equilibration of cognitive structures.* New York: Viking.

Vygotsky, Lev S. 1962. *Thought and language.* Cambridge, MA: MIT Press.

Evaluation of Students:
Evaluation of Teachers

The power of evaluation in whole language classrooms lies in the process of becoming—the changes or moves that people make from what they are to what they come to be. These moves are important not just for students but equally for the professional development of teachers and the dynamic nature of the ongoing curriculum. As we begin a dialogue on evaluation among teachers, administrators, and teacher educators, it may be helpful to consider the concept of reflection and the mirror image as a metaphor. In our classrooms, as we critically examine what students do in order to help them grow as educated human beings, we become consciously aware that at the same time we are seeing a reflection of ourselves. We keep in mind that teachers are prime movers in organizing the environments in which learning takes place. Our planning and organization influence the classroom environment in so many ways that the evaluation of students becomes an evaluation of ourselves and of the curriculum. Seeing ourselves reflected in our classrooms and in the responses of our students helps us to understand the nature of language learning and at the same time helps us become aware of our influences on that learning and on the relationships between teaching and learning. The dynamic transaction between teachers and students results in change in all the actors and actions involved in the teaching/learning experience. Evaluation—the

Originally published in *The Whole Language Evaluation Book,* edited by Kenneth S. Goodman, Yetta M. Goodman & Wendy J. Hood (Portsmouth, NH: Heinemann, 1989). Reprinted with permission.

examination of that change—reveals the development of the learning, the teacher, and the curriculum. At the same time that we look into the mirror to see the reflection of our teaching in the students and their learning, we also take advantage of what we see to reflect on our own professional development as teachers.

Evaluation: An Integral Part of Curriculum

Evaluation is part of curriculum: it cannot be divorced from classroom organization, from the relationship between teachers and students, from continuous learning experiences and activities. To think about and plan for evaluation, it is necessary to keep in mind the classroom community and its organization. There is no way to separate the role of evaluation from the dynamic teaching/learning transaction.

Whole language teachers value the social community of the classroom. Respect for all the members of the learning community suggests that each plays a role in teaching, each is involved in continuous learning, and therefore each has a role in the evaluation process. The classroom belongs to the community that lives there, with the teacher providing the major leadership role but respecting the students' ideas about how the classroom can be organized to be an effective place in which to live and to learn. In planning for evaluation, we must understand and utilize the power of the social group. The classroom community is part of the larger community in which teachers and students live and communicate daily. It is therefore also important to involve other teachers, administrators, and parents in the evaluation process.

Whole language classrooms are rich in resources and opportunities. Students are enabled to use language in all its forms. Students are trusted to care for a variety of resources, which are available and accessible. The social community in the classroom is organized so that every member knows the responsibilities and privileges of access to the tools of learning. In whole language programs, students learn in an environment that invites them to participate in all the activities in the classroom and to make choices about the kinds of experiences in which they participate.

Functional and authentic experiences are planned by both teachers and students. That means that students see the potential in their experiences to solve their problems and to gain the knowledge they need as citizens in a democracy. As members of the learning community plan together, they include opportunities for the evaluation of their own experiences.

Building a Professional Sense

Teachers continuously monitor the development of their students during their daily contacts. Thinking as parents about our own kids at home will help us explore this idea. How do we know when our kids have grown physically, intellectually, and emotionally? I remember having to buy them larger-sized clothes, spending more money on food. The doctor would measure and weigh my kids, but the figures simply confirmed what I already knew as an observant and caring parent and what the children knew about themselves. The measurements were only additional bits of statistical information. All the other important information had already let me know that my kids were growing up, how they were changing, what they knew, and how much they cared.

I remember sitting at the dinner table and looking across at my eldest daughter and suddenly realizing that I was looking straight into her eyes; I was not looking down at her anymore. I was evaluating her growth with a practiced eye. When your son or daughter walks into the house from school, you can often tell whether something terrible or wonderful happened that day. And then you confirm your initial judgment by gathering new information. First you sense the change, then you find ways to confirm what you sense.

When children begin to ask questions about people's health or their economic condition, we begin to see growth in their empathy for others. When they join in conversations about current events, we realize that their interests and knowledge base have changed. As parents we use all of our developing senses to make decisions about the growth of our children. Those senses often called common sense aren't common to all. They are common to parents who build their parental sense over a period of time.

Teachers build similar senses, but I prefer to identify these as professional senses. Teachers not only build these senses through their interactions with and reflections about students but also professionalize their senses by confirming their judgments through their reading and continued scholarship in areas such as human development, language learning, and practices in effective schooling.

Initially, professional senses are intuitive. Beginning teachers are often unaware that they are thinking intuitively, using their background knowledge whenever they have to make decisions such as whether a student is a good reader, which are the appropriate ways to make presentations to the class, and what their students understand about scientific of mathematical concepts. Once teachers begin to take account of what they know about learning, language, and conceptual development, however, they then build confidence in their ability to make judgments about students' growth. Their reflective thinking grows and takes on new dimensions.

It is crucial to legitimize the power of the professional intuition of teachers, which has largely been ignored for at least two reasons. The first reason, I believe, is related to a lack of respect for teachers as thinkers and decision makers. Therefore as a profession we avoid giving voice to this power. It is not discussed much in the educational literature or in preservice or inservice teacher programs. Although scholars such as John Dewey (Archambault 1964) and Eliot Eisner (1976) have explored the significance of reflective thinking, educational connoisseurship, and criticism for teachers, the educational establishment does not seem to respect the thinking abilities of teachers enough to give the concept of a developing professional sense legitimacy. Eisner states:

> What I believe we need to do with respect to educational evaluation is not to seek recipes to control and measure practice but rather to enhance whatever artistry the teacher can achieve. . . . Good theory in education . . . helps us to see more; . . . theory provides some of the windows through which intelligence can look out into the world. (p. 140)

The second reason why the professional sense of teachers has not been adequately explored may be an unexamined belief in statistical information. Because numbers take on an aura of objectivity, *which they do not intrinsically deserve,* statistical test data are equated with the development of knowledge and are valued more highly than the sense of an informed, committed professional who uses knowledge about students, the community, and the context to make judgments.

Of course educators need to know the limitations of their professional sense and discover a variety of ways to confirm their intuitions. But when the power of professional intuitions is denigrated with comments such as *It's just subjective* or *Test scores are better than nothing,* we cannot develop the forum in which to discuss both the power and the limitations of professional judgments and explore the legitimate uses of the professional sense of teachers. Whole language teachers who know they are competent are willing to assume responsibility for their judgments and have no difficulty being accountable to their students, to parents, and to other professionals in their schools and districts.

Professional sense comes from the interplay of what teachers know about language and learning, what they observe in their relationships with students, and the knowledge that is built on those relationships. The professional sense becomes more focused as teachers seek opportunities to raise their intuitions to a conscious level.

Building a Knowledge Base

In order to evaluate language and conceptual development as well as the physical and emotional growth of students, it is necessary for teachers to be lifelong learners. As a result, the professional sense of whole language teachers develops continuously. Whole language teachers learn from their students through the evaluation process; they learn from their interactions with other practitioners as they share ideas and problems; and they learn from child-study groups organized within the school by resource teachers or principals. They attend classes and become active in professional organizations. They attend workshops and conferences not only to hear from other knowledgeable professionals but also to present their ideas in order to think them through and get responses from others. They read the latest scholarship in professional journals and books about their subject-matter specialties, about the kinds of kids they work with, and about language and learning. They critique research about language and cognitive development and relate it to their classroom setting, and they participate in action research in their own classes to learn more and to see if research they think has merit rings true for their own kids. Building a knowledge base becomes the foundation on which professional sense grows. John Dewey suggested that genuine freedom comes from reflective thinking that interacts with an everdeveloping knowledge base,

> the power of thought, an ability to turn things over, to look at matters deliberately, to judge whether the amount and kind of evidence requisite for decision is at hand, and if not, to tell where and how to seek such evidence. If . . . actions are not guided by thoughtful conclusions, then they are guided by inconsiderate impulse, unbalanced appetite, caprice of the circumstances of the moment. (Archambault 1964, pp. 258–59)

Thinking reflectively about a knowledge base in order to build a professional sense cannot be accomplished quickly. The process is cumulative over a professional lifetime. We can't hurry learning in kids, and we can't hurry learning in ourselves as teachers. Whole language teachers have to be as patient with themselves as learners as they are with their own students.

The Double Agenda of Evaluation

Evaluation is part of the double agenda in the whole language classroom. As shown in Figure 1, the right side of the agenda, *Students' Learning*, indicates where the students and teacher are busily and ac-

Figure 1.
The Double Agenda

Teacher's Evaluation	Students' Learning
Teachers are involved	Kids and teachers are involved
Evaluation of Language development Cognitive development Curriculum	Learning about their world Answering their questions Solving their problems Evaluating their own learning through language use
A continuous ongoing integral process	Reading Writing Speaking Listening

tively involved: in reading to solve problems, to add to their scientific knowledge and their aesthetic pleasure; in writing to express their meanings, to discover what they know, to create artistically, and to take care of everyday business; and in using oral and written language to learn about the world. The left side of the agenda shows that while the classroom community is engaged in learning, the *Teacher's Evaluation* is monitoring the goals of language learning and conceptual development.

Evaluation doesn't get in the way of the kids' learning. At the same time that students are involved in the plans for the day as one part of the double agenda, evaluation is a constant part of the other aspect of the agenda. Teachers are involved in evaluation during all aspects of the curriculum. It is a continuous, ongoing, integral process.

Whole language teachers don't decide to think about evaluation in June; they don't start to focus on evaluation in order to get ready for report card time or for parent conferencing. Whole language teachers know that evaluation is going on all the time; it is built into the plans every day. It is integral to the process of teaching and learning, not a separate, discrete activity. As the kids and the teacher are involved in learning about their world, answering their questions, and solving their problems, another part of that learning is to answer other kinds of questions: What am I learning? How are things going?

Who is getting things done? How are students' concepts and hypotheses changing? Who seems confused? How did things go in our discussion group? Did we do an adequate job of cleaning up after our art activity today? Did I organize the writing area so those who wanted to continue to write could do so?

Observing, Interacting, and Analyzing

A few years ago a group of whole language teachers in Tucson, Arizona, began to explore the issues of evaluation in their classrooms. They were involved in a variety of kidwatching activities and wanted to share what they were doing with other teachers, especially those new to whole language. They realized that kidwatching activities usually occur in three different ways. They became aware that they were evaluating whenever they were observing, interacting with, and analyzing students (Marek et al. 1984). These became categories that proved useful in thinking about whole language evaluation.

Observation includes examining what students are doing as the teacher stands on the sidelines. The teacher may choose to observe one student working alone, a student as a member of a group, all the members of a small group, or the class as a whole to make judgments about language use, problem solving, leadership, and collaborative capabilities.

Interaction includes ways in which a teacher converses or conferences, participates in discussions, interacts in journals, and raises questions with students in order to discover what students know and to encourage or challenge students to explore beyond what they are thinking at the moment.

Analysis includes eliciting information in ways such as the reading of a story, a written response to a book, a composition, or an oral conversation on tape, and then using psycholinguistic and sociolinguistic knowledge to analyze in depth what students know about language and how they show development in their language use.

Like so many other aspects of whole language, these three types of evaluation are separated for purposes of spotlighting the importance of each, but in most cases when these are in practice they are overlapping and integrated. They are strong evaluation tools, especially when they are used in concert. Each can help confirm the information gained from the use of the others.

Figure 2 shows aspects of observation, interaction, and analysis within the classroom setting. Each may be done formally: for example, records kept of an activity following a particular procedure at regular intervals. Or each may be informal and occur at any time the

Figure 2.
Evaluation in Whole Language Classrooms

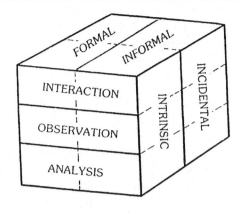

teacher and the student or students come in contact. Observation, interaction, and analysis may occur incidentally, whenever the teacher perceives that the students are engaged in an activity that will reveal important understanding about a student's learning or development. Or it may be part of a planned activity with a variety of forms and materials at hand to assist in the collection and analysis of the information. I will discuss each with relevant examples.

Observation

Confident and knowledgeable teachers are often able to sense whether a student's staring into space means that he or she is deep in concentration, involved in some painful thoughts, or daydreaming about some activity not directly related to the work at hand. Of course the professional verifies such observational judgments through interacting, by engaging the student in conversation or asking a question, or through more formal evaluation if warranted. The use of such professional hunches followed by appropriate confirmations is a legitimate part of evaluation. Initial judgments based on observation are helpful in gaining insight into the learning processes of particular students.

Informal observations, which most often take place as the teacher moves around the classroom, build an intuitive sense of an individual or a group of students. Teachers are watching and listening to discussions of small groups; they're noticing students engaged in reading or writing, working on scientific experiments, researching for reports, or solving math problems; teachers are becoming aware of the interactions taking place and how the interactions relate to the tasks at hand. The teacher may keep a notebook or two in a few strategic places in the classroom to jot down general impressions by noting key words, dates, and names. At a critical moment, when something important happens that provides significant evidence about development, it may not be convenient to write a complete anecdotal record, but a few notes in an "Impressions Notebook" can be used later at a more convenient time to stimulate the memory in order to record more formal and long-lasting records.

Formal observations can be made by keeping anecdotal records of a very specific nature. These are dated, the names of the students are recorded, and these records are kept in a student's portfolio or permanent file. Some teachers are careful to observe every student at least once every two weeks. Other teachers find it best to do such recordings once a month or twice a semester. Teachers who find formal anecdotal entries useful are careful to rotate around the room at different times of the day or week, making sure to record appropriate information about each student working in different subject-matter areas and different settings in the classroom and participating in different activities such as silent reading, journal writing, collaborations, small-group discussion, and so on. These formal entries, of course, are supplemented by less formal observations.

Teachers who use formal observations may do so for the first few months of the year only. Then the teacher may add informal observations to the anecdotal records file on a less regular basis as important new information arises. As the teacher comes to know the students better as the semester goes on, less formal observations are made when the teacher recognizes information that may add to the profile of the student's development and evaluation. At the end of the semester or year or near the time for reporting to parents, the teacher finds it helpful to reread earlier entries, discuss them with the student, and then observe more intently for a period of time in order to illuminate a student's development and add a few more formal entries on each student.

Any time any of these recording devices seems not to be working for the teacher, it is helpful to experiment with new ways of observing. A system that has outgrown its usefulness simply becomes a chore and loses its power as an evaluation tool. Formal methods of observation may include check sheets for different subject-matter areas as well as written narratives about a student's development. Perhaps some day teachers will have machines on which to record oral information on students regularly. The tapes will then be given to the school secretary, who will type up the transcripts and add them to the students' files.

Interaction

Interaction with students may be the most powerful aspect of the process of evaluation in whole language classrooms, because of its immediate relationship to instruction. As teachers interact with students, they are not just discovering what students know about any particular learning but are also using the moments of interaction to question the student, to encourage, to stimulate, and to challenge.

The power of the interacting aspects of evaluation and their relationship to curriculum are supported by the work of many scholars in education, ethnography, psycholinguistics, and sociolinguistics. Vygotsky explores the *zone of proximal development* (1987), Bruner (1978) discusses the importance of *scaffolding,* and Halliday (1980) talks about the role of *tracking.* Piagetians have built into their research design the method of clinical exploration (Ferreiro & Teberosky 1982).

These scholars have theoretical differences concerning language and learning, but they have important thoughts in common in relation to the notion of interaction that informs whole language evaluation. They all suggest that two heads are better than one, that students learn more and can do more with the support of others, especially a knowledgeable teacher, than they are often capable of doing by themselves. These interactions lead to the critical teaching moments when the teacher learns that the student knows more than the teacher expected or shows creative thinking that is not along the lines of conventional adult forms. The teacher not only evaluates at these moments but uses them to plan immediate or future lessons or experiences to capitalize on the intellectual functioning of the student.

Carefully considered and appropriate questions at such moments gently push kids to consider greater, conflicting, or different information and become powerful in moving students toward moments of disequilibrium so they have to reorganize their concepts and rethink their ideas. Such questions can be specific to a particular task. For example, Ferreiro and Teberosky (1982) explored with children why Spanish speakers say the word for *chicken* in different ways. (The *ll* in the word *pollo* can be pronounced three different ways in the area in Argentina where this study took place.) The researchers questioned the children in such a provocative way that they were able to come up with some profound conclusions about dialect variations. One child concluded her discussion by saying, "Yes, but there are other countries where they speak different and they have to say it how they say it. They're not going to start to talk . . . as if it was wrong. We're not going to have to teach them, no. They teach them like they know" (p. 254).

In more general ways teachers can encourage kids to examine their statements and their knowledge base critically with open-ended questions such as: Why do you think so? Is it possible? What if we tried this instead? What if I said . . . ? I wonder if. . . . If teachers help students believe that they really expect explorations in their interactions with the objects of learning, then the evaluation of students takes on new and exciting dimensions. Students become aware that a focus on single correct answers is not what is valued, and their learning changes qualitatively to a more critical analysis of whatever they are studying. Students begin to reflect on their own learning, which results in self-evaluation on the part of the learner.

Interaction has its informal moments through daily conversations and discussions, the teacher's movements in and out of small groups of students working together, and the times when the teacher's authentic questions and wonderments are shared with students.

Interactions can be formally planned to be intrinsic to curriculum activities as part of reading and writing strategy lessons. A well-designed selected slotting or cloze passage is an example of such a strategy. Two students work together. The teacher participates, especially the first time the students work at this kind of lesson. For the most part, however, the students take the lead. As they discuss which linguistic units belong in particular blank spaces, the students often comment on what kinds of language are appropriate for particular slots. The teacher listens and discovers what students know about language as well as about the content of the material. The teacher evaluates what the students know and also helps students become more consciously aware of what they know about language. This aids in building confidence and provides opportunities for student self-evaluation. Notes may be kept of such interactions to show how students' problem-solving strategies change over time. In addition to strategy lessons, regularly planned individual or small-group reading and/or writing conferences also provide opportunities for formal evaluation through interactions. Teachers keep formal records of their reading and writing conferences with their students. Formal interactions can also take place in written form through dialogue journals or learning logs kept between students and the teacher.

Analysis

Teachers use many analytical tools that have been developed over years of research as formal devices for evaluating the reading and writing processes. As teachers become competent in the use of such formal tools, they can eventually be used informally. Teachers who have done a great deal of formal miscue analysis (Goodman, Watson

& Burke 1987) build a strong understanding of the principles underlying miscues in reading and are always in a position to evaluate miscues as they listen informally to kids reading during an individual conference. Those who have carefully analyzed the spelling or punctuation development of their students using linguistic insights (Read 1971; Wilde 1986/1987) understand the developmental moments in the spelling and punctuation of their students and can eventually point out a student's development by informally examining the student's composition.

There are many teachers, schools, and school districts that have developed writing and reading portfolios to keep files of students' work so as to allow for formal analysis of that work at any time. Students can be involved in such record-keeping procedures. They can help select the pieces of writing that will be collected weekly or monthly for the portfolio. They can record the names of the books they have read. If teachers have children read from a selected text and then retell onto an audio tape at intervals during the year, this account can also be kept in a student's evaluation or reading portfolio. These materials can be evaluated using many different kinds of analytical procedures, depending on the knowledge of the teacher and the particular focus a teacher wants to take at different times during the school year.

If the school faculty has worked together to develop a language policy, then a committee of teachers may decide what aspects of analysis to focus on for a particular year, depending on the teachers' concerns, their knowledge about language, and the concerns of the parents, the community, and the students. Holistic scoring procedures, analysis of story grammar, variation and flexibility in styles of writing and genres of reading, interests, spelling and punctuation development, and qualitative miscue changes all lend themselves to in-depth analysis.

Self-Evaluation

The ultimate goal of the evaluation process in whole language classrooms is self-evaluation for both the teacher and the student. Professional development is continuous when teachers assume responsibility for decision making in the classroom. Whole language teachers do so confidently. At the same time the teachers are in the position to help students assume responsibility for understanding, capitalizing on their strengths and finding ways to diminish and overcome their areas of weakness.

Through self-evaluation the teacher involves the kids in serious examination of such questions as: How am I doing? Are things going as I planned? What can I do to see that things go better next time? Students help by keeping records about their own learning experiences and meet with the teacher in conferences to evaluate what they have accomplished and what goals they hope to achieve, planning with the teacher how these are to be met. In this manner the teacher helps the kids learn about themselves and their capabilities. Simultaneously teachers reflect on their own development as they see their practices and plans reflected in their students' responses to learning. If individual learners are confident and knowledgeable enough, they will know how their own learning is working for them. Reflecting on their own learning is empowering. John Dewey says:

> By putting the consequences of different ways and lines of action before the mind, it enables us to know what we are about when we act. It converts action that is merely appetitive, blind, and impulsive into intelligent action. . . . Only when things about us have meaning for us, only when they signify consequences that can be reached by using them in certain ways, is any such thing as intentional, deliberate control of them possible. (Archambault 1964, pp. 212–13)

While the teacher is evaluating students and involving them in their own self-evaluation, there is constant opportunity for self-reflection on the part of the teacher. How students do is strongly influenced by the kinds of interactions the teacher has with students. Opportunities kids have to learn, their access to resources, and the support and encouragement they have from teachers will determine how students *see* themselves as invited into or excluded from the "literacy club" or the learning club (Smith 1986).

As teachers examine the ways in which they invite their students to learn, they are reflecting on their own teaching—self-evaluating—and informing their own teaching practices.

Working with colleagues in study or support groups also provides teachers opportunities for critical self-evaluation. As teachers talk about the forms they want to develop, the portfolios they plan to keep, and their plans to change and improve what they are doing in the classroom, opportunities for self-reflection are heightened. Social interaction with other teachers allows for critiquing, team learning, sharing, and many other means of examining one's teaching.

References

Archambault, R. C. 1964. *John Dewey on education*. Chicago: University of Chicago Press.

Bruner, Jerome S. 1978. The role of dialogue in language acquisition. In R. Jarvella, A. Sinclair & W. Levelt (Eds.), *The child's conception of language* (pp. 241–56). New York: Springer-Verlag.

Eisner, Elliott W. 1976. Educational conssoisseurship and criticism: Their form and functions in educational evaluation. *Journal of Aesthetic Education, 10,* 135–50.

Ferreiro, Emilia & Teberosky, Ana. 1982. *Literacy before schooling.* Portsmouth, NH: Heinemann. (Original work published 1979)

Goodman, Yetta M., Watson, Dorothy J. & Burke, Carolyn L. 1987. *Reading miscue inventory: Alternative procedures.* New York: Richard C. Owen.

Halliday, M. A. K. 1980 Three aspects of children's language development: Learning language, learning through language, learning about language. In Yetta M. Goodman, Myna Haussler & Dorothy Strickland (Eds.), *Oral and written language development research: Impact on the schools* (Proceedings from the 1979 and 1980 IMPACT Conferences) (pp. 7–19). Newark, DE & Urbana, IL: International Reading Association & National Council of Teachers of English. (ERIC Document Reproduction Service Document ED 214 184)

Marek, Ann, et al. 1984. *A kidwatching guide: Evaluation for whole language classrooms* (Occasional Paper No. 9). Tucson: Program in Language and Literacy, College of Education, University of Arizona. (ERIC Document Reproduction Service Document ED 277–978)

Read, Charles. 1971. Preschool children's knowledge of English phonology. *Harvard Educational Review, 41,* 1–34.

Smith, Frank. 1986. *Insult to intelligence: The bureaucratic invasion of our classrooms.* New York: Arbor House.

Vygotsky, Lev S. 1987. *Thought and language* (2nd ed.). Cambridge, MA: MIT Press.

Wilde, Sandra. 1987. An analysis of the development of spelling and punctuation in selected third- and fourth-grade children. (Doctoral dissertation, University of Arizona, 1986). *Dissertation Abstracts International, 47,* 2452A.

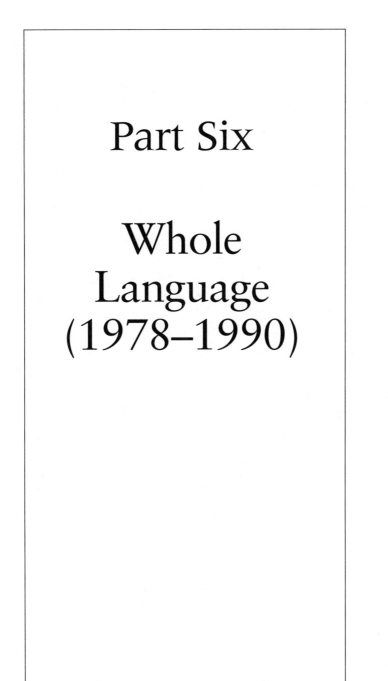

Part Six

Whole Language (1978–1990)

Being part of the whole language movement in the 1980s and 1990s has meant coming full circle for me historically. I am where I began, having passed through an elongated spiral as I visit and revisit the principles and ideas that are most informative to me about teaching and learning. My own teacher education in Los Angeles, during the late 1940s and 1950s, was strongly influenced by the philosophy and pedagogy of scholars such as John Dewey, Hilda Taba, Helen Heffernan, and other progressive educators in California.

Language experience, a holistic teaching practice, was the reading instruction I used, especially with my struggling readers. I remember Bill Driver, one member of my "lowest" reading group of six males in sixth grade, writing nonfiction reports on rocks that he turned into a rock dictionary. Karl Ehlers, another member of the group, was interested in why the Los Angeles River was without water and we found answers to the questions he and the others posed. Carlos Peña wrote stories and poems about his mother, whom he had not seen in years. After a field experience with the content we were exploring, I scribed their stories and reports and we made books and a magazine that became the reading material we used in class.

Although I used basal readers selectively with my more proficient readers, I never was controlled by the scripted teachers' manuals. I remember Rita Hanson, my language arts methods instructor at Los Angeles State College, suggesting that we mine the enriched sections of three or four different teachers' manuals for good ideas and forget the other "stuff." I've suggested that to my own language arts methods classes for years.

I participated in a schoolwide inquiry unit on sex education with my sixth graders. For the first time, we kept boys and girls together for this topic, saw professionally developed films, and talked about issues that the children raised. Parents were involved in the planning and supported the work. Action research was conducted on the unit, and one conclusion I remember was that the kindergarten and first graders were serious and became involved in the study very quickly. My sixth graders, on the other hand, giggled and acted silly because of their embarrassment at discussing such issues in school.

Another year, my class of eighth graders wrote a cantata on the history of the first Intermediate School in Redondo Beach, California. We were the first class to be in that school. We interviewed administrators and teachers to find out why such an intermediate school was organized and the purposes it served. We debated the pros and cons of self-contained and departmentalized schools. We interviewed parents, grandparents, and educators in different positions to understand the criticism of the establishment of junior high schools. We wrote a series of songs, poems, and vignettes that represented the history of the school, and presented our cantata as a choral reading to the school community.

I share these short, selected vignettes to indicate that whole language was where I was at in my early teaching career. We called it integrated language arts, progressive education, social studies and science at the center of the curriculum, or multitext curriculum at that time.

Many of my questions about the teaching and learning of reading and writing came from seeing my students expand their reading and writing proficiency at the same time as they were involved in answering questions relevant to their world. I realized that kids spelled differently during testing situations and during composing time. I understood that my students were often involved in reading and writing, while denying that they could read and write.

My questions about teaching and learning come from my experience as a classroom teacher, and as I entered graduate programs, I began to answer some of my questions; the research I read in turn informed my pedagogy. During the 1960s and 1970s, intense research in both oral and written language development by many scholars provided the knowledge for why holistic practices in teaching were important in learning language. It was from this transaction between theory and practice that whole language emerged in the 1970s. It is important to see whole language in its historical setting in order not to dismiss it as a fad or newfangled idea. It is the cyclical extension of pedagogical principles explored by scholars and researchers and put into practice by teachers for a number of centuries.

We know more now about why these ideas work as well as they do, but the pedagogy informs the research as much as the research informs the practice. It is not a one-way direction from research to practice. It is a powerful transaction that needs to be acknowledged.

Respect for the
Language Learner

Ever since I knew that I would become president of the National Council of Teachers of English, I've been wondering who would be more surprised to find this out: my immigrant mother, who never learned to speak English comfortably herself, or a number of my language arts and English teachers. To my mother, education was the most prized possession. She used to tell me stories about hiding behind her house in a small *shtetl*, or village, in Russia, learning to read Yiddish from her self-taught sister. They couldn't go to school because they were Jews and girls. My mother tried hard to become literate a number of times during her life but never fully succeeded.

My English teachers would have been surprised for other reasons. A number of them warned me during my school career that bilingual children had weak vocabularies so that I'd never pass the tests necessary to get into college. My grammar, my vocabulary, my command of English certainly were seldom deemed good enough by teachers to give me any feelings of confidence in my own language learning. But because I assimilated my mother's strong belief that education was of great value and because of a few teachers who helped me believe in myself as a learner, I rejected the statements of those who told me I could never get through college.

Building a belief in myself was not a quick process: it took many years. Perhaps the greatest contribution to my becoming comfortable

Presidential address presented at the November 1978 annual meeting of the National Council of Teachers of English, Kansas City, Missouri, as excerpted in NCTE to You, *Language Arts* (January 1979), 91–95. Reprinted with permission.

as a speaker of English came from my interaction with my own pupils. They laughed good naturedly when I used to tell them to "open" or "close" the lights. We learned to cherish the ways we used the English language, and we communicated.

So when I learned that the year of my National Council of Teachers of English presidency was also to be designated the International Year of the Child by UNESCO and that UNESCO's stated rights of children included that of education, I decided to relate my theme of the year to this basic right. The right to an education for children and youth must include the right to an environment conducive to learning, free from ridicule and scorn. People—as infants, children, and developing adults—are always trying to make sense out of the universe, to organize and conceptualize the surrounding world. Only if this search or inquiry can be supported, nurtured, helped along in a positive way, will the learner want to continue learning from those of us educated to show others the way. This takes respect on our part for the learning capacity of every human being.

More is known about learning, about language, and about language learning than ever before. The National Council of Teachers of English should focus its energies on finding ways to disseminate this rapidly growing knowledge to the general population as well as other teachers. Our profession's goals center on helping others use language. Let us also use language to help others understand what we have come to know.

My simple theme is Respect for the Learner. Such a theme shouldn't need to be highlighted. It should be basic to the education and philosophy of every teacher. Yet as I read newspapers, visit classrooms, and hear the cry from many about our schools, our youth, and our language, I realize that my simple message is urgent. We may have little impact on those who are shouting for some romantic past that never existed or for some abstract perfection that can never be. However, if we can be of some support to teachers who believe in kids and learning, and if we can band together to help young people develop positively in a different world, then this focus will be of some value.

Is it possible that as professionals we do little to dispel the myths that are so prevalent about education? Why is it that the myths about learning and language as preached by the John Simons, the Edwin Newmans, and the Hyman Rickovers are readily believed?

The back-to-basics forces want to control the learning and the thinking of young people by controlling our teaching. If schools' total energies go into minimum competencies, then there is little need to worry about a growing body of informed, literate adults who question what they hear and what they read, who become actively involved in the major issues of a democracy. These issues were addressed years ago when Earl Kelly, a prominent humanist in education who promoted the workshop technique in secondary schools, wrote *In Defense of Youth* (1962). His central idea was that the general public, including the professional education establishment, rejects the young. He warned, "To continue to do so will destroy us." Kelly suggested a number of ways that we were rejecting the young: "Parts of the curriculum enjoyed most by youth are being cut out, leaving only the parts young people dislike. . . . Excessive testing is one of the most highly developed forms of rejection that has so far been invented."

Kelly's book was written in response to the Sputnik period—the back-to-basics movement of the fifties and sixties. He described what happened to young people then: "When Russia launched her first satellite . . . it . . . hurt our pride almost beyond repair. . . . When we looked around for someone to blame, we did not see the Pentagon . . . Congress . . . . Whom did we see? We saw our youth! Here was the perfect scapegoat—perfect because youth has little power to strike back."

Kelly's book foreshadowed new changes. The civil rights movement brought together forces that turned our focus toward the educational needs of the poor and the disenfranchised. This drive—education for all—produced results in terms of growing numbers of all levels of society being educated.

Yet the movement of the post-Sputnik era to educate all and to innovate in order to foster greater opportunity for all Americans has given way to a 1970s back-to-basics movement. The reasons are complex. The backlash against minority progress, the tax rebellion, post-Vietnam conservatism, confusion over changing lifestyles, and many other factors helped to usher in yet another period of overt rejection of the young. The scapegoating started again. "Is anyone out there learning?" asked CBS as they painted a picture of surly, ignorant, uninterested learners led by incompetent, self-serving teachers.

I believe that we have educated more people to higher levels than ever before. But the levels of educational expectation have also risen. When I was a child, my friends and I were not surprised that our parents were illiterate. We often had to read contracts, translate for them during business transactions, and tell our parents what to sign and where. We did not respect our parents any less because of this. We did not consider them unwise because they were unschooled. They sent us to school to become literate because they had never had such opportunities. Such situations have become rare now. So rare indeed that if someone does admit to being illiterate, a feature article or TV spot can be devoted to the problem.

We ought to be proud of where we are educationally as a nation. But there are many who insist that equal education means equal performance as measured by some standardized test. An early purpose of testing, as Earl Kelly said, was to screen out undesirables. Testing is even more of a rejection device than ever before. We now deprive young people of high school diplomas they have spent twelve years pursuing while being taught by professional educators. We will punish them for our shortcomings.

Such a negative and rejecting attitude toward youth and their learning is in and of itself a powerful force against learning. In my own research exploring how children learn to read and write, I have discovered that there are many students who believe they cannot read or write despite the fact that they actually do. People's belief in their own ability to learn often reflects the views of others. Respect for the language learner is not simply a lovely moral issue. Self-confidence is basic for learning to occur.

Why, then, isn't respect a part of every teacher's response to learners? Do we fear that youth will come to know and understand more than we do as our attitudes, values, and wisdom become obsolete?

There are teachers who believe that only we have knowledge to impart to others; such an attitude is found among some of my colleagues at the higher end of the educational scale, although it can be found even among some preschool and kindergarten teachers. How can we, as teachers, hope to share our culture, knowledge, and values with large numbers of others if we disdain our students? In a democratic society such a position is not popular and so it becomes disguised. Instead of saying we don't want them to learn, we say they can't learn.

Yet in spite of the current back-to-basics movement, the hopes of the sixties have not died. Educational reform of that period awakened in many the belief that it was indeed possible for all members of this society to learn to achieve, to grow intellectually, to expand language effectiveness. In schools everywhere there is evidence that minority people will not be turned back by the system. We still have a long way to go to equalize educational opportunity, but we cannot go back to a time when higher education was for a handful of social, economic, or educational elite. And the key is respect. Students can learn. Students usually want to learn, but they must be in a language environment that helps them believe in themselves as learners. NCTE must continue to lead the way. We understand how to organize an environment in which learning is nourished and cherished.

Some teachers believe that this means lowering our standards. The issue isn't standards. It never was. All of us as English teachers share the desire that every learner should achieve powerful control over language and a love and appreciation of its finest glories. But that must be built on a base of pride and self-confidence in each learner, which can come from their perceiving our respect for them. We must help our colleagues understand this. We can learn from each other.

We can also learn from our pupils. The roles of teacher and pupil are not mutually exclusive. Within every adult, I believe, is a constant state of being a learner, and within the child is a developing state of being a teacher. Within all teachers is the ability to interact with children in order to learn from them: Are the perceptions of the young the same as mine? Are the differences in perception a matter of time or age or culture? What marvelous new knowledge can we add to our own? But this can happen only if we truly believe that we can learn from others—those poorer than ourselves, those less educated, those younger than we are. Humility about our own achievements does not diminish them. Rather, it keeps us open to new learning.

I don't mean to oversimplify and suggest that if teachers change their attitudes toward students, learning will automatically occur. Learning is too complex, and it would be naive to believe that respect for learners is all that is needed. But respect is foundational. When a learner believes that he or she is respected, there is reason to continue to learn, reason to reach out, to share what others have to offer.

I wish to close with the words of one of the great artists of our time, who seemed to understand my theme. Pablo Casals said:

> Each second we live is a new and unique moment in the universe. A moment that never was before and never will be again. And what do we teach our children? We teach them two and two makes four. When will we also teach them what they are? We should say to each of them: You are a marvel. You are unique. In all the world, there is no child exactly like you, and when you grow up can you then harm another who is, like you, a marvel? You must cherish one another. You must work, we must all work, to make this world worthy of its children. (Quoted in Kirk 1974, pp. 551–52)

References

Kelly, Earl. 1962. *In defense of youth.* Englewood Cliffs, NJ: Prentice-Hall.

Kirk, H.L. 1974. *Pablo Casals.* New York: Holt, Rinehart & Winston.

Exploring the Power of Written Language Through Literature for Children and Adolescents

Isn't it ironic that we encourage children and young people to consider so many issues—ecology, nuclear war, the stock market, the seven basic foods—yet we lack curricula to help them explore issues related to something as basic as reading and writing.

Despite the paucity of such curricula, professional writers provide many ways for children and young people to explore the power of written language. In their narratives, poems, and essays, they artistically demonstrate the impact that writing and reading have on their lives and on the lives of those they bring to life in their writing. Through their literary creations, they express their views of literacy in the world today. Some authors explore the influences of literacy on their own lives; others examine the nature of literacy and the many functions and purposes it serves for society. Others focus on the implicit and explicit political and intellectual power of reading and writing.

Exploring Issues About Literacy

Adolescent's and children's literature provide many opportunities to help students think about the power of literacy for their own devel-

Previously published as a Practical Reflections column in *The New Advocate* 1 (1988), 254–65. Copyright by Yetta M. Goodman.

opment and at the same time discuss significant issues about literacy in school and society. Because authors and poets are themselves immersed in reading and writing and are professionally concerned with the role of literacy in society, many of them explore how reading and writing can be painful, pleasurable, and powerful.

As they work with literature that reflects literacy issues, teachers can involve students in examining people's use of literacy in society and how it affects their lives. In this way, students discover differing beliefs about the importance of literacy and about how reading and writing are learned and used. Students will then be able to participate knowledgeably and actively in the debates surrounding literacy.

Researchers in linguistics, psychology, and education are exploring the significance of readers and writers becoming consciously aware of their own processes. The phrase *metalinguistic awareness* refers to the knowledge people have about how they read and write, the processes of learning to read and write, and the ability to discuss people's use of everyday reading and writing (Goodman 1980). Through experiences with literature, students can explore the strategies they themselves use in seeking to become literate, the mundane and esoteric uses of literacy, and the benefits and dangers literacy poses in a democratic society.

Central to becoming literate is learning why and how people read and write and the discovery of the pitfalls of becoming literate. Students need to understand that literature can indoctrinate with the same kind of intensity with which it can liberate. Students can recall negative as well as positive experiences in learning to read and write. Here, it is essential that all viewpoints be examined and that romantic and simplistic notions about how becoming literate produces successful and happy people not be fostered. Through open and honest discussion about how authors and literary characters reflect on literacy and literacy learning, students gain confidence in their own literacy learning.

Active Involvement in Reading and Writing

Jean Piaget (1952) highlighted the significance of the learner's involvement in generating hypotheses and developing concepts—being actively engaged in his or her own learning. By exploring autobiographical material, students have the opportunity to think about what excites people about reading and writing and what stimulates their involvement in becoming literate. Nobel laureate Isaac Bashevis Singer (1984) recalled the impact books, magazines, and family controversy had on his own aspirations when he was about five or six years old.

My brother Joshua bought the Yiddish newspaper every morning and I tried to read this, too. My father maintained that all the secular writers were unbelievers, liars, mockers. Their writings were an abomination. About the Yiddish theater my father said that charlatans sit there all day long, eat pork, play around with loose women and speak profanities. But my brother said that the theater was a part of culture. He praised the Yiddish writers . . . and brought home translations . . . of Tolstoy, Dostoyevsky, Turgenev, . . . Mark Twain. He called their writings literature and he said that to write the way they do, one must have talent and great knowledge of the human soul.

I craved learning how to read these newspapers and especially the books whose writers had all the knowledge about the human soul. . . .

I absorbed all this information and strange words with a decision to always retain them. I fantasized about becoming a second Edison or a writer of books. (pp. 15–16)

As middle or secondary school students read, or have read to them, this and similar material, they can explore matters such as the kinds of settings that nourished Singer's stimulation and involvement with his own literacy learning, the sources of his ideas, and the relation of reading to his growth as a writer. Students might consider whether such opportunities are available to them and whether they would or would not make decisions similar to Singer's.

Such discussions can provide opportunities for students to realize the ways in which they can take charge of their own learning. Developing readers and writers need to understand that people learn from newspapers as well as from books and that the world awaits exploration by hungry minds. They also need to understand the role of controversy between generations and how young people must decide which authority to believe, which drummer to follow.

Older students might also read Claude Brown's memoir, *Manchild in the Promised Land* (1965). Brown describes coming of age in an environment and through experiences that are radically different from Singer's. He is befriended by the wife of the superintendent of a prison facility who shares books with him about the lives of Mary McLeod Bethune, Jackie Robinson, Sugar Ray Robinson, and Albert Einstein.

Then I read a book by Albert Schweitzer. He was another fascinating cat. The man knew so much. I really started wanting to know things. I wanted to know things and I wanted to do things. It made me start thinking about what might happen if I got out of Warwick and didn't go back to Harlem. But I couldn't really see myself not going back to Harlem. I couldn't see myself going anyplace else, because if I didn't go to Harlem, where would I have gone? That was the only place I ever knew. (pp. 156–57)

Claude Brown's involvement with his own reading, and his thoughts about the ideas of the authors he read, helped him extend his thinking and learning. He discusses his interest in reading, his choices in deciding what to read, and how these led him to make significant life choices, not all of them successful.

Adolescents can compare their own literate environments and their interest or lack of interest in reading and writing to those of Brown, Singer, and other authors. As students talk about how professional authors respond to encounters with books and reading, they can begin to legitimize their own personal responses to literature. Both Singer and Brown related their reading to their own lives—to their fears, hopes, and developing beliefs. Adolescents need to know that they can respond in similar ways to their reading.

Elementary school children may also explore the importance of authors and illustrators being personally influenced by literacy experiences through a book such as *Once Upon a Time*, published in 1986 in honor of the twentieth anniversary of Reading Is Fundamental. Through poetry, illustration, personal narrative, folktale, and fiction, authors and artists such as Jack Prelutsky, Leo and Diane Dillon, and Virginia Hamilton reflect on their earliest encounters with books. Students can be encouraged to discuss or record their personal responses to the words and illustrations of these popular authors and illustrators.

Louise Rosenblatt (1978) makes it clear that readers respond to literature personally, based on their own knowledge and experiences. Legitimizing such personal responses helps students believe that they not only have a right to such responses but that all good readers have such rights. In traditional classroom settings, where the focus so often is on single correct answers or interpretations, students learn not to trust or value their own responses and come to believe that only the teacher or critic can understand literature well enough to state personal opinions about literary works. Through honest open-ended discussions, students can learn that people respond differently to the same information, that variations in response are the result of the different knowledge and background each reader brings to the reading experience. Through such discussions students build the shared meanings of a community and learn to trust their opinions and to value and understand the opinions of others.

Learning to Read

Discussions about how literacy is reflected in literature should begin very early, with the many appropriate books and illustrations for young children.

Cartoonists such as Bill Keane and Charles Schulz regularly explore such issues in their work. Kindergarten and first-grade children, in response to such cartoons, can discuss how and what people read, and why reading is important. In the process, teachers can gain important insights into the beliefs that young children have about learning to read and write.

A series of books by Miriam Cohen, illustrated by Lillian Hoban, celebrate humanistic teachers who explore learning to read, taking tests, and programs for the gifted. These books are warmly received by kindergartners and first graders and should be shared with parents and administrators as well. In *First Grade Takes a Test* (Cohen 1980), the children discover there are many things more important than being the best on a standardized test. As their teacher says:

> The test doesn't tell . . . all the things you can do! You can build things! You can read books! You can make pictures! You have good ideas! And another thing. The test doesn't tell you if you are a kind person who helps your friend. Those are the important things. (pp. 17–18)

In *When Will I Read?* (Cohen 1977), Jim worries about when he will learn to read. His teacher is patient, knows how to capitalize on teachable moments, and after a variety of literacy events in the classroom, says to Jim:

> "I told you it would happen. . . . You can read."
> "I can?" Jim said.
> "Yes," said the teacher.
> "That was reading. You really read the sign."
> Jim and the teacher put the new sign on the hamster's cage.
> "I waited all my life," said Jim. "Now I can read." (pp. 27–28)

Books of photographs such as *Signs* (Goor & Goor 1983), *I Walk and Read* (Hoban 1984), *I Read Symbols* (Hoban 1983b), and *I Read Signs* (Hoban 1983a) explore the world of environmental print, including signs, names, logos, and so on. These books help primary-grade children to become aware of their own significant beginnings in literacy development. Young children initially can spend time examining these books independently or in small groups. Later, the teacher can lead discussions about why print exists and can lead children in brainstorming ideas about the various functions print serves and the importance of reading signs. Children can discover that written language enters their lives from every corner of the waking world. Such books stimulate a variety of literary experiences that might culminate in a *What I Can Read* book produced by each class member. Children can take photographs of all the signs that they can read, and write an accompanying narrative or a caption for each picture. Children can explore how all-encompassing reading is, and how many opportunities they have to read. Children thus realize that they are already readers and writers, that learning to read and to write are not mysterious or very hard, and that school and teachers are there to help them expand and build upon what they already know.

Troubled Readers

There are many books that deal with children who have trouble learning to read and write. These books can be read aloud a chapter at a time in upper-grade classrooms and accompanied by appropriate discussion. Or teachers may obtain sets of books to be used by groups or an entire class.

In *Goodnight Mr. Tom* (Magorian 1981), Willie has trouble with reading, writing, and schooling in general. Forced to leave London for the more peaceful countryside of England during World War II, Willie and Mr. Tom, the recluse he comes to live with, learn to reach out for each other as Mr. Tom reads to him and supports Willie's effort to learn to read and write.

Another moving story dealing with the theme of literacy learning for troubled readers is *The Lottery Rose* (Hunt 1976). This story often brings tears to the eyes of its readers or listeners as Hunt explores issues related to battered children. Georgie hadn't learned to read, school was intimidating and irrelevant, and life with an alcoholic mother was traumatic. Through a number of experiences, Georgie finds himself in a new school where he meets Mr. Collier, a retired education professor, who helps him learn to read.

> He and the grandfather had worked . . . during the weeks of early spring and summer . . . . They wrote stories together which Georgie read aloud and then listened happily as the grandfather praised him.
>
> By midsummer Georgie was able to read simple stories and he was happy to read aloud to anyone who would listen. He read to his rosebush, to Mr. Collier, to some of the nuns who were his special friends. (p. 109)

Upper elementary and middle school students can discuss their own difficulties in learning to read and write and the importance of a warm supportive environment as an aid to literacy development. They can discuss their responsibility as a community of readers and writers in the classroom in helping to establish such an environment for themselves.

A Variety of Literacy Experiences

Authors explore many of the functions of reading and writing in their works. Some authors place their characters in libraries where they find the resources needed to solve their problems. Others involve characters in writing letters, cryptic notes, poems, stories, and community newspapers, which have impact on their own lives as well as those of friends or family. Some characters keep diaries or are affected by their reading of major authors or poets. Students of all ages can relate such experiences to their own lives and begin to understand that reading and writing involve a good deal more than simply reading fiction or writing stories.

The Jolly Postman (Ahlberg & Ahlberg 1986) explores various kinds of mail. There is a book contract from Peter Piper that Cinderella must consider, a postcard from Jack to the giant, and a note of apology from Goldilocks to the three bears, among many other personal and business letters, notes, and cards. The pages in the book are envelopes, and young readers participate eagerly in opening the envelopes, drawing out the letters and cards, and reading a variety of styles of writing and different print forms. There are no limits to the discussions that elementary school children can have about the kinds of mail they receive, why people get mail, how people respond to mail, and the kinds of mail they can generate. The classroom or the school can be turned into a post office, or the students can study the practices of the community concerning mail. In addition, a book such as Ezra Jack Keats's *A Letter to Amy* (1968) can be shared with primary students at the opportune moment when they need to invite someone to their classroom or to a birthday party.

In *The Knight and the Dragon* (1980), Tomie de Paola shows through words and pictures how both of the main characters solve their own problems through the use of the library. The knight finds out "how to fight dragons," while the dragon discovers information about "the art of tail swishing." In response to such a book, young children can explore the variety of resources they have available to solve their own problems and to answer their own questions.

Leigh Botts, the main character in Cleary's *Dear Mr. Henshaw* (1983), helps middle-grade children and teachers see that when letter and diary writing are undertaken for authentic and personal reasons, the quality of writing improves and the reasons for writing become very important. Early in the book, Leigh reluctantly writes to an author because of his teacher's assignment.

> Dear Mr. Henshaw,
> I am the boy who wrote to you last year when I was in the second grade. Maybe you didn't get my letter. This year I read the book I

wrote to you about called *Ways to Amuse a Dog.* It is the first thick
book with chapters that I have read. . . .
   If you answer I get to put your letter on the bulletin board.
   Your friend, Leigh (Lee) Botts
   (p. 2)

Later in his diary Leigh has become personally involved in reading and writing and tells of the excitement of meeting and talking to
a real author:

"Oh!" said Mrs. Badger. "So you're the author of *A Day on Dad's Rig!*". . .
"I just got honorable mention," I said, but I was thinking, She
called me an author. *A real live author called me an author.*
"What difference does that make?" asked Mrs. Badger. "Judges
never agree. I happened to like *A Day on Dad's Rig* because it was
written by a boy who wrote honestly about something he knew and
had strong feelings about. You made me feel what it was like to ride
down a steep grade with tons of grapes behind me. . . . You wrote
like you, and you did not try to imitate someone else. That is one
mark of a good writer. Keep it up." (pp. 118–20)

After reading the book, students might discuss the degree to
which Leigh's reactions parallel their own involvement with keeping
journals or writing compositions.
   A character in S. E. Hinton's *The Outsiders* (1967) writes a response
to a high school English class assignment. In it, Ponyboy refers to a
Frost poem after experiencing a sunrise. In response, Ponyboy's friend
Johnny says: "That sure was pretty . . . the mist was what was pretty
. . . all gold and silver . . . too bad it couldn't stay like that all the
time." Ponyboy, a sensitive young "greaser," responds:

"Nothing gold can stay. I was remembering a poem I'd read once. . . .
Robert Frost wrote it. He meant more to it than I'm getting, though.
. . . I always remembered it because I never quite got what he meant
by it." (p. 69)

Later, in a note Johnny writes to Ponyboy, this teenager who
found it so difficult to relate to adults says:

"That poem, that guy that wrote it, he meant you're gold when
you're a kid, like green. When you're a kid everything's new, dawn.
It's just when you get used to everything that it's day. Like the way
you dig sunsets, Pony. That's gold. Keep that way, it's a good way to
be." (p. 154)

Hinton provides a vehicle through which adolescents can explore
how language can be used by even the toughest teenagers to think
through the significant problems they must confront as they grow up
in a complex and confusing world.

The Power of Language

Students can explore the power of language and speculate on their ability to harness that power. Students can come to understand their own use of language—learning to express their thoughts through discussion, conversations, reading, and writing—which gives them the opportunity to control their own learning and thought processes. There is an old German folk song "Die Gedanken Sind Frei" (Thoughts Are Free)(1956):

> My thoughts give me power
> No scholar can map them, No hunter can trap them,
> My thoughts will not cater to duke or dictator,
> No man can deny . . . *Die Gedanken sind frei.*

In discussing the power of language, students need to explore both the strengths and possibilities for harm of literacy. There are many books for upper elementary and middle school readers that can facilitate such exploration. For example, in *The Present Takers* (Chambers 1983), the notes that young adolescents write to and about each other both harm and charm. *Harriet the Spy* (Fitzhugh 1964) loses her friends and gets in trouble with her parents and school officials as she continues to write in her notebook pursuing what she believes to be the truth. Ole Golly, the housekeeper she loves, eventually helps Harriet face some important truths about life and the power of written language. Ole Golly advises Harriet about the power of language:

> "Naturally, you put the truth in your notebooks. What would be the point if you didn't? And naturally those notebooks should not be read by anyone else, but if they are then, Harriet you are going to have to do two things: . . . 1) . . . apologize . . . 2) lie . . .
> "Remember that writing is to put love in the world, not to use against your friends. But to yourself you must tell the truth." (p. 123)

Elizabeth Speare's *The Sign of the Beaver* (1983) provides an opportunity to explore the relation between critical reading and the power of language. In this story two adolescents, Attean, a Penobscot Indian, and Matt, a white settler in the Northeastern United States, discover they have much to learn from each other. As Matt is reading to Attean from *Robinson Crusoe*, Attean reacts with great hostility when Crusoe indicates that Friday's bowing down to him was "a token of swearing to be my slave forever." Attean responds, "Not kneel down . . . Not be slave. Better die." This causes Matt to rethink his interpretation of *Robinson Crusoe*.

> He had never questioned that story. Like Robinson Crusoe, he had thought it natural and right that the wild man should be the white

man's slave. Was there perhaps another possibility? The thought was new and troubling. (pp. 42–44)

Crucial to becoming a critical reader is having the opportunity to read an exciting book, to explore the notion that different people from different backgrounds have varying responses to the same information.

The power of language is obvious as students explore and debate issues and controversies concerning censorship and libel in relation to freedom of the press, the right to read and to learn to read.

There Was Once a Slave (1947), Shirley Graham's biography of Frederick Douglass, describes the young slave learning to read at the same time as his small master. But when the head of the household finds out, he storms:

> It's against the law. . . . Learning will spoil the best nigger in the world. If he learns to read he'll never be any good as a slave. The first thing you know he'll be writing, and then look out. A writing nigger is dangerous! (p. 79)

Students need to know why people through the ages have thought it dangerous to allow the disenfranchised of society to become literate and consider whether this is still the case in the world today.

In the Hands of Professionals

I believe that no published program can teach children to read or write, nor can one help students become aware of the power of language. It is only as students become actively engaged in wondering why and for what reasons people read and write and how such processes affect their own lives that the power of language will take on meaning.

The books I have suggested are simply examples of many books for children and young people that include such themes; not every such book need be examined so diligently. The knowledgeable, committed professional should know

- how and where to find such books;
- how to adjust the uses and presentations of the books to the age and interest level of the students;
- how to organize opportunities for students to explore such themes;
- how to organize reading and follow-up discussions and experiences so that students become aware of how they can and do control their reading and writing and understand how powerful that control can be.

That is where the art of teaching becomes the key to students' learning. I'm sure that Leland Jacobs would not mind if I extended his statement that "reading is caught, not taught" to a statement that reading and writing—literacy learning—are caught

- in an environment that excites and stimulates;
- in an environment that encourages students to select what they intend to read and write;
- in an environment that fosters appreciation of students' personal responses to their literary explorations.

E. B. White has helped young and old alike to sense the power of language—language that in his case included well-turned phrases, significant ideas, and words such as *Some Pig, Terrific,* and *Humble.* In *Charlotte's Web* (1952), White uses a spider and a pig to help us all see how language learning is part of our everyday lives. Charlotte is the great teacher, finding the critical moments to help Wilbur understand his complex and difficult world. White explores the troublesome nature of language at the same time that he exposes its powerful influences. But in the end, both language and personal relationships enrich Wilbur's life.

> Wilbur never forgot Charlotte. Although he loved her children and grandchildren dearly, none of the new spiders ever quite took her place in his heart. She was in a class by herself. It is not often that someone comes along who is a true friend and a good writer. Charlotte was both. (p. 192)

In this examination of the role that literacy learning plays in literature, I have attempted to help teachers become more conscious of the opportunities available for children to wonder and reflect on the nature of reading and writing. Having opportunities for such inquiry will help all of our students discover the writers who will become trusted friends who can lead them onto the road of lifelong literacy.

References

Ahlberg, Janet & Ahlberg, Allen. 1986. *The jolly postman, or other people's letters.* Boston: Little, Brown.

Brown, Claude. 1965. *Manchild in the promised land.* New York: Macmillan.

Chambers, Aidan. 1983. *The present takers.* New York: Harper & Row.

Cleary, Beverly. 1983. *Dear Mr. Henshaw.* New York: Morrow.

Cohen, Miriam. 1977. *When will I read?* New York: Greenwillow.

Cohen, Miriam. 1980. *First grade takes a test.* New York: Greenwillow.

de Paola, Tomie. 1980. *The knight and the dragon*. New York: Putnam.

"Die Gedanken sind frei." 1956. *Let's all sing* (p. 98). New York: Jewish Music Alliance.

Fitzhugh, Louise. 1964. *Harriet the spy*. New York: Harper & Row.

Graham, Shirley. 1947. *There once was a slave: The heroic story of Frederick Douglass*. New York: J. Messner.

Goodman, Yetta M. 1980. The roots of literacy. In Malcolm P. Douglass (Ed.), *Claremont Reading Conference, 44th Yearbook* (pp. 1–32). Claremont, CA: Claremont Colleges.

Goor, Ron & Goor, Nancy. 1983. *Signs*. New York: Crowell.

Hinton, S. E. 1967. *The outsiders*. New York: Viking.

Hoban, Tana. 1983a. *I read signs*. New York: Greenwillow.

Hoban, Tana. 1983b. *I read symbols*. New York: Greenwillow.

Hoban, Tana. 1984. *I walk and read*. New York: Greenwillow.

Hunt, Irene. 1976. *The lottery rose*. New York: Scribner's.

Keats, Ezra Jack. 1968. *A letter to Amy*. New York: Harper & Row.

Magorian, M. 1981. *Good night, Mr. Tom*. New York: Harper & Row.

Once upon a time: Celebrating the magic of children's books in honor of the 20th anniversary of Reading Is Fundamental. 1986. New York: G. P. Putnam's Sons.

Piaget, Jean. 1952. *The origins of intelligence in children*. New York: International Universities Press.

Rosenblatt, Louise. 1978. *The reader, the text, the poem: The transactional theory of the literary work*. Carbondale, IL: Southern Illinois University Press.

Singer, Isaac B. 1984, September. Literature. *Moment, 4*, 13–16, 58–61.

Speare, Elizabeth G. 1983. *The sign of the beaver*. Boston: Houghton Mifflin.

White, E. B. 1952. *Charlotte's web*. New York: Harper.

Roots of the Whole Language Movement

In the first picture book made for children and the most popular text-book in Europe at the time, the most eminent educator of the seven-teenth century, John Amos Comenius, wrote: "It is a *little Book*, as you see, of no great bulk, yet a brief of the whole world, and *a whole language:* full of Pictures, Nomenclatures, and Descriptions of things. . . . We have filled this first book . . . with the chief of things and words, or with the grounds of the whole world, and the whole language, and of all our understanding about things" (Comenius 1887, pp. xiv, xvii, first italics in original, second, mine). Although Comenius did not have the same concept of whole language as we do today, important characteristics in his concern for children and learning tie seven-teenth-century pedagogy with whole language as we know it today.

Comenius believed that children can discover new information by being introduced to what is familiar to them within their life experiences, by being able to manipulate the concrete objects being studied, and by using their native language to talk about what is being learned. These beliefs are similar to those held by whole language advocates.

Common Ties to Earlier Educational Movements

Philosophical ties to Comenius and advocates of other educational movements must be considered in understanding the evolution of

Previously published in *Elementary School Journal* 90 (1989), 113–27. Copyright 1989 by the University of Chicago Press. Reprinted with permission.

whole language and why it has emerged and flourished. The common ties between whole language and its antecedents include views of the learner, views of the teacher, and views about language.

The view of the learner is reflected in an often-used term—the learner-centered or child-centered curriculum. Comenius believed that in order to learn, children need to enjoy their learning experiences. "To entice witty children to [the book], that they may not conceit a torment to be in the school, but dainty fare" (Comenius 1887, p. xv).

The focus of the whole language curriculum is not on the content of what is being studied but on the learner. This does not minimize the importance of content; rather, it represents the belief that content can only be understood and seriously studied when learners are actively involved and interested in learning, are participating in deciding what will be learned, and are relating what they are learning to what they already know. Learners are viewed as always actively involved in their learning, especially when they are immersed in an environment organized to show respect toward all members of the learning community with the expectation that learning will occur.

The teacher is viewed as a colearner with the students. The environment is a democratic one in which the teacher and the learners collaboratively set agreed-on goals. Teachers are knowledgeable about students as well as content, but their major commitment is to plan learning experiences that build on the background and experience of the learners. Teachers strive to understand the needs and expectations of students, their cultures, and the communities in which they live. Teachers organize a rich literate environment that invites learners to take part in the social community of the classroom, taking into consideration all that they know about the learners. I am not sure that Comenius had envisioned a democratic classroom, but he did believe that teachers had to know enough about their students to assure that their teaching "will be *clear*, . . . if whatever is taught and learned be not obscure, or confused, but apparent, distinct, and articulate; . . . will be *true*, if nothing be taught but such as is beneficial to one's life" (p. xiii).

Teachers are aware that what they are teaching is not always what students learn. They realize that teaching and learning are not isomorphic but, rather, that they are symbiotic, each strongly influencing the other. Recognizing this essential relationship between teaching and learning is one of the major characteristics in whole language and reflects one of the constant battles in education. There is no one-to-one correspondence between what is taught and what is learned. Whole language educators and their predecessors believe that learners ultimately are in control of what they learn regardless of what is being taught.

Although the view of language in the present whole language movement is most influenced by twentieth-century scientific investigations into language learning, even Comenius believed that unless learning is meaningful to students, it has no place in school, and he therefore recommended that children begin their learning in school in their vernacular language: "that it be bound up in their native tongues only" (p. xvi). Comenius was reacting to the use of Latin as the language of instruction in schools. "We can neither act nor speak wisely, unless we first rightly understand all the things which are to be done and whereof we are to speak. Now there is nothing in the understanding, which was not before in the sense" (p. xiv).

Whole Language: The Concept and the Term

Whole language is a grass-roots movement. Many groups of teachers, administrators, teacher educators, and researchers are participating in a network of study and discussion groups, raising questions, researching, writing articles, and coming to conclusions resulting in a dynamically conceived conceptualization and definition of whole language.

It is most likely that the popular use of the term *whole language* came from teachers who were becoming aware of the knowledge explosion surrounding oral and written language development and the reading and writing processes. Later sections of this article, as well as an article by Kenneth Goodman (1989), explore the research influences on the knowledge explosion that derive from studies on composition and reading instruction. With this new knowledge, teachers who were developing insights about language learning in school realized that students needed to use language to solve problems that were significant and meaningful to their daily lives in order to take charge of their own learning (Goodman et al. 1987). At the same time, they realized that they had to change their views about how language was learned and their role as teachers of language. Teachers, administrators, and teacher educators used the term casually in daily discussions about classroom practices before it was taught in organized preservice or inservice programs; before it was used in curriculum guides, newsletters, professional articles, or books; and before it became a descriptor in reference guides.

Those of us who have been close to the emergence of the present use of the term *whole language* may find it interesting to uncover its origins. Jerome Harste and Carolyn Burke (1977) described how teachers developed a theoretical view of the reading process, and one of the paradigms was called a whole language view of reading. In 1978, Dorothy Watson and others in Columbia, Missouri, formed the first teacher-support group to meet under the organizational name Teachers Applying Whole Language (TAWL). Ken Goodman and I wrote a paper in 1979 entitled "A Whole Language Comprehension-centered Reading Program." Orin Cochran, Ethel Buchanan, and a teacher–support group in Winnipeg, Canada, called CEL (Child-centered, Experience-based Learning) began to present workshops about whole language teaching and learning in 1980. The early users of the term were not consciously naming a new belief system or movement. We were talking about some new ideas about language, about teachers and learners, and what these meant in terms of implementation, and we needed new language to express our new meanings. It is not important to identify who used the term first or from which individuals or groups it came. What is important is how the whole language movement has influenced pedagogy, research, and teacher-education programs, and the positive effect it has had on the changing nature of teaching and the learning of students in whole language classrooms. As the historian of whole language for the purposes of this article, it is important that I state explicitly that I am actively involved with the development of whole language. In order to expose my biases, I will share not only my professional views of whole language but my personal history as well.

Pedagogical Influences on Whole Language

In this examination of the influences on whole language from scholars and earlier movements, I have tried to select the greatest contributors from my vantage point, but any omissions or oversights on my part should not be used to evaluate the contributions of those who may be inadvertently left out. Any other whole language historian would have included the names of others and excluded some of those I discuss.

Major Theorists

John Dewey is a major twentieth-century philosopher who provides a theoretical rationale for understanding the power of reflective teaching, learners' being at the center of the process of curriculum development, and the integration of language with all other studies in the curriculum. Dewey's work raises significant curricular questions about the nature of the child in the school setting. He explores the significance and the roles of experience, democracy, and activity as the child inquires into significant issues and problems. Dewey (1943) discusses the importance of the integration of curriculum, arguing that

> we do not have a series of stratified earths, one of which is mathematical, another physical, another historical, and so on. . . . All studies grow out of relations in the one great common world. When the child lives in varied but concrete and active relationship to this common world, his studies are naturally unified. . . . Relate school to life, and all studies are of necessity correlated. . . . If school is related as a whole to life as a whole, its various aims and ideals—culture, discipline, information, utility—cease to be variants. (p. 91)

Dewey envisioned classrooms as laboratories with "the materials, the tools with which the child may construct, create, and actively inquire" (p. 32), and he included language as one of the tools.

> The child who has a variety of materials and facts wants to talk about them, and his language becomes more refined and full, because it is controlled and informed by realities. Reading and writing, as well as the oral use of language, may be taught on this basis. It can be done in a related way, as the outgrowth of the child's social desire to recount his experiences and get in return the experiences of others. (p. 56)

Dewey (1938) was concerned that students of all ages participate in their own learning by solving real and important problems that they are concerned with at the moment.

The work of the epistemologist Jean Piaget has also influenced the whole language movement. Throughout his life, Piaget explored a major question with great implications for education: how people come to know concepts, ideas, and moralities. With his colleagues, he developed and used the clinical methodology approach to research the genesis of thought. Piaget and his co-researchers show how children are actively involved in understanding their world and in trying to answer their questions and solve the problems that the world poses for them. Children do not wait for someone to transmit knowledge to them but, rather, learn through their own activity with external objects and construct their own categories of thought while organizing their world. Children develop their own conceptualizations, which often are at odds with adult versions of the world. Piagetians have highlighted the importance of the different views of the world that children hold (Duckworth 1987). Thinking children play an active role in learning, and they learn both written and oral language in similar ways (Ferreiro & Teberosky 1982).

Vygotsky (1986), a Russian psychologist, aids whole language educators in exploring the relation between the learning of the individual student and the influences of the social context. Vygotsky's *zone of proximal development* emphasizes the important role teachers play in students' learning, even though learners are ultimately responsible for their own conceptual development. The student does not learn in isolation but is supported, and, unfortunately, sometimes thwarted, in language and thinking development by others in the school environment. Vygotsky also explores the important social aspects of the role of peers as well as activity such as play in the development of intellectual functioning, factors that have long been a major concern of scholars in the field of early childhood. "Play creates a zone of proximal development of the child. In play a child always behaves beyond his average age, above his daily behavior; in play it is as though he were a head taller than himself. As in the focus of a magnifying glass, play contains all the developmental tendencies in a condensed form and is itself a major source of development" (1978, p. 102).

M. A. K. Halliday, a systemic linguist, provides ways of understanding the power of the context situation on learning and on language use. Discussions by whole language teachers about what kinds of instructional experiences constitute functional and natural language use in classrooms are supported by questions explored by Halliday (1975). He has developed a system of functional grammar that relates the study of language to the actions within the situational context and to the relationship of the actors involved. Halliday contends that at the same time as learners are using language, they are learning language, learning through language, and learning about language. This notion has had a strong impact on the integration of language arts and other subjects in the development of whole language curricula (Pinnell & Matlin 1989).

Influences from the Field of Reading

In addition to theorists from psychology, linguistics, and philosophy, many educationists have made major contributions to the field of education in general and have also affected the issues discussed among whole language advocates.

Some of the beginnings of whole language are traced to research on the reading process, especially the work of Kenneth Goodman and Frank Smith, from as early as the 1960s, and to the subsequent move to apply their research findings to reading instruction (Smith & Goodman 1971). Smith and Goodman, working from different perspectives, developed the theory and research that established the notion of a unified single reading process as an interaction between the reader, the text, and language.

Much earlier, Louise Rosenblatt applied John Dewey's concepts to reading and literature in her now classic book *Literature as Exploration* (Rosenblatt, 1938/1976). She was the first to describe reading as a transaction between the reader and the text, establishing the rights of readers to their own meanings. Influenced by an additional work by Rosenblatt (1978), whole language incorporated the term *transaction* to represent a rich and complex relation between the reader and the text.

The views of reading proposed by Goodman and Smith and the concept of transaction provide a sound rationale for literature- and language experience–based reading programs. These kinds of reading programs were well developed and popular prior to the 1960s. Research and theoretical support for the seemingly simplistic notion that people learned to read through reading helped to explain much of the success of programs that immersed students in reading real books and explained why children who were read to early in the home tended to be successful in learning to read. They also helped to explain why children were so successful in learning to read when they read materials in their own language based on participation in experiences relevant to their daily lives. At the same time, the theory and the research raised some questions about the direction various programs were taking.

The language experience approach to reading became part of the reading instruction literature when Lillian Lamoreaux and Dorris Lee (1943) wrote *Learning to Read Through Experience*. The theory and approach were updated in 1963 by Lee and Roach Van Allen, who were instrumental in the popularization of language experience based on a definition that reading is "developing meaning from patterns of symbols which one recognizes and endows with meaning. Reading arouses or calls up meanings. It does not provide them" (p. 2).

Language experience emphasized the "all around development of the child," which involved the learner in a wide range of experiences including excursions; group activities that focused on science, social studies, or math; discussions; storytelling; drama; music; and art. The experiences were to be accompanied by all kinds of language that would result in charts, lists, menus, plans, magazines, newsletters, and books that would become reading materials for children. There is much in whole language that is similar to language experience views of instruction, and, indeed, many whole language educators, including myself, were initially advocates of language experience.

Some supporters of the language experience approach may believe that whole language is simply language experience with a new label because the basic tenets of the two are compatible. The focus on language learning taking place in relation to a variety of experiences, all language and content experiences being integrated for instructional purposes, and students being excited about and interested in what they are learning are certainly important aspects of both views. However, language experience became a variety of approaches and, for some educators, the original philosophical beliefs about language learning and child development became secondary to the procedures themselves. For others, the approach was reduced to an activity that was done simply to get children to write down something that they then could read. As the language experience approach was popularized and often misapplied, some of us believed that the label *language experience* had lost the power of its original conceptualization.

In addition, new knowledge generated about the nature of written language raised questions about the relation between oral and written language. As it became more obvious that written language took forms and served functions not directly related to oral language, concerns were raised about how children came to understand the nature of written language as different from oral language if their oral language was a major source of written language. Teachers and researchers developing new knowledge about the writing process wondered how children became independent writers when the teacher did so much of the scribing. Charles Read's (1975) discovery that children invented spelling provided a strong rationale for children to generate their own writing to a greater degree than was generally acceptable within the language experience approach.

With a holistic and progressive educational policy, New Zealand, influenced by John Dewey, disseminated a view of reading instruction that has had a lasting influence on the teaching of reading in the whole language movement (Penton 1979). Don Holdaway (1979) developed the concept of shared book experience and promoted literature-based reading programs that were supported by the research of Marie Clay (1980). Teacher-produced Big Books of children's favorite stories that they asked to have read over and over again, a strong focus on reading books to children, and the immersion of children in reading books and magazines became the commonplace reading instructional program in New Zealand (New Zealand Department of Education 1972, 1985).

Based on the work of New Zealanders such as Sylvia Ashton-Warner (1963), Jeanette Veatch (1964), long an advocate of choice in reading, raised questions about the nature of packaged programs and basal readers and urged that reading instruction focus on the growing market of trade books for children. She popularized individualized reading instruction in the United States.

With Leland Jacobs (1965) in the lead, many experts in children's literature wrote about the power of trade books in individualized or literature-based reading programs. Charlotte Huck (Huck & Kuhn 1968), Martha King (1985), Bill Martin, Jr. (1966), and others legitimized the effect of children's literature and the development of narrative on the development of reading in children. This has been supported by a strong rationale from researchers and theorists who have studied the nature of storytelling and narrative and how children's language development is influenced by their being read to (Applebee 1978; Rosen 1984; Wells 1986).

Influences from the Field of Composition

Scholars such as Alvina Burrows in *They All Want to Write* (Burrows, Jackson & Saunders 1939) urged that young children should be able to express themselves in their own voices in writing from the very beginning of schooling. During the first half of this century, she informed elementary school teachers that kids had to write about their own experiences. Burrows's work was supported in the 1970s by the research of Don Graves (1983), who has clearly documented that children learn to write and that their writing continues to develop when they have opportunities to write in a supportive environment. Graves's work was part of a knowledge explosion in the field of composition that has greatly influenced whole language.

The focus on writing during the 1970s and 1980s was welcomed by whole language advocates and was supported not only by those working in elementary schools, such as Graves and his colleagues, but also by the work of secondary school English teachers and professors of English and English education involved with the National Writing Project, whose headquarters are at the University of California, Berkeley. The National Writing Project has been instrumental in involving teachers in becoming writers themselves, sharing their writing with others, discussing successful ways of teaching writing, and learning about theory and research in the field of composition.

The work of these English educators has been influenced by the work of James Britton, Nancy Martin, Harold Rosen, and others (Britton et al. 1975) from the London Institute of Education. The concept of language across the curriculum was popularized by language scholars from the London Institute and is reflected in *A Language for Life* (Bullock 1975). This report was commissioned by the secretary of state for education and science in the United Kingdom and influenced not only the teaching of composition but also the teaching of English and language arts in all English-speaking countries. Whole language has benefited from the innovations taking place in English-speaking countries that focused on integrating the English language arts with all subjects and using writing and reading for functional and varied purposes (Goodman & Goodman 1983).

Whole language has been enriched by research and writing in the fields of both reading and composition that have taken place since 1960. Although some advocates of these works stressed either reading or writing, whole language educators have organized research and curriculum to capitalize on the integration of all the language areas and to study and understand the relations between them. Questions are being raised about expanding functions of reading and writing beyond books, narratives, and reports, and about the effects this will have on curriculum. Educators are exploring ways to integrate reading and writing into all areas of the curriculum and are exploring the authenticity of the reading and writing events themselves (Edelsky 1987).

Influences from Early Childhood Education

Educational influences from England came not only from secondary educators concerned with language matters but also from educators concerned with school beginners in the British infant schools. Early childhood education in the United States was greatly influenced by the British Infant School movement, which, at the same time, was being influenced by the progressive education of John Dewey (Featherstone 1967, 1968, 1969). Following the child's lead in planning curriculum, starting where the child is and expanding from that point in order to encourage problem solving, and seeing play as the building blocks of intellectual development are all theoretical notions that whole language advocates and early childhood educators have in common. It is understandable that early childhood educators find it easy to support and participate in developments in whole language (Loughlin & Martin 1988).

Influences from Advocates of Integrated Curriculum

The concept of integrated language arts was also influenced by the concept of the integrated day, or integrated curriculum, that was being actively promoted by curriculum theorists during the 1940s and 1950s. Integrated programs were being developed not only for the elementary schools but also for junior high, middle, and secondary schools through the integration of language arts and social studies, social studies and humanities, and often science and math programs. The artificial isolation of content, which seemed appropriate for the purposes of research and scholarship in postsecondary education, did not seem appropriate for growing children and adolescents.

In the post-World War II years, organizations such as the American Council on Education (ACE) and the Association for Supervision and Curriculum Development (ASCD) were actively involved in discovering the best ways to organize integrated curricula. With students representing an ever-widening range of race, ethnicity, nationality, linguistic background, and socioeconomic status among those entering and staying in schools and moving on to higher education, educators were discussing ways of making education relevant to all students in all walks of life. Hilda Taba expressed this concern. "The problem, then, is that of developing ways of helping individuals in this process of creating a unity of knowledge" (1962, p. 299).

The concern for integration of curriculum was influenced not only from the point of view of the unity of knowledge through the integration of subject matter but also included a concern for the integration of attitudes and values with the development of knowledge necessary for members of a democratic society. The ties to attitudes and values and the philosophy of John Dewey are again evident. The ACE commissioned a number of educators to debate, discuss, and develop integrated curriculum with a focus on intergroup education (Taba 1950). According to Taba, Brady, and Robinson (1952),

> a person who knows all the facts but whose feelings are limited is likely to have a 'so what?' attitude. . . . One who can sympathize . . . with others but has neither conceptual framework nor basic facts . . . is likely to be a sentimental idealist. . . . Those untrained in sound reasons will not be able to apply knowledge . . . [and those without social skills will] be frustrated in practical situations and unable to behave accordingly. (p. 51)

Building on Kilpatrick's (1918, 1936) project method (Hines 1972), teachers and curriculum specialists were developing units of work or thematic strands of study to help students relate what they were learning to other areas of the curriculum as well as to their own lives.

The ASCD also commissioned a number of books and monographs on curriculum, including an impressive volume entitled *Perceiving, Behaving, Becoming* (Combs 1962). Although *Perceiving, Behaving, Becoming* focused on how teaching and schooling could be organized to facilitate the "truly adequate person" (defined variously as sufficient, fully functional, and self-actualizing), group discussion and collaboration among students were viewed as significant aspects of the development of individuals.

Taba (1962) supports the importance of social interaction as she reminds her readers "that the so-called child-centered school was always in a measure also a society-centered school" (p. 30). She also argues, "The learning process is primarily social. The innate tendencies of an individual are modified, suppressed or encouraged according to social demands" (p. 131).

The dynamic activity centered on the integrated curriculum and the concern for the development of the self-actualizing personality in collaborative group settings diminished in 1955 because of a national concern that the United States was lagging behind the Soviet Union in scientific progress. Sputnik was launched, and this important date in history had an equally significant impact on education. The focus in curriculum turned toward improving math and science education, supporting gifted students, and promoting "excellence" and individual competitive achievement.

Within the next decade, however, due largely to the civil rights movement, the focus of schooling once again turned to equal educational opportunity for all students—the development of all human potential. The effects of curriculum development of the forties and fifties and the concern for the development of individual potential could be seen as groups of educators came together to discuss issues such as the integration of curriculum and individual differences, especially those of linguistic and cultural minorities.

In the early 1970s a group of educators formed the Center for the Expansion of Language and Thinking (CELT) whose first president was Ken Goodman. Its main purpose was to develop a network of teacher educators and educational researchers to provide a forum for continual discussion; to identify ways of informing and involving classroom teachers, curriculum specialists, and administrators in the new knowledge coming from linguistics, psycholinguistics, and sociolinguistics that could be applied to education; and to work collaboratively in various research endeavors. CELT members are actively involved in the development and dissemination of whole language.

Concerned with organizing environments to provide activity-oriented curriculum for all children, Lillian Weber called for expanding beyond the walls of the classroom when necessary to facilitate talk, problem solving, role-playing, and simulations. Weber established the Workshop Center for Open Education to support teachers, administrators, paraprofessionals, and parents who were interested and involved in open education in New York City. The philosophy of the Workshop Center includes beliefs similar to those of whole language. "We . . . wanted to make provision for individual differences. We wanted to provide for the diversity of the participants' interests, needs, and stages of development. We wanted to provide for browsing, for free exploration, for talk, for direct demonstration. We wanted to share with others the account of our difficulties and successes in change" (Weber 1973, p. 2).

The center provided opportunities for teachers to come together to explore issues and to discover ways to exist in schools when there was little support for their innovations and experimentation.

In 1972, educators met at the University of North Dakota "to discuss concerns about the narrow accountability ethos that had begun to dominate schools and to share what many believed to be more sensible means of both documenting and assessing children's learning" (Perrone 1977, front matter). Thus the North Dakota Study Group was formed. Its goal, "to provide materials for teachers, parents, school administrators and governmental decision makers that might encourage re-examination of a range of evaluation issues and perspectives about schools" (front matter), has influenced the direction whole language educators are taking to discover new ways of evaluating both teachers and students in whole language programs (Goodman, Goodman & Hood, 1989).

In the late 1970s, groups of teachers began to meet together to discuss many issues about the teaching and learning of language, building on the new insights about language and learning that I have been sketching. This was the beginning of the whole language teacher-support groups that Dorothy Watson (1989) has discussed. Originally there were small groups in California, Arizona, Missouri, Manitoba, and Nova Scotia. These groups have grown to over one hundred at this writing and were organized as a confederation of support groups, the Whole Language Umbrella, at a whole language conference in Winnipeg in February 1988.

All the groups found the need to establish communication in order to respond to the growing imposition of rigid and narrow educational practices from some administrators, academics, and members of the general public who are calling for a stronger-than-ever focus on accountability by standardized tests, a prescribed curriculum often driven by narrowly conceived textbook programs, and a back-to-basics curriculum based on unenlightened views about reading, writing, learning, and language. The development of whole language teacher-support groups shows the discontent teachers have felt with traditional education and suggests professional educators' need for collegial support, communication with like-minded colleagues, and professional development. I believe it is from this need that whole language emerged and grew. Its dissemination became the focus of teachers' search for ways to be responsible and knowledgeable professionals.

Whole language is a new response to an old argument. In the 1920s and 1930s a movement variously called *the new education* and *progressive schools* emerged as a "product of discontent with traditional education. In effect it is a criticism of the latter" (Dewey 1938, p. 18).

Dewey expresses this discontent: "The traditional scheme is, in essence, one of imposition from above and from outside. It imposes adult standards, subject matter and methods upon those who are only growing slowly toward maturity" (pp. 18–19).

The history of whole language shows that many groups and individuals have made continual attempts to consider issues such as curriculum; individual differences; social interaction; collaboration; language learning; the relation between teaching, learning, and evaluation; and their influences on the lives of teachers and students. At the core is the belief that decision making must be placed in the hands of teachers and learners.

The development of whole language has been reflected in innovative practices: the collaboration between teachers of math and science working with scientists to help students build conceptual understanding; teachers filling their classrooms with tools such as blocks, easels, autoharps, and woodworking equipment; teachers and students building replicas of communities, space satellites, stock markets, and colonial kitchens in order to study their problems and ways of solving them and at the same time integrating social studies, science, math, and language arts; teachers using photographs, paintings, and literature to help students raise questions and solve problems through discussion and argumentation; English teachers organizing ways to allow students choice in courses and materials; and teachers organizing experiences so that students will need to read and write in a wide range of genres in response to real and functional experiences. At the same time, those involved in these developments have been concerned with basing them on research that is compatible with the theory on which whole language is built (Goodman 1989).

Becoming a Whole-Language Professional: A Personal History

The history of a movement is dynamic and is best understood not only by examining the academic roots of its major ideas but also by examining the histories of the individuals who are involved in the development of the movement. Those of us who consider ourselves active participants in the development of whole language have come to our decisions along different paths. Whether as members of whole language support groups or as individuals, we have our own personal histories of ideas, beliefs, and knowledge about teaching and learning and about language that inform what we know, what we believe, and what we do as whole language practitioners. The different paths we took and the similar conclusions we came to are important to understanding the whole language movement.

As I look back on the history of my own teaching and learning, I realize that I was involved in some of the antecedent movements that influenced whole language from the beginning of my career. My professors still commonly used the term *progressive education* when I was in my teacher-education program at Los Angeles State College from 1949 to 1952. A number of ideas from this program strongly influenced my early teaching.

I valued the language experience approach, which stressed the significance of children's having personally meaningful experiences surrounded by rich oral language opportunities prior to reading and writing and related this to integrating subject matter with the language arts through the use of thematic units. Both of these influences were supported by two principles: that the needs of the child were central to all curriculum planning and that children needed to be actively involved in their own learning. I knew the names of John Dewey, Roach Van Allen, Hilda Taba, Alice Miel, Leland Jacobs, and Dorris Lee, among others, but I did not fully appreciate their influences on my teaching at that time.

My developing professional beliefs were also influenced by some negative learning experiences from my personal history as a student. As I grew up, I had no sense of being a learner. I was convinced by most of my teachers that, as a bilingual working-class kid, I had a weak vocabulary and that my quite average grades were evidence that I would have little success in scholarly pursuits. I would not be capable of attending a university.

Eventually, I proved them wrong, but it took a number of forces to convince me that I was capable of becoming a learner. I came to believe that when children are respected as learners, they recognize themselves as learners. They become members of the "learning club" by joining those whom they admire the most who are also learners. Smith (1986) has popularized the "club joining" concept: "Children join the . . . club . . . with the implicit act of mutual acceptance: 'You're one of us.' 'I want to be just like you.' There are no special admission requirements, no entry fees" (p. 37).

When I started to teach, the positive and supportive responses of my eighth-grade students helped me sense my potential success as a teacher, and my growing self-confidence made me believe that perhaps I might be a capable learner. I learned that developing a child-centered curriculum meant that kids needed to make choices, to discuss and ask questions about topics that were of interest to them. Although I used basal readers and had at least three reading groups, I did not introduce the basal until the students and I had participated in some active experience accompanied by a good deal of oral language. These experiences related to the stories we were going to read and also to what the kids knew and cared about. Using the basal was a small part of our reading program. We had trade books in the classroom and made extensive use of libraries so that students could select their own books to read. We often had small-group discussions about the same book after three or more of the students had read it. We used nonfiction trade books related to science and social studies units. My students who were having difficulty with their reading were writing stories about their personal interests, and these became part of a literary magazine and were used as the material we read together in reading groups. Students' assignments involved reading the newspaper or listening to reports on the radio and leading discussions about current events to start each day. When I introduced choral reading and role-playing, I learned that as students worked together toward a presentation, they became a more cohesive group, concerned for each other and tolerant of each other's inadequacies. Not only did my classes perform poetry and readers' theater for other classes and parents but, as the oldest kids in the school, they also produced a cantata of their own history in the school to be performed at eighth-grade graduation.

Individual students were encouraged to become experts on a topic of their own choosing and of interest to them. As a class, we studied a variety of issues during the year. The great waves of migration to California during that time were a natural focus for us as we explored together our own immigration from other states to California and the immigration of parents and grandparents from Mexico or Europe. Led by a dynamic and wise principal, and with wide community support, parents and teachers planned a schoolwide unit about sex education.

Another important influence on my view of whole language came from my summer work as a counselor and later as director and overall coordinator for the Los Angeles Jewish Community Center Day Camps. These camps had a social group work philosophy that recognized the impact of collaborative learning and problem solving on the growth and development of children and youth. I observed youth becoming effective and efficient learners about their environment and about themselves as they interacted with others of varying ages in collaborative group settings. I incorporated this social-group work philosophy into my developing beliefs about learning in classroom settings.

As I look back at my early experiences in teaching and outdoor education, I know there are things I did that I do not consider compatible with a whole language philosophy. The Spanish-speaking children in my classroom were not encouraged to use their native language. I maintained my reading groups throughout the year despite the progress my students were making. I called what they wrote as stories "creative writing" and did not relate the reports they were doing in social studies and science to the composing process. I had the students participate in "fun" games and activities that isolated sounds and words because they enjoyed them. I never considered the ways in which these activities related to what students already knew about language.

Not until my graduate studies with progressive educators who encouraged students to participate actively with them in theoretical discussions, research, and writing did I become reflective about my beliefs about teaching and learning. My own research in miscue analysis, early literacy development, and the writing process put me in a position to observe learners while they were using language, and I began to discuss with others the concept of "kidwatching" (Goodman 1978, 1985). During this time I was also fortunate to be part of a learning community of teacher educators, researchers, and teachers with whom I continue to collaborate, to reflect, and to wonder in order to articulate a philosophy about teaching and learning.

Within a Context of Science and Humanism

In addition to influences that relate present-day whole language to the personal and pedagogical histories that preceded it, whole language is embedded in the traditions of science and humanism. What we take from humanism is respect for and positive attitudes toward all learners regardless of their ages, abilities, or backgrounds. What we take from science are the discoveries in psychology, linguistics, psycholinguistics, and sociolinguistics that are part of the current knowledge explosion concerning how students learn, how they learn language, how they use language to learn, and the influences of the individual, peers, teachers, and various cultural institutions on language learning and on using language to learn.

What whole language teachers, administrators, teacher educators, authors, and publishers are doing is substantially different from the foundation on which the whole language movement has been built. There is greater respect for the power of language, greater understanding of the importance of children's being actively involved in their own learning, and greater understanding that children learn language best as they use it for real and functional purposes. Whole language educators realize that for teachers to improve learning experiences for students, teachers must believe that they have the responsibility and power to make decisions, and they need to be knowledgeable to do so. Finally, there is more awareness of the importance of taking into consideration the social community of the classroom and its influences on learning language. These new understandings are part of the debate within whole language.

How should classrooms be organized to capitalize on the new knowledge and developing belief systems? The articles in this issue[1] concerned with classrooms and school-based whole-language programs explore the ways some practitioners have considered such a question.

How should professional education be organized to provide opportunities for teachers and researchers to become more reflective about their roles in the teaching and learning processes? Several of the articles in this issue address this question. Ken Goodman raises issues that researchers must consider as they study whole language classrooms. Short and Burke examine issues that teacher educators must consider if preservice programs are to include opportunities for self-reflection on the part of future teachers. Watson looks at the present state of whole language and how teachers are involved in continuous self-development.

What kinds of activities are real and functional and purposeful for the learner? With the learner at the center of concern for whole language educators, it is not surprising that a number of the articles in this issue focus on the learning environment that allows learners the opportunities for educational growth.

How do we evaluate growth to show parents and students—as well as skeptics—that what happens in whole language classrooms supports students' learning? Teachers are expressing in their own voices ways for schools to plan for appropriate evaluation of whole language programs (Goodman, Goodman & Hood 1989).

As concepts grow and develop, it is helpful to have terminology to explore the new aspects of the concepts. That is why I believe the term *whole language* has grown in the present climate. However, if the term *whole language* remains static and does not reflect the dynamic changes that are emerging from the continual debate and exploration currently taking place, then the label may be supplanted by another. Regardless, the educational theories and beliefs that represent what whole language is today will be foundational to educational practices of the future. In the same way that those of us who call ourselves whole language proponents today discover our roots in the humanistic and scientific beliefs of those who came before, any movement

---

[1] This article was part of a special issue of *Elementary School Journal* focused on whole language.

built on similar humanistic and scientific beliefs will discover its roots in the dynamic debate going on today within the movement called whole language.

References

Applebee, Arthur N. 1978. *The child's concept of story: Ages 2 to 17.* Chicago: University of Chicago Press.

Ashton-Warner, Sylvia. 1963. *Teacher.* New York: Simon & Schuster.

Britton, James, Burgess, T., Martin, Nancy, McLeod, Alex & Rosen, Harold. 1975. *The development of writing abilities (11–18).* London: Macmillan.

Bullock, Alan. 1975. *A language for life.* London: Her Majesty's Stationery Office.

Burrows, Alvina T., Jackson, Doris C. & Saunders, Dorothy O. 1939. *They all want to write: Written English in the elementary school.* Hamden, CT: Library Professional Publications.

Clay, Marie. 1979. *Reading: The patterning of complex behavior.* Portsmouth, NH: Heinemann.

Combs, Arthur (Ed.). 1962. *Perceiving, behaving, becoming: A new focus for education* (ASCD Yearbook). New York: Association for Supervision and Curriculum Development.

Comenius, John A. 1887. *The orbis pictus.* Syracuse, NY: C. W. Bardeen. (Reissued in1969, Detroit: Singing Trees Press)

Dewey, John. 1938. *Experience and education.* New York: Macmillan.

Dewey, John. 1943. *The child and the curriculum* and *The school and society.* Chicago: University of Chicago Press. (Original works published 1902 and 1915)

Duckworth, Eleanor. 1987. *The having of wonderful ideas and other essays on teaching and learning.* New York: Teachers College Press.

Edelsky, Carole. 1987. *Writing in a bilingual classroom: Había una vez.* Norwood, NJ: Ablex.

Featherstone, Joseph. 1967, September 2. How children learn. *The New Republic, 57,* 17–21.

Featherstone, Joseph. 1968, December 18. Experiments in learning. *The New Republic, 59,* 23–25.

Featherstone, Joseph. 1969, January 1. Why so few good schools? *The New Republic, 60,* 18–21.

Ferreiro, Emilia & Teberosky, Ana. 1982. *Literacy before schooling.* Portsmouth, NH: Heinemann. (Original work published 1979)

Goodman, Kenneth S. 1989. Whole language research: Foundations and development. *Elementary School Journal, 90,* 207–21.

Goodman, Kenneth S. & Goodman, Yetta M. 1979. *A whole language comprehension-centered reading program* (Occasional Paper No. 1). Tucson: Program in Language and Literacy, College of Education, University of Arizona. (ERIC Document Reproduction Service Document ED 210 630)

Goodman, Kenneth & Goodman, Yetta. 1983. Reading and writing relationships: Pragmatic functions. *Language Arts, 60*, 590–99.

Goodman, Kenneth S., Goodman, Yetta M. & Hood, Wendy J. (Eds.). 1989. *The whole language evaluation book*. Portsmouth, NH: Heinemann.

Goodman, Kenneth S., Smith, E. Brooks, Meredith, Robert, & Goodman, Yetta M. 1987. *Language and thinking in school: A whole language curriculum* (3rd ed.). New York: Richard C. Owen.

Goodman, Yetta. 1978. Kidwatching: An alternative to testing. *National Elementary Principal, 57*, 41–45.

Goodman, Yetta M. 1985. Kidwatching: Observing children in the classroom. In Angela Jaggar & M. Trika Smith-Burke (Eds.), *Observing the language learner* (pp. 9–18). Urbana, IL & Newark, DE: National Council of Teachers of English & International Reading Association.

Graves, Donald. 1983. *Writing: Teachers and children at work*. Portsmouth, NH: Heinemann.

Halliday, M. A. K. 1975. *Learning how to mean: Explorations in the development of language*. New York: Elsevier.

Harste, Jerome & Burke, Carolyn. 1977. A new hypothesis for reading teacher research: Both the *teaching* and *learning* of reading are theoretically based. In P. David Pearson (Ed.), *Reading: Theory, research, and practice* (Twenty-sixth yearbook of the National Reading Conference) (pp. 32–40). Clemson, SC: National Reading Conference.

Hines, Vynce A. 1972. Progressivism in practice. In James R. Squire (Ed.), *A new look at progressive education* (ASCD Yearbook) (pp. 118–64). Washington, D.C.: Association for Supervision and Curriculum Development.

Holdaway, Don. 1979. *The foundations of literacy*. New York: Ashton Scholastic.

Huck, Charlotte S. & Kuhn, Doris Y. 1968. *Children's literature in the elementary classroom*. New York: Holt, Rinehart & Winston.

Jacobs, Leland B. (Ed.). 1965. *Using literature with young children*. New York: Teachers College Press.

Kilpatrick, W. H. 1918. The project method. *Teachers College Record, 19*, 318–34.

Kilpatrick, W. H. 1936. *Foundations of method*. New York: Macmillan.

King, Martha. 1985. Language and language learning for child watchers. In Angela Jaggar & M. Trika Smith-Burke (Eds.), *Observing the language learner* (pp. 19–38). Urbana, IL & Newark, DE: National Council of Teachers of English & International Reading Association.

Lamoreaux, Lillian A. & Lee, Dorris. 1943. *Learning to read through experience* (2nd. ed.). New York: Appleton-Century.

Lee, Dorris & Allen, Roach V. 1963. *Learning to read through experience*. New York: Appleton-Century-Crofts.

Loughlin, Catherine E. & Martin, Mavis D. 1987. *Supporting literacy: Developing effective learning environments*. New York: Teachers College Press.

Martin, Bill, Jr. 1966. *Sounds of language*. New York: Holt, Rinehart & Winston.

New Zealand Department of Education. 1972. *Reading: Suggestions for teaching reading in primary and secondary schools*. Wellington, NZ: Department of Education.

New Zealand Department of Education. 1985. *Reading in junior classes*. Wellington, NZ: Department of Education.

Penton, J. 1979. *Reading in NZ schools: A survey of our theory and practice*. Auckland, NZ: Department of Education.

Perrone, Vito. 1977. *First California conference on education evaluation and public policy*. Grand Forks, ND: North Dakota Study Group on Evaluation.

Pinnell, Gay S. & Matlin, Myna. 1989. *Teachers and research: Language learning in the classroom*. Newark, DE: International Reading Association.

Read, Charles. 1975. *Children's categorization of speech sounds in English* (Research Report No. 17). Urbana, IL: National Council of Teachers of English.

Rosen, Harold. 1984. *Stories and meanings*. Portsmouth, NH: Boynton–Cook.

Rosenblatt, Louis. 1976. *Literature as exploration* (3rd ed.). New York: Noble & Noble. (Original work published 1938)

Rosenblatt, Louise. 1978. *The reader, the text, the poem: The transactional theory of the literary work*. Carbondale, IL: Southern Illinois University Press.

Short, Kathy G. & Burke, Carolyn L. 1989. New potentials for teacher education: Teaching and learning as inquiry. *Elementary School Journal, 90*, 193–206.

Smith, Frank. 1986. *Insult to intelligence: The bureaucratic invasion of our classrooms*. New York: Arbor House.

Smith, Frank & Goodman, Kenneth S. 1971. On the psycholinguistic method of teaching reading. *Elementary School Journal, 71*, 177–81.

Taba, Hilda. 1950. *Curriculum in intergroup relations*. Washington, D.C.: American Council of Education.

Taba, Hilda. 1962. *Curriculum development: Theory and practice*. New York: Harcourt, Brace & World.

Taba, Hilda, Brady, Elizabeth H. & Robinson, John T. 1952. *Intergroup education in public schools*. Washington, D.C.: American Council on Education.

Veatch, Jeannette. 1964. *How to teach reading with children's books*. New York: Richard C. Owen.

Vygotsky, Lev S. 1978. *Mind in society: The development of higher psychological processes*. Cambridge, MA: Harvard University Press.

Vygotsky, Lev S. 1986. *Thought and language*. Cambridge, MA: MIT Press.

Watson, Dorothy J. 1989. Defining and describing whole language. *Elementary School Journal, 90*, 128–41.

Weber, Lillian. 1973. *Notes from Workshop Center for Open Education* (New York: City College), *2*.

Wells, Gordon. 1986. *The meaning makers: Children learning language and using language to learn*. Portsmouth, NH: Heinemann.

Vygotsky in a Whole Language Perspective

(with Kenneth S. Goodman)

The best method [for teaching reading and writing] is one in which children do not learn to read and write but in which both these skills are found in play situations. . . . In the same way as children learn to speak, they should be able to learn to read and write.

—Lev Vygotsky

Centrifugal Force and Centripetal Force: Personal Invention and Social Convention

A common interpretation of Vygotsky's view of language development is that social experience is internalized and social language shapes the language of the individual. Though there can be no doubt that eventually the language of each individual must fall within the norms of the

These excerpts are from a longer article about relationships between the whole language model of education and the work of Lev S. Vygotsky, the influential Soviet psychologist who is best known for the term *zone of proximal development*. The article was originally published in *Vygotsky and Education: Instructional Implications and Applications of Sociohistorical Psychology*, edited by Luis C. Moll, pp. 223–50 (New York: Cambridge University Press, 1990). Copyright 1990 by Cambridge University Press. Reprinted with the permission of Cambridge University Press.

social language and that the way society organizes meaning and represents it strongly shapes the way the individual makes sense of the world, we believe that language is as much personal invention as social convention. Human learners are not passively manipulated by their social experiences; they are actively seeking sense in the world. The individual and society both play strong roles in language development.

Vygotsky (1986) describes the process of internalization: "An operation that initially represents an external activity is reconstructed and begins to occur internally" (pp. 56–57). We don't disagree with this concept of internalization. But we believe that there are also internal efforts to represent experience symbolically and that the reconstruction of external activity is simultaneously a reconstruction of internal activity.

There are two seemingly opposing forces shaping the development of language in individuals and in communities. Although they are opposing in a sense, they operate in an integral fashion. The metaphor we use to describe these forces comes from the concept of centrifugal and centripetal forces of physics. If a ball is twirled on a string, there is a centrifugal force pulling it away from the center. The string, however, transmits an opposing, centripetal force pulling it back toward the middle. As long as these are in balance, the ball will orbit the center.

In language, the centrifugal force is the ability of people individually and collectively to create semiotic systems, to invent new language, to deal with new experience, feelings, and ideas. This creative force produces change and makes it possible for language continuously to meet the developing and changing needs of its users. But if this force were unchecked, language would expand so rapidly and diversely that it would lose its social utility. People would soon be unable to understand each other at all.

The centripetal force that provides the counterbalance and relative stability is the social nature of language. If language were static and unchanging it would quickly inhibit its users in learning and in communicating their responses to new experiences. Change in language, whether temporary or permanent, may be initiated by individuals, but it must be understood and accepted by others in order for language to be effective. To serve its functions it must be comprehensible by others, not just by the speaker or the writer. In social transactions with others, learners experience the conventions of the social language. When language changes there is always balance between the creative force and the need to communicate. So the inventor moves toward the social forms and uses social resources in making new inventions. Thus there is a centripetal force that balances the outward thrust of personal language.

Language development, then, can be viewed as being shaped by these two forces. There is an almost explosive force from within children that propels them to express themselves, and at the same time there is a strong need to communicate that pushes the direction of growth and development toward the language of the family and community. This shaping is accomplished through the myriad language transactions that involve children with others. The language is generated by the child, but it is changed in transactions with others by their comprehension or lack of comprehension and by their responses. Thus parents, teachers, caregivers, siblings, peers, and significant others play vital roles in the language development of children. They are essential communicative partners, less role models than respondents, less to be imitated than to be understood and understanding.

Another way to view these two opposing forces shaping language is as a balance between invention and convention. Both invention, personal creation of language, and convention, the socially established systems and norms, are necessary for learning. Language is not learned by imitating adults or learning rules out of the context of language use. It is invented by each individual, and in the context of its social use it is adapted to social conventions. Every language must have within it devices for change, but innovators must use the devices for change the language provides or risk not being understood.

Learners are not resistant to the social force in language. In fact, language comes about at least partially as a means of social participation. Infants sense the social functions of language before they understand the communicative functions. As they begin to represent their own needs and experiences symbolically, they are eager to be understood and to understand others. So they are accepting of the social conventions of language. But these conventions are implicit, not explicit. The rules by which language is governed can be inferred by learners, but they are never directly observable, never imitatable. Any attempt by well-meaning adults to make the rules explicit can actually inhibit learning. Rather, the child keeps inventing rules and trying them out until they work—until they come into balance with social conventions.

We believe that maintaining the balance between invention and convention in developing reading and writing is a major factor in whether pupils come to consider themselves as insiders or outsiders, members of the literacy club or excluded from club benefits (Smith 1988). If all students are subjected to rigid curricula and interventionist teaching, some will survive and make their way into the club anyway. As they do they will be permitted more latitude in their reading and writing and will be able to balance their inventive energy against the conventions they find in their authentic literacy events. Because they belong to the literacy club, their in-school activities begin to look more like what they do outside of school. Other pupils, defeated by the rejection of their inventions, will be confused by the rigid conventions of textbooks and by the inflexibility of prescriptive language rules. These pupils will be excluded from the literacy club. The less they succeed, the less authentic will their experiences be and the less control will they be permitted. School life becomes alien to their out-of-school experiences. Ironically, the interventionist program is given credit for those who make it into the literacy club whereas the pupils who do not make it are blamed for their own failure.

Society values the inventions of some but not others. Established artists, writers, and scientists are supported. Art shows and book, drama, and concert reviews often praise the creative aspects of artistic works or performances. New discoveries of scientists are extolled on the front pages of newspapers. But a scientist whose discovery breaks with the dominant paradigm will not be easily accepted by his or her peers. Which concepts are scientific is not self-evident. Consider how long it took for Darwin's ideas about the scientific nature of biology to become established. The French Impressionists were vilified and unappreciated because they broke with the conventions of their time. Eventually their inventive energy was so strong, and they themselves so persistent, that new conventions emerged. The fact that these artistic nonconformists were also nonconformist in their life-styles did not help their acceptance.

To this day, we are likely to reject and minimize the creative invention of some groups more than others. Poor people, minorities, teenagers, those from cultures outside the mainstream, and nonconformists in general are not expected to contribute in valued ways. Their lack of conformity to some social conventions as defined by reference to the dominant culture is interpreted as ignorance, incompetence, or antisocial behavior.

The inventive abilities of young people of all ages are often treated as disruptive and antisocial. So school practice in all respects has tended to treat difference as deficiency and inventive strength as random weakness. Instead of understanding the ability of all pupils to learn and the need for them to make their own way to an equilibrium between invention and convention, we treat some as lacking in the requirements for admission to the literacy club, and use interventionist strategies that become self-fulfilling prophecies. Eventually many accept the view of themselves as incapable; those that don't rebel or drop out.

The process of balancing invention and convention works better for young people outside of school than in the traditional school setting. Schools have traditionally narrowly defined conventions of behavior, of learning, of language, of thinking, even of dress. We believe that the difference between learning in school and out of school is largely an imposed one and an undesirable one. It ought to be easier to learn in school than out of school because in school there are professional teachers to mediate the learning. But instead of adjusting school to learners we require learners to adjust to the school.

Scientific concepts can be considered a type of social convention; they are conventional views shared by the best informed and most enlightened within the society. The process by which concepts are validated as scientific is itself highly conventionalized. The status of scientists gives their concepts a special status in society. But that also makes those concepts resistant to displacement by better, alternative concepts, which may have to break with or defy the conventions. We believe scientific concepts are learned in the same way as other concepts, through the push and pull of personal invention and social convention.

Vygotsky certainly recognized the tensions between the individual and society. Wertsch (1985) says Vygotsky discusses the child's cultural development on two planes. "First it appears between people as an interpsychological category and then within the child as an intrapsychological category." We see this as more a transaction than a one-way sequence with the social first and the personal following. Rather, the child invents in the context of authentic social experiences in which conventions are implicit. Over time the inventions come to conform to the social conventions.

Aaron, at age four, provided a powerful example of invention when he wrote his "GRAPA GHNE" a birthday card. The card contains much evidence to support our contentions about the relationship of invention to convention, including his awareness of card giving for birthdays and the general form of birthday cards. But his spelling of GRAPA GHNE is a very strong example of how invention works in language development. What he is inventing is a spelling for *Grandpa Kenny*, his most common name for his grandfather. English spelling does not represent the aspiration of /k/ in the initial position in *Kenny* (contrast the breathiness of the /k/ in *Ken* with the /k/ in *skill*). Aaron perceives this aspiration and draws on his knowledge of how it is represented in his own last name, *Hood*. At the same time as he invents the spelling GHNE, he shows his knowledge of a number of phonological and orthographic conventions.

Traditional methods in schools may get willing students to echo verbalizations of language conventions and scientific concepts and even to manipulate them in narrow and controlled contexts. But for these to become internalized and operationalized by learners—for the social to become the personal—there must be room to invent, to test out, to experiment, and to reach personal-social equilibrium.

The Teacher's Role in Balancing Invention and Convention

Teachers have traditionally been seen as agents of conformity in the language use of their pupils. This role must be reconsidered to give sufficient room for invention and to let learners become aware of convention as it exists in social language. Too often teachers have rewarded conformity, punished experimentation and risk taking, and confused learners about conventions just as they are building some sense of them.

In fact, the rules taught in school are based on authority, a set of arbitrary rules established by textbooks or teachers, and not on scientific concepts about language in use. Learners often find it hard to apply the rules or confirm them in their own language experiences. For example, teachers have sometimes taught pupils that *and* and *but* may not be used to start sentences. *But* pupils have often found examples of sentences that do start with these words in their reading. Too much intervention and direction by others, particularly teachers, can minimize invention and focus excessively and prematurely on the need for conventionality.

Everything we learn involves imperfection and error as we gain competence. Support for mistake making and hypothesis testing is one way teachers can mediate the balancing of invention and convention. "To err is human" is an old folk saying that illustrates how long people have been aware that error is a normal part of human learning. If language learning were purely imitative or purely innate it would be hard to explain the pervasiveness of error. But if we understand the role of invention then we can understand that as people move into equilibrium between invention and convention their errors reflect their progress. The two-year-old who says "I taked it" has moved to a rule for past tense that is partway between his early inventions and the convention of adult grammar.

The six-year-old who invents the spelling WAT for *went* has invented the alphabetic system whereby letter sequences represent sound sequences. Her spelling represents what she hears and her own articulatory system. The /n/ in *went* is usually a nasalized vowel, a feature that does not fit the stop-consonant phoneme she normally represents with *n*. But spelling conventions in English do not represent all phonetic features, and therefore standard spellings cannot be dependably generated. For the sake of standardizing spellings across pronunciation, the system sacrifices conformity to rules. Invented spellings represent the child's control over the basic principles of the orthography but not the many exceptions.

If the teacher treats all nonstandard spellings as equally wrong the insight into the learner's control of English spelling is lost. If the teacher insists on conventional language at all stages of development and during every phase of the composing process, then the whole balance between invention and convention is destroyed and the strength and creativity of the pupils in language learning is neutralized.

No invention is wholly the creation of the inventor. Every invention, whether one by a famous scientist that has broad impact on society or the child's invention of something known to every adult in the community, is built on transactions with others. Vygotsky (1978) emphasized the child's development from the outside in. Our view, supported by literacy development research in the last decade and a half, shows how children's inventions based on social transactions transform written language and are modified until they coincide with the social conventions of written language (Ferreiro & Teberosky 1982; Goelman, Olberg & Smith 1984; Goodman & Altwerger 1981; Teale & Sulzby 1986). Thus the social becomes the personal through the tension between invention and convention.

Eleanor Duckworth (1987) comes to similar conclusions regarding personal invention:

> I see no difference in kind between wonderful ideas that many other people have already had and wonderful ideas that nobody has yet happened upon. That is, the nature of creative intellectual acts remains the same, whether it is an infant seeing things and reaching for them . . . or an astronomer who develops a new theory of the creation of the universe. (p. 14)

Collaboration in Whole Language Classrooms

In whole language there is a reciprocal, transactional view of teaching and learning. Using *transaction* as Dewey did implies that in classroom transactions teachers and learners are changed. Wertsch (1985) quotes Vygotsky on this change in learners: "Internalization transforms the process itself and changes its structure and functions" (p. 81). The traditional idea that teaching can control learning or that each act of teaching results in a reciprocal act of learning in each learner is too simplistic. Teachers learn and learners teach, and as they transact each is changed. Both can resist this change by not committing themselves to the transactions. Whole language teachers recognize the power of classroom transactions and plan for them.

One key to teachers' success is building an atmosphere of mutual respect in their classrooms. These become social communities where teachers value each learner, help the learners to value themselves and each other, and win the respect of their students.

Whole language teachers don't abdicate their authority or responsibility. But they lead by virtue of their greater experience, their knowledge, and their respect for their pupils. They know their pupils, monitor their learning, and provide support and resources as they are needed. They recognize that there must be collaboration between themselves and their pupils if an optimal learning atmosphere is to be created. Whole language teachers believe that experiences and literacy events must be as authentic in the classroom as they are outside of it. Pupils must feel a sense of purpose, of choice, of utility, of participation, and of shared ownership in their classrooms and in what happens there. Even as young beginners they need to participate in decision making and see relevance in what they are doing. The tenor of relationships between teachers and learners becomes one of trust and collaboration rather than conflict and domination.

New Roles for Teachers

In whole language classrooms teachers are empowered. They are not reduced to powerless technicians administering someone else's work sheets, skill drills, and basal readers to powerless pupils. In turn they empower learners by valuing who they are and what they know, do, and believe. They support learners in solving their problems and pursuing knowledge. The learners are involved and committed to the ongoing learning events in their classrooms because these events are authentic and relevant and because the learners are empowered participants.

The teacher is an initiator. Whole language teachers are initiators. Their roles are in no sense passive. They create authentic contexts in their classrooms and participate with their students in order to stimulate learners to engage in solving problems and identifying and meeting their own needs. As they do so they insightfully observe the learners so that they can recognize and even anticipate their potential. These teachers know how to create conditions that will cause learners to exhibit and make the most of their zones of proximal development.

The teacher is a kidwatcher. The whole language teacher is skilled at observing kids at play and at work, knowing where they are developmentally, and seeing the naturally occurring zones of proximal development. We believe it is a mistake to think that teachers can control or even create zones of proximal development in learners. But whole language teachers know how to detect the evidence of what learners are ready to do with support. If the teacher is not a successful kidwatcher the zones will be missed, and so will opportunities for growth and learning.

The teacher is a mediator. Redefining learning requires us to redefine teaching. Optimal learning requires teaching that supports and facilitates it without controlling, distorting, or thwarting the learning. Vygotsky's (1978) concept of mediation is a useful way to view a major component of optimal teaching. The learner is in a situational context in which problems need to be solved or experiences understood. The teacher is present as the learning transaction takes place but in the role of mediator—supporting the learning transactions but neither causing them to happen in any direct sense nor controlling the learning. In this way the forces of invention and convention are unfettered, and the teacher supports the learner in achieving equilibrium.

In defining themselves as mediators, whole language teachers understand that less can be more. They realize that helping a learner solve a problem is better than giving him or her an algorithm or a solution. In reading and writing, teachers interfere as little as possible between the text and the reader. Teachers mediate by asking a question here, offering a useful hint there, directing attention to an anomaly, calling attention to overlooked information, and supporting learners as they synthesize what they are learning into new concepts and schemata. They provide just enough support to help the learner make the most of his or her own zone of proximal development. Whole language teachers do assume, as Vygotsky (1978) said, that "what children can do with the assistance of others might be in some sense even more indicative of their mental development than what they can do alone" (p. 85). But whole language teachers also know that assisting pupils in doing something is different from doing it for them or controlling what they do. Consider two classroom episodes:

1. A group of black inner-city fourth-grade pupils have read Langston Hughes's poem "Mother to Son" (Hughes 1963, p. 67). The pupils discuss the poem. The classroom procedure involves a pupil leading the discussion; the teacher is a codiscussant. The teacher wonders what they think about the mother's saying "Life for me ain't been no crystal stair." Some of the pupils point out other references to stairs in the poem. The teacher shares with them her knowledge of the author's life and political beliefs. She suggests that the stairs represent the author's view of this woman's attempt to raise herself up from her difficult con-

ditions. One boy asks, "She talkin' 'bout climbin' up to heaven?" They decide that the mother is contrasting her hard life to the religious idea of life as a beautiful crystal stair leading to heaven. In doing so they draw on their own knowledge of the likely experiences and religious beliefs of the mother. They share stories of their own mothers. "I never thought of this poem in quite that way," says the teacher.

2. An eighth-grade group in a working-class suburb plans a unit on evolution. The discussion and webbing of their knowledge of the concept introduce the controversy over the biblical view of creation. Two weeks after the unit begins one student tells the teacher that his minister would like to come in and debate evolution with the teacher. The teacher declines, explaining that studying a theory is different from advocating it. The class discuss the situation and reaffirm that they are studying evolution as a theory. They decide to explore the role of theory in science and the difference between established fact and theory. The student is encouraged by the teacher and his classmates to bring into the study literature from creationists on the subject. The ensuing study is enlivened. The pupils search avidly for resources not only on evolution but on the history of the theory and the controversy over it. One group of students reads Irving Stone's 1979 biography of Charles Darwin and shares their responses.

In both of these examples, the teacher plays a crucial but not controlling role. The teacher is an initiator, selecting a poem to be shared, planning a unit, providing time for pupils to pursue a spontaneous question. The teacher is a kidwatcher who considers not only where the pupils are but where they are capable of going in their learning. So one teacher is supportive and receptive as pupils relate their own schemata to Hughes's poem. The other teacher welcomes the fundamentalist challenge to the scientific concept. These teachers are not intervening in learning, they are mediating it. The role of the teacher as mediator is an active one and reflects the teacher's understanding that teaching supports learning; teaching can't force learning to happen.

In areas of controversy the teacher is not afraid to express belief, but shows respect for the developing beliefs of the learners, whether they are based in personal, public, or scientific concepts. The teacher shares knowledge but knows that when learners can relate the new knowledge to what they already know and what they need to know, they will understand why the knowledge is important, and they will be able to integrate the new knowledge with their existing schemata and conceptual systems. In building comprehension, the teacher knows that pupils' development of their own strategies is more important than whether they agree with the teacher. So the teacher helps the pupils to examine the available facts, to evaluate their own beliefs, and to find more information as they need it.

The teacher is by no means the only mediator in the whole language classroom. By providing opportunities for pupils to self-evaluate, the power of reflective thinking as a mediating force is revealed. Reflecting on one's own learning is necessary for both the teacher and the learner. Dewey, in his concern for reflective thinking, says: "Thinking enables us to direct our own activities with foresight and to plan according to ends-in-view, or purposes of which we are aware" (Archambault 1964, p. 212).

The teacher is a liberator. There is a vital difference between mediation and intervention. This difference controls whether the teacher liberates or suppresses learners. In intervention the teacher takes control of learning, knows with great certainty in advance what learning will be acceptable, and thus undermines learners' confidence in themselves; the teacher becomes the determiner of social conventions and the suppressor of invention. When invention is inhibited, risk taking is limited and zones of proximal development are unlikely to be revealed or explored.

Paolo Freire (1970) contrasts "banking" views of pedagogy with liberating views. The banking view treats learners as empty vessels. Teachers deposit bits of learning into their heads. Learners have no control over the process, nor are their needs or interests considered. Liberating pedagogy sees learners in a power relationship to society. If education is to help them to liberate themselves it must be empowering. Learners must own the process of their learning. They must see learning, including literacy and language development, as part of a process of liberation. Freire was successful in helping Brazilian peasants to become literate by using the ideas and concepts of their political lives in the texts they used in learning to read.

In a broader sense Freire was recognizing that learners learn best when they are free to control their own learning. This liberation is neither romantic nor abstract. Teachers cannot liberate pupils from society nor from the constraints of social transactions. But they can remove the artificial controls of traditional schooling. They can encourage pupils to enter freely into speech and literacy events, authentic social transactions, in which language is a tool for communication. They can make their classrooms communities of learners in which a full range of language genres occur naturally and in which their own language and the language of their home cultures are completely accepted. In such a community pupils are free to invent ways of dealing with their functional needs and free to discover the conventions in authentic social language transactions.

Freeing pupils to take risks is a major concern of whole language classrooms. In traditional classrooms, not only are pupils required to stay within arbitrary conventions in their oral and written expression, but they are penalized for their errors. Whole language classrooms liberate pupils to try new things, to invent spellings, to experiment with new genres, to guess at meanings in their reading, to read and write imperfectly, to challenge textbooks, to pursue inquiry.

Our research on reading and writing has strongly supported the importance of error in language development (Goodman & Gollasch 1982; Goodman & Wilde 1985). Miscues represent the tension between invention and convention in reading. They show the reader's use of existing schemata in attempting to comprehend texts. They also show how the text itself mediates learning. In whole language classrooms risk taking is not simply tolerated, it is celebrated. Learners have always been free to fail in school. However, in whole language classrooms they are free to learn from their failures with the support of their teachers.

Dewey relates failure to the power of thought:

> While the power of thought, then, frees us from servile subjection to instinct, appetite, and routine, it also brings with it the occasion and possibility of error and mistake. In elevating us above the brute, it opens the possibility of failures to which the animal, limited to instinct, cannot sink. (Archambault 1964, p. 217)

References

Archambault, R. C. 1964. *John Dewey on education*. Chicago: University of Chicago Press.

Duckworth, Eleanor. 1987. *The having of wonderful ideas and other essays on teaching and learning*. New York: Teachers College Press.

Ferreiro, Emilia & Teberosky, Ana. 1982. *Literacy before schooling*. Portsmouth, NH: Heinemann. (Original work published 1979)

Freire, Paolo. 1970. *Pedagogy of the oppressed*. New York: Seabury.

Goelman, Hillel, Olberg, Antoinette A. & Smith, Frank (Eds.). 1984. *Awakening to literacy*. Portsmouth, NH: Heinemann.

Goodman, Kenneth S. & Gollasch, Fred. 1980. Word omissions: Deliberate and nondeliberate. *Reading Research Quarterly, 16*, 6–31.

Goodman, Yetta M. & Altwerger, Bess. 1981. *Print awareness in preschool children: A study of the development of literacy in preschool children* (Occasional Paper No. 4). Tucson: Program in Language and Literacy, College of Education, University of Arizona. (ERIC Document Reproduction Service Document ED 210 629)

Goodman, Yetta M. & Wilde, Sandra. 1985. *Writing development in third and fourth grade Native American students: Social context, linguistic systems, and creation of meaning.* (Occasional Paper No. 14). Tucson: University of Arizona, College of Education, Program in Language and Literacy. (ERIC Document Reproduction Service Document ED 278 017)

Hughes, Langston. 1963. Mother to son. In Arna W. Bontemps (Ed.), *American Negro poetry* (p. 67). New York: Hill & Wang.

Smith, Frank. 1988. *Joining the literacy club: Further essays into education.* Portsmouth, NH: Heinemann.

Stone, Irving. 1980. *The origin: A biographical novel of Charles Darwin.* New York: Doubleday.

Teale, William & Sulzby, Elizabeth (Eds.). 1986. *Emergent literacy: Writing and reading.* Norwood, NJ: Ablex.

Vygotsky, Lev S. 1978. *Mind in society: The development of higher psychological processes.* Cambridge, MA: Harvard University Press.

Vygotsky, Lev S. 1986. *Thought and language.* Cambridge, MA: MIT Press.

Wertsch, James V. 1985. *Vygotsky and the social formation of mind.* Cambridge, MA: Harvard University Press.

Coda

Lucy Sprague Mitchell:
A Woman's Language Story

The role of women in language arts education deserves careful exploration by elementary school teachers and others with an interest in elementary education. By considering aspects of the life of Lucy Sprague Mitchell and her female colleagues who were a force in language arts education during the first half of this century, elementary and middle school teachers may find new ways to evaluate their own roles in language arts education in the 1990s.

The first time I read Lucy Sprague Mitchell's biography, written by Joyce Antler (1987), I reacted emotionally to much of what I was reading. Lucy Sprague Mitchell, humanist and scientist: she was what we might now call a whole language teacher of young children, a whole language teacher educator of preservice and inservice teachers, a researcher, teacher-researcher, research collaborator with other teachers; an author of research reports, journal articles, and books for teachers; an author of social studies and reading material for children; and at the same time, a woman and a wife with four children.

As I read about her life I felt a wellspring of pride for Lucy Sprague Mitchell and for myself, because there are so many overlaps in what we believe and what we hope to contribute to the lives of teachers and children. She was concerned with the improvement of the classroom environment not just for children but for teachers as well. She believed that the more teachers knew about language and learning, the arts, and social and political issues, the more enriched life in the classroom would be. She supported teachers' self-reflection on their own practices and helped teachers become observers of children, discovering insights into their development of language and thinking.

But as I read, I also was often angry. How many of you have heard of Lucy Sprague Mitchell? How many of you know of her contributions to the field of education and reference her work when you write about teacher researchers, research on teaching, language learning, children's literature, integrated curriculum, or social studies and reading instruction? I have been in education for at least forty years. In addition to my teaching, during those years I have been researching aspects of the reading process and the roles of learning and teaching, especially in relation to literacy learning and development. I've received advanced degrees in curriculum and teacher education. Why was I just now becoming aware of Lucy Sprague Mitchell and her work? Her name was vaguely familiar and I knew that she had something to do with Bank Street College, but I never knew that her work should have been informing my own work over the years.

Another emotion I experienced as I read was empathy with the appreciation and love that were evident among the women in Lucy Sprague Mitchell's professional learning community. I kept thinking about my warm feelings toward my colleagues in professional organizations with whom I have argued and agreed and cried and laughed about the state of education. So many of them are women who have stimulated my own inquiry into the field of language arts.

And I must admit to one other emotion: conviction, a conviction that the kind of educational experiences and quality of life in every school every day that most of us are working toward for our children and our grandchildren need continual vigilance and support. Like Lucy Sprague Mitchell, we are strong advocates for students and for classroom teachers, and we are not embarrassed to admit to such bias.

I want to explore the issues that emerged from my reading and rereading about Lucy Sprague Mitchell and her colleagues by first recognizing the right to take my emotional responses into consideration whenever I address questions regarding language and language learning. Actions, inquiry, hard work, and conviction come out of our beliefs, which are directly tied to our emotions. When we think logically we must come to the conclusion that there is no way to separate the cognitive from the affective, the intellectual from the emotional. When we don't recognize how interrelated these are, we ofttimes forget that all of our actions come out of what we feel and what we believe. As thinkers we need to take all of our reactions under consideration. We don't need to cover up our passion in jargon that some like to call objectivity. The more we recognize our biases, the more we explore the language learning and thinking of those for whom we are advocates, the more likely we are to know why we respond in the ways that we do and the greater will be our contributions to those we work so hard for—whether they are teachers or children or both.

So I let those initial feelings, those emotions that I had in reading this biography the first time, inform my questions: Why don't more of us today know about and talk about the work of Lucy Sprague Mitchell? How can her convictions, and the hard work and caring of the group of women she worked with for a period of more than twenty years, be called on even today to help us maintain our morale and to inform our own research and our work? Are there lessons to be learned from this story about the life of Lucy Sprague Mitchell that can help us sustain some of the forward steps we are making to improve the lives of teachers and students as they are immersed in language learning and teaching?

Lucy Sprague Mitchell and Her Colleagues

Let me first tell you a little more about Lucy, and then I will tie aspects of her life to the questions that I have just raised. (When I call her Lucy, I do so in order to build our personal connection with her.)

Lucy Sprague Mitchell was a woman before her time, but of course she was also a woman of her time. Perhaps the phrase *before her time* reveals a lack of insight into educational history. Now that I have discovered Lucy for myself, I wonder whether there are other women in earlier centuries who need to be unearthed and discovered. The examination of Lucy's personal and professional history reveals the life of an educator during the early part of this century, concerned with issues of humanism and science that are most compatible with the concerns that face whole language educators today. At the same time, it also provides an exemplary profile for the active involvement of teacher educators in developing supportive and healthy educational lives for children and teachers.

Lucy Sprague Mitchell was appointed in 1906 as first dean of women and the first woman on the faculty at the University of California at Berkeley. She was concerned with women's issues on many fronts in that position, but then she made a move that may have diminished her contributions in the eyes of some feminists. She married Wesley Clair Mitchell in 1912 and left her position in California, moving to New York and subsequently giving birth to four children. As she moved into her married life, her concerns about education and humanism took her in a new direction. Instead of looking to professionalize herself as part of a male-dominated university faculty, she became an elementary school teacher, a researcher, an innovator in integrated educational experiences for children, a teacher of teachers, and an author of works for children and educators.

Lucy taught all the elementary grades as well as preschool because she was in need of appropriate schooling experiences for her own children at the same time that she was professionally involved in educational research and development. She was a teacher and an educational adviser to more than a dozen experimental schools; she documented the experience of twelve experimental schools in New York City (Mitchell 1950); she was instrumental in the establishment of Bank Street College (originally known as the Bureau of Educational Experiments), dedicated to the teaching of teachers, as well as the establishment of school workshops to facilitate collaborative relationships between teachers, researchers, parents, and children.

Lucy and her female colleagues were interested in experiences for children that would capture their interests and expand their worlds. They explored the significance of play in children's learning and created materials that would enhance children's intellectual inquiries. They studied children's language and conceptual development, collecting well over a thousand pages of transcripts of children's language, and used this information to write developmentally appropriate books for children. They organized preschool and elementary school programs for children from all socioeconomic backgrounds in both private and public sectors. They wrote about play, social studies education, the teaching of geography, teacher education, and child language development. They organized a writers' workshop for authors of children's books.

Antler captures this time period in her powerful biography, showing how Lucy touched the lives of others, influencing their development as they influenced hers. Lucy was a contemporary of and collaborated with Margaret Wise Brown, the children's author who started her writing in a Writer's Laboratory organized at Bank Street College; Caroline Pratt, founder of the City and Country School in New York and involved in the development of the play school movement with a focus on preschool and early childhood education; Elisabeth Irwin, the organizer of the Little Red School House; Harriet Johnson, the first director of the Bank Street Nursery School, who was concerned with scientific research on child development; Julia Richman, committed to public education and a concern for the education of the "whole child"; Evelyn Dewey, a major voice in the organization of progressive schools; Jessie Stanton, who was able to see the world through the eyes of children; Barbara

Biber, who built bridges between the fields of psychology and education; Agnes Snyder, who collaborated with Mitchell on a social studies series for children; and those (including many of the above) who established Bank Street College to provide a supportive and cooperative working environment for teaching, writing, and research. Jane Addams and Lillian Wald, the major social reformers of the day, were also important influences on Lucy's life. It is wonderful to be immersed in a book on education concerned with beliefs that I treasure.

The Politics of Referencing

So why don't we know more about Lucy Sprague Mitchell and her colleagues?

This question comes out of the anger I have over my ignorance about this woman, the group of outstanding female educators with whom she collaborated, and the contributions she made to literacy education during the first half of this century. It is sad that although I was vaguely familiar with some of their names, I never became aware of the influence these women had on progressive, humanistic, and holistic education. But I was very aware of the contributions of John Dewey, G. Stanley Hall, William Kirkpatrick, George Counts, and Edward Thorndike, who were contemporaries and influenced Lucy in various ways. She, no doubt, influenced their work as well, but they probably didn't reference her work as much as she referenced their work and they referenced each other's.

Let me digress to explore the politics of referencing as it relates to sexism and to the elitism of supposed researchers over supposed practitioners. (I say supposed because all of these women were involved in researching children in home, school, and play settings). As I examine the bibliographies of men in the field, there is a great tendency to reference each other and to ignore the work of practitioners and teacher-researchers. There no doubt needs to be more careful research to document my cursory examination of this. However, my suspicions can be documented by an argument between John Dewey and Charles Hubbard Judd at the University of Chicago early in this century. Although Dewey saw teachers and researchers as more alike than different, Judd believed that teachers should be transmitters of subject matter, organizing classrooms by applying the knowledge produced by researchers. Because of this separation of functions, Judd also believed that teachers should be female without graduate education while researchers should be males with Ph.D.s (Lagemann 1989).

The reason such "politics of referencing" needs careful consideration is that there is a good deal of similar research going on in educational settings today. There are many teacher educators and researchers who never want to escape the classroom and children to move to clinical settings for experimentation. They (and I include myself among them) collaborate, interact, and work with teachers and children within school settings. Similarly, many teachers, a large number of them female, are actively involved in classroom research in various ways. Teachers are once again finding their voices and writing for each other in newsletters, magazines, and books. The National Council of Teachers of English honored the research of Nancie Atwell, a middle grade teacher, with the David H. Russell Research Award in 1990. It is important to consider the possibility that these educators of the 1980s and 1990s might also become invisible when the history of this period of time is written. Perhaps more historians like Antler will help keep women educationists visible. (Leonard Markus [1992] has recently written a biography of Margaret Wise Brown.) But female teachers and researchers must reference more carefully, keeping an eye on our own influences and stature. Also, as we write the history of our own time or look into history to understand our present, let's look for and remember the women who have made significant contributions to the understanding of the role of language and thinking in schools. Of course I want to read and understand and I want my students to know and reference the work of James Britton, Brian Cambourne, Ken Goodman, Donald Graves, Michael Halliday, Jerome Harste, Harold Rosen, and Frank Smith, but I don't want to lose sight of the work of Nancie Atwell, Alvina Burrows, Lucy Calkins, Eleanor Duckworth, Anne Haas Dyson, Carol Edelsky, Emilia Ferriero, Ruqaiya Hasan, Charlotte Huck, Sarah Hudelson, Martha King, Mary Kitagawa, Clotilde Pontecorvo, Louise Rosenblatt, Margaret Spencer, Dorothy Watson, and on and on . . . the list is substantial.

Was I more aware of the males in educational history because of sexism or because of status differences between those considered "theorists and researchers" and those considered "practitioners"? Probably a bit of both. There is considerable evidence that to this day the work of theorists and researchers is considered to be of greater prestige than the work of practitioners. Since the majority of practitioners are female, such beliefs about the relationship between researchers and practitioners need to be examined from a feminist perspective. I am very aware of the growing female presence at professional conferences and in graduate classes in education. We can't escape the role of women in teaching, teacher education, and research in language and learning development and language arts education.

Lessons from Lucy Sprague Mitchell

So what are the lessons that we can take from the time of Lucy Sprague Mitchell that inform today's issues and struggles?

Lucy and her colleagues were advocates for teachers and children without the need to apologize for their passions. They were concerned about the immigrants from all lands who were pouring into this country. They were affected by poverty, illness, and unemployment, but saw eager children wanting to learn. I wonder if they were responsible for the fourth-grade teacher I had in 1940 who let us read real books with stories and poems. I wonder if they were responsible for the kindergarten teacher who took my classmates and me to the public library to sign us up for library cards.

Here are Lucy Sprague Mitchell's own words about learners:

> What, then, is a good life for children? An active, a full, a rich life of meaningful experiences at each stage of their development. It is a sound humanitarian impulse to give children such lives. But it is more than that. A good life is a life in which one keeps growing in interests, in breadth of emotions and powers of expression, in depth and extent of human relations. Growth in all one's powers . . . leads on to an adulthood which is not static, completed, but still retains the capacity and the eagerness to grow. Adults, for good or bad, retain in their very fiber the results of their childhood experiences. Children's best chance to be learners, doers, creative, constructive members in the society they live in as adults is to have lived lives which gave these qualities a chance to grow steadily. . . . A good life for children is, above all, a chance to keep growing as 'whole children.' (1950, p. 14)

Lucy believed that learning experiences had to be integrated and related to the child's daily life. She wrote about how she and her colleagues organized curriculum to make a good life for children:

> We discussed what happens to curriculum building if children are planned for as organically whole people instead of as bundles composed of bodies and brains and membership in a society and an outfit of emotions, each to be attended to one at a time. . . . We find ourselves discarding such traditional school thinking and practices as separate courses of study, confining body activities to recess, separating pleasure from learning, as inappropriately trying to teach split-up children; and accepting . . . thinking and practices which give children experiences in living situations which will develop them as whole, fully functioning persons. (p. 190)

Lucy wrote about how teachers at a Bank Street workshop responded to the question, What is a curriculum built out of? "The needs of children. . . . Subject matter related to the children's own lives. . . . Experiences which help children to understand the world they live in—the work aspects, for instance. . . . Also, the physical world, which is explained by science. . . . Expression through the arts" (pp. 188–89).

Many of us are concerned about the shallowness of whole language education when the focus is on activities and not on the quality of life in the classroom. Lucy Sprague Mitchell provides a historical backdrop for the need for self-reflection on the part of teachers—their need to examine the quality of life in classrooms for themselves as well as for their students. She illuminates issues concerning the quality of life for teachers. She made it clear that the quality of life for children depended on the quality of life for teachers. She was an advocate for teachers as well as for children:

> Schools and communities are leaving the attitude that teachers are somehow set apart from other human beings in their personal lives; that they should see all sides of a question but have no convictions; should refrain from entering into politics; that they should always be serious, dignified; be respectful to superior officers and follow their instructions unquestioningly; that women teachers should not marry; that teachers should find their satisfactions only through the respect of the community and devotion to the job even if personal sacrifices are involved. Schools and communities are far more than formerly thinking of teachers as normal human beings who need adult satisfaction both in their professional and in their personal lives, . . . realizing that the more teachers have rich, satisfying personal lives the more they have to give to children of what children need and the greater their capacity to take from children what children need to give—in short, that well-rounded human beings are the most likely to build a well-rounded rich group life with children. Schools are more and more realizing that professional satisfactions for teachers come only from carrying genuine professional responsibilities . . . for planning, for thinking, for experimenting within their classrooms, also for sharing the responsibility of planning. . . . So, more and more of the school's job as it concerns teachers becomes one of changing their status from docile followers to constructive creative initiators and thinkers. (pp. 28–29)

Lucy believed that such a quality of life came from building a community of learners. First a community of learners with the children in the classroom:

> The teacher/child and child/teacher relationship is a close one in a more significant way than spending hours each day together in the same room. There must be a sharing of interest, a sharing of planning, a sharing of putting interests into action. The teacher remains

an adult though she becomes a member of the group. Her role is different from the role of the children. But it remains true that teacher and children must have a good life together or neither will have a good life. (p. 17)

I would add that teachers also need to be part of a community of learners with other professionals.

The biggest impact on me from the work of Lucy Sprague Mitchell has been the recognition it brought me of the power of collaborative groups. Throughout her life, Lucy gave credit to the influences of others, including her husband and John Dewey. But the group of women with whom she interacted had the greatest influence on her professional life and was important both in the exploration of her ideas and how they could be put to use in schools with children and in the documentation of the kinds of impact her ideas were having. Lucy focused much of her energy toward collaborative work. "She led her colleagues toward 'joint thinking' and a 'group focus.' 'Relatedness,' a central feature of her management style as well as of her educational theory and practice, was her favorite word" (Antler 1987, p. 364).

I now understand the importance of groups of people with like minds who come together to support each other and develop social meanings about schooling. I appreciate the importance of the Impact of Child Language Development Research conferences held by the National Council of Teachers of English and the International Reading Association in 1979 and 1980 (Goodman, Haussler & Strickland 1980; Pinnell & Matlin 1989), organized by a committee of mainly women language arts educators in order to discuss, present, and explore the growing knowledge and research about child language development. (It is gratifying to see such an exploration continuing in 1994–1996, organized by Myna Matlin and David Bloome.) The importance of collaboration helps explain the spread of whole language support groups throughout the United States, Canada, and other countries at the present time. Teachers have come to understand that support groups are important enhancements to their own professional development. The importance of working in groups to disseminate issues and findings of theory and practice explains the popularity and the impact of the National Writing Project and other writing workshops organized and maintained by those interested in the composing process. When I was researching the history of the whole language movement for the November 1989 issue of the *Elementary School Journal* (Goodman 1989; the article is reprinted in this volume), I discovered many other professional collaboratives: Lillian Weber's group at City University in New York concerned with involving parents and teachers in schooling issues; the North Dakota Study group concerned with exploring issues of testing and how teachers can support the role of active inquiry on the part of students; the Literature Connection in Columbus, Ohio, examining the important role of children's and adolescent literature as the focus of the reading program; and the Center for the Expansion of Language and Thinking, founded to establish a network of people interested in collaboratively exploring psychosociolinguistic aspects of language learning and their impact on professional development.

Our lives are enriched by our coming together to share meaning, to try to understand where we are coming from, to build a learning community, and to nurture one another. Learning is lifelong for professionals as well as for students. As we become professionals, we must hold on to our nurturing natures. We must become involved with others in the educational community to build support groups and network groups at many levels. As I work with whole language teachers in support groups, I am impressed with the significant self-reflection and professionalization taking place as teachers come together to share meaning with each other. I am impressed with the respect and admiration that they extend to each other as well.

In writing about the life of Lucy Sprague Mitchell, Joyce Antler credits Lucy for many of the ideas we are working so hard for today: "If education . . . is committed in our time to a concern for individual development, to the encouragement of curiosity and understanding rather than rote learning, to acquainting children with their environment—above all to a respect for the child's own pleasure in activity—very much credit must go to the institution and programs Lucy Sprague Mitchell created; they played a major role in bringing these 'progressive' notions into the mainstream of education" (pp. 364–65).

In this vein, we need to build our connections with women in other academic fields so that they can understand the role of female educationists and classroom teachers working to establish thinking human beings. Perhaps in this way we won't have female professors putting down future teachers in ways that are much too common in academic circles. We can challenge their views by raising the issue of feminism in relation to such attitudes.

Interestingly, Joyce Antler gives Lucy a good deal of credit for maintaining a female presence in the world of education: "During these post-Progressive years, often considered a time of decline in women's professional achievements, Bank Street and other institutions in the experimental education movement sought quiet ways to remake the world according to democratic, humanistic principles. In their ideals and programs, the activism common to women during the Progressive Era was sustained. I see their work as a continuation of the social reform movements of this earlier period, transformed by modern currents of social science and professionalism" (p. xix).

It is abundantly clear to me that all work related to teaching is concerned with women's issues. The quality of life in classrooms impacts teachers, the majority of whom are women. The quality of life in classrooms impacts students who are connected to working women outside the home; it impacts the lives of the next generation of women.

I wish to conclude with Lucy's words, words that sound so similar to statements we are making today:

> Critical times are questioning times. We feel confused and without direction when our old ways do not work. We feel something has gone wrong somewhere in our basic cultural patterns and attitudes that we were not able to prevent a new crisis or are not better able to handle it when it comes. And we wonder what we should do about it. It is so today in these critical worrying times. One of the questions many people are asking is, "How can our schools be improved—how can they develop people equal to the problems that their own lives and the times bring to them?" This question is asked . . . in the hope that if we find an answer, we may get nearer to the solution of some of our social problems. (Mitchell 1950, p. xxiii)

What makes this quote so important is that we must carefully examine why we are no nearer to solutions of our social problems than we were in the twenties, thirties, and forties. The quality of life for most kids and teachers in classrooms is no better today. So many of the kinds of practices we have worked so hard to put into place in schools—integration of language arts with social studies and science; a concern and knowledge about the environment in which we live; a love for art and music; a delight in literature; opportunities to read and to write; real experiences that are meaningful and important to the lives of students; opportunities to grow in language use through problem solving and rich experiences—were all discussed and put into practice by Lucy Sprague Mitchell and the colleagues with whom she worked. There are many forces that keep us from reaching these goals. Let us use the history of our past, let us look to our roots in order to help us move forward in search of better schools and better lives. Let's find many ways to talk seriously with each other and the colleagues with whom we work. Let's do something in an action-oriented way today. I don't want to wait another fifty years before such good sense becomes professional wisdom in schools.

References

Antler, Joyce. 1987. *Lucy Sprague Mitchell: The making of a modern woman.* New Haven: Yale University Press.

Goodman, Yetta M. 1989. Roots of the whole language movement. *Elementary School Journal, 90,* 113–27.

Goodman, Yetta M., Haussler, Myna & Strickland, Dorothy (Eds.) 1980. *The relationship between oral and written language: The children's viewpoints. Oral and written language development research: Impact on the schools* (Proceedings from the 1979 and 1980 IMPACT Conferences) (pp. 47–56). Newark, DE & Urbana, IL: International Reading Association & National Council of Teachers of English. (ERIC Document Reproduction Service Document ED 214 184)

Lagemann, Ellen. 1989. The plural worlds of educational research. *History of Education Quarterly, 29,* 185–214.

Markus, Leonard. 1992. *Margaret Wise Brown: Awakened by the moon.* Boston: Beacon Press.

Mitchell, Lucy S. 1950. *Our children and our schools.* New York: Simon & Schuster.

Pinnell, Gay S. & Matlin, Myna. 1989. *Teachers and research: Language learning in the classroom.* Newark, DE: International Reading Association.

Afterword

It is gratifying to reflect on the writing I have done during the more than three decades I have been involved with teaching and teacher education. Writing has never been easy for me, so to consider the influences my writing may have had on the thinking of other researchers and teachers in education is not something that I take lightly. Often when I write, struggling with what I am trying to mean, I wonder a great deal about the writing process. I consider carefully the language choices I make. I want to state my beliefs with conviction but without sounding arrogant. I want my audience to be aware of my advocacy for kids and my support for the empowerment of teachers. I want my readers to come to appreciate the political restraints in education that often keep teachers from believing in their own abilities to affect the environments in which they and their students live and work.

Another concern I have about my writing is the acknowledgment of how my ideas have been influenced by others. I often discuss the professionalism and politics of referencing with students and colleagues. In academic circles, we are all too susceptible to placing a stamp of personal ownership on our own thinking without considering where our ideas come from. There are those who write about education without doing the necessary homework to discover the origins of their ideas or to cite scholars who had similar ideas in the past. In addition, it is sometimes more important to such writers to cite authors who are perceived as more prestigious and therefore better for their own career advancement, rather than those who may have influenced their thinking but have less prestige in the field. It is not easy in the competitive world of academia to realize that much of what we know is established by the professional community in which we work. This tension of deciding where our ideas come from, which ideas we call uniquely our own and whose ideas we are building on, is not something we discuss often in the academic community.

Regardless, I want to make it clear that so much of who I am as a writer, a researcher, and a professional educator is the result of the intellectual community in which I work. That community includes my husband, Ken Goodman; my daughters, Debra Goodman, Karen Goodman, and Wendy Hood; my personal friends and professional colleagues in my twenty-five-year-old support group, CELT (The Center for the Expansion of Language and Thinking); my professional colleagues in the International Reading Association, the National Council of Teachers of English, and the National Reading Conference and at the University of Arizona; and certainly not least the conscientious, intellectually curious, and innovative doctoral students and classroom teachers with whom I have been fortunate to work. My writings are also influenced by those with whom I disagree because they push my thinking into areas I might not otherwise travel. And under the influence of all the members of my professional community (my thought collective, as Jerome Harste likes to call it), I plan to continue to write and contribute to the complex teaching and learning issues that we will continue to face.

My responses to the selected writings in this volume are reflected in the introductory notes to each section. Sandra Wilde organized this work to reflect the themes she found in my writing. Rather then react specifically to each piece of writing, I decided to share some of the history that has influenced these themes as well as the ideas that I am still considering. At this point, I want to thank Sandra Wilde, who is a colleague in research and writing as well as a committed teacher educator concerned with many of the issues that have influenced the direction of my work. I am grateful. Without her interest and concerns, this volume would not have become a reality.

Yetta M. Goodman:
A Brief Curriculum Vitae

Experience In Teacher Education

University or Arizona, College of Education, 1975–present. Professor, Regents Professor.

University of Michigan-Dearborn, Division of Urban Education, 1967–1975. Assistant Professor, Associate Professor.

Wayne State University, College of Education, 1963–1967. Professor Intern.

Education

Wayne State University. Ed.D. (Curriculum Development) 1967.

Los Angeles State College. B.A. (History) 1952, M.A. (Elementary Education) 1956.

Honors and Awards (selected)

Elected into the Reading Hall of Fame, 1994.

National Council of Teachers of English, Distinguished Service Award, 1994.

University of Arizona, Regents Professor, 1991.

International Reading Association and Merrill Publishing Co., Outstanding Teacher Educator in Reading Award, 1983.

University of Arizona Faculty Achievement Award, 1987.

Books Published (selected)

Goodman, Yetta M. & Burke, Carolyn L. 1972. *Reading Miscue Inventory manual: Procedures for diagnosis and evaluation.* New York: Macmillan.

Goodman, Yetta M. & Burke, Carolyn. 1980. *Reading strategies: Focus on comprehension.* New York: Holt, Rinehart & Winston.

Goodman, Kenneth S., Smith, E. Brooks, Meredith, Robert & Goodman, Yetta M. 1987. *Language and thinking in school: A whole language curriculum* (3rd ed.). New York: Richard C. Owen.

Goodman, Yetta M., Watson, Dorothy J. & Burke, Carolyn L. 1987. *Reading miscue inventory: Alternative procedures.* New York: Richard C. Owen.

Goodman, Kenneth S., Goodman, Yetta M. & Hood, Wendy J. (Eds.). 1989. *The whole language evaluation book*. Portsmouth, NH: Heinemann.

Goodman, Yetta M. (Ed.). 1990. *How children construct literacy: Piagetian perspectives*. Newark, DE: International Reading Association.

Goodman, Kenneth, Bird, Lois B. & Goodman, Yetta. 1991. *The whole language catalog*. Santa Rosa, CA: American School.

Goodman, Yetta M., Hood, Wendy J. & Goodman, Kenneth S. 1991. *Organizing for whole language*. Portsmouth, NH: Heinemann.

Goodman, Kenneth, Bird, Lois B. & Goodman, Yetta. 1992. *The whole language catalog: Supplement on authentic assessment*. Santa Rosa, CA: American School.

Goodman, Yetta M. & Wilde, Sandra (Eds.). 1992. *Literacy events in a community of young writers*. New York: Teachers College Press.

Bird, Lois B., Goodman, Kenneth & Goodman, Yetta. 1994. *The whole language catalog: Forms for authentic assessment*. New York: Macmillan/McGraw-Hill School.

Goodman, Yetta M. & Marek, Ann. 1996. *Revaluing readers and reading: Retrospective miscue analyis*. Katonah, NY: Richard C. Owen.

Goodman, Yetta M., Watson, Dorothy & Burke, Carolyn. 1996. *Reading strategies: Focus on comprehension* (2nd ed.). Katonah, NY: Richard C. Owen.

Whitmore, Kathryn F. & Goodman, Yetta M. (Eds.). 1996. *Whole language voices in teacher education: Practicing what we teach*. York, ME: Stenhouse.

Offices in Professional Organizations

Center for Expansion of Language and Thinking: President, 1975–79; Board of Directors, 1972–present.

International Center for the Study of Literacy Processes, University of Rome, Italy: Board of Directors, 1991–present.

International Reading Assocation: Board of Directors, 1994–97.

National Council of Teachers of English: President, 1979–1980; Executive Board Member, 1976–1980.

University of Arizona Association of Faculty Women: President, 1986–1987.

Consultant and Speaker

Yetta Goodman has spoken at conferences and universities, conducted workshops, and provided consultation to school districts and departments of education in most states of the United States and provinces of Canada, as well as numerous other countries, including Australia, China, Denmark, Mexico, New Zealand, and Venezuela.